Kurdistan on the Global Stage

Kurdistan on the Global Stage

Kinship, Land, and Community in Iraq

DIANE E. KING

RUTGERS UNIVERSITY PRESS

NEW BRUNSWICK, NEW JERSEY, AND LONDON

LIBRARY OF CONGRESS CATALOGING-IN-PUBLICATION DATA

King, Diane E., 1966–
    Kurdistan on the global stage : kinship, land, and community in Iraq / Diane E.
King.
      pages cm
    Includes bibliographical references and index.
    ISBN 978-0-8135-6353-4 (hardcover : alk. paper) — ISBN 978-0-8135-6352-7
(pbk. : alk. paper) — ISBN 978-0-8135-6354-1 (e-book)
    1. Kurdistan (Iraq)—Politics and government.   2. Kurdistan (Iraq)—Social
conditions.   3. Kurds—Iraq—Politics and government.   4. Kurds—Ethnic identity.
I. Title.
    DS70.8.K8K55   2014
    956.7'2—dc23

                                             2013010360

A British Cataloging-in-Publication record for this book is
available from the British Library.

"Candy Shop," Words and Music by Curtis Jackson and Scott Storch. Copyright
© 2005 50 CENT MUSIC PUBLISHING, SCOTT STORCH MUSIC, and TVT MUSIC INC.
All Rights for 50 CENT MUSIC PUBLISHING Controlled and Administered by
UNIVERSAL MUSIC CORP. All Rights Reserved. Used by Permission. Reprinted
with Permission of Hal Leonard Corporation.

Visit our website: http://rutgerspress.rutgers.edu

Manufactured in the United States of America

For the atrocity and war survivors of Kurdistan and Iraq.
May they find not only safety, but a just abundance.

CONTENTS

ILLUSTRATIONS

Figures (Charts and Maps)

Photographs

ACKNOWLEDGMENTS

My research would have failed without a warm welcome from people in both diasporic and homeland Kurdish communities starting in the mid-1990s, who endured, in almost all cases cheerfully, my endless questions. When research participants may come into harm as a result of their participation in the research, university Institutional Review Boards (in the United States) require that they be protected through the use of pseudonyms and other means. Successive IRBs have expressed what I believe are appropriate concerns for my interlocutors. Because of these concerns, and even more so due to my own concern that no one be endangered or embarrassed by my research, there are many people to whom I owe a debt of tremendous gratitude, but cannot name. I thank you, even though my thanks cannot be public. My special thanks goes to my host families, especially the one that long ago "adopted" me and has still not changed its mind. You are delightful, all of you.

I value very highly, and am grateful for, the freedom I have in Kurdistan to talk to seemingly anyone, a freedom I exercise every time I am in the field. Especially when I think of Iraq's totalitarian past, and the present in much of the territory surrounding Iraqi Kurdistan, I do not take it for granted. I thank the Kurdistan Regional Government for its openness, trust, and support. Asmat M. Khalid, current KRG minister of higher education and founder and former president of Dohuk University, and Nesreen Barwari, former KRG minister of reconstruction and development and Iraq minister of municipalities and public works, deserve special mention. I also thank Stafford Clarry, KRG humanitarian affairs adviser.

Over the years I have hired a number of research assistants. Four became integral to my work: Nazira Mehsin Shamdeen, Zhiyan Rozh,

Elie W. Mouchrik, and Erin Richter. I also thank Janet Johnston for her logistical help.

I stole away and wrote parts of this book in two homes, those of Kippy Gambill and the late Del Gambill, and Art Miley and Babs Miley. Thank you for your generosity.

I am profoundly indebted to Linda Stone for her mentorship, encouragement, and friendship over nearly two decades.

For their input on the manuscript I thank M. Cristina Alcalde, Nicholas Bailey, Francie Chassen-Lopez, Kristin Monroe, Lien-Hang T. Nguyen, Karen Petrone, Ana Rueda, Linda Stone, and Mark Schuller and his students at York College CUNY. I also thank participants in the Second International Conference on Kurdish Studies at Exeter University.

I am grateful to the anonymous reviewers for Rutgers University Press for their very helpful feedback. Marlie Wasserman, the press's director, and her associates were wonderful to work with.

My research and writing have been supported by the Wenner-Gren Foundation, the Hewlett Foundation, the Howard Foundation (of Brown University), and the British Council. Three universities have also supported my work: Washington State University, American University of Beirut, and University of Kentucky.

I believe in intervention by the divine in human events. Several times during my research, I have been the beneficiary of small miracles, and I imagine there were more of which I was not aware. I am grateful.

NOTE ON TRANSLITERATION, PRONUNCIATION, AND PROPER NOUNS

The Kurdish language is written in a number of different scripts. The Arabic script is most common in Iraq, followed by the Latin script. Because of its similarity to English, I use the romanized script in this book. I render many Kurdish words, and words from neighboring languages such as Arabic, Turkish, and Persian that are used in spoken and written Kurdish, in their most common English spelling, even if such a spelling is not standard in the romanized Kurdish script. Examples include "Zakho," the name of a town that in Kurdish is spelled "Zaxo," and "peshmerga," the word for resistance fighters that in Kurdish is spelled "pêşmerge." In other cases, I retain the spelling in English that is closest to the Kurdish spelling, but without Kurdish diacritics. An example is "Silemani," the name of a city that in Kurdish is spelled "Silêmanî" (and this city is often referred to by other authors writing in English by a transliteration of its Arabic pronunciation, such as "Sulaymaniyah"). When quoting another author, I leave spellings as they are in the original.

Kurdish encompasses several significant dialects and many sub-dialects. Most of the colloquial Kurdish featured in this book is from the Behdini Kurmanji dialect.

Some places have multiple names that are derived from different languages or different historical periods. For example, the capital of the Kurdistan Region is the city that is known as "Hewler" (Hewlêr) in Kurdish but "Erbil" in Arabic. The latter tends to be more common in English-language sources. I favor the former in this book, but also use the latter.

Pronunciation Guide for the Kurdish Roman Alphabet

A, a   a in father

C, c   j in June, jar

Ç, ç	ch in church
E, e	e in bet
Ê, ê	a in bake
G, g	g in go
Ḧ, ḧ	"heavy" h
I, i	i in kit
Î, î	ee in seen
J, j	s in vision
O, o	o in oat (but shorter)
Q, q	phryngeal q
R, r	flapped r
RR, rr	trilled r
Ş, ş	sh in shop
U, u	u as in put, a short vowel
Û, û	oo in soon, a long vowel
X, x	as ch in Scottish "loch" (sometimes rendered "kh")
Ẋ, ẋ	as in "X, x," but voiced
'	glottal stop
'	ayin, a guttural sound

Kurdish has fourteen additional letters. These particular letters are listed either because they differ from English, or because if used in English they could signify more than one sound.

Kurdistan on the Global Stage

1

Kurdistan Glocal

Kurdistan Parliament passed Domestic Violence Law; making Female Genital Mutilation criminal offense, prohibiting forced marriages, child labor.

—Barham Salih via Twitter, 2011

In 1991, hundreds of thousands of people fled up the soggy, freezing mountainsides of Kurdistan, the Kurdish homeland that spans Turkey, Syria, Iraq, and Iran, to escape attacks by the Iraqi military. The attacks were ordered by Iraqi leader Saddam Hussein, one of the world's most brutal dictators, in response to an uprising by three main categories of Kurdish fighters: the *chete* (çete) tribal mercenaries who had been on the government's payroll, and long-standing government adversaries the KDP (Kurdistan Democratic Party, Partî Dêmokratî Kurdistan) and PUK (Patriotic Union of Kurdistan, Yeketî Niştîmanî Kurdistan), whose fighters are called *peshmerga* (pêşmerge) "those who face death." Enraged that the three Kurdish groups had united to challenge him, and hoping to use the fog of the waning Gulf War with the United States as a cover, the Iraqi leader sent his well-equipped army charging toward the Kurdish-populated area of Iraq, Iraqi Kurdistan. Desperate people streamed into the mountains toward Turkey and Iran. With little food and spending nights outside without adequate shelter, young, old, and vulnerable people began to die. At the Turkish border, many tried to cross and a few succeeded, but Turkish soldiers beat most people back. Although those particular attacks by Iraq were contextualized as a by-product of the Gulf War between the United States and Iraq, they followed many years of conflict in which Kurds had fought for autonomy and the central Iraqi government had done its best to crush them, using chemical weapons, mass deportations and executions, and all manner of terror.[1]

In the pages to come, I will describe a Kurdistan in Iraq that is, as Michael Gunter puts it, "ascending" (2008). The Kurdistan Region now projects the image of a rising, peaceful democracy where Kurdishness is celebrated. That image may be problematic, but this is Iraqi Kurdistan's new image nonetheless. This is a visage that goes against history and is counterintuitive for the region's neighbors, elites and nonelites alike. Iraqi Kurdistan is surrounded by troubled states with troubled bodies politic in which Kurdishness is unwelcome or at minimum suppressed. Yet, somehow, at this juncture of history in the early twenty-first century, the Kurds of Iraq have found a way to stand tall in the Middle East, becoming increasingly famous for defying the odds. I will also describe a Kurdistan that is resolutely itself, with social forms that are highly local. While this book makes arguments about collective identity and the global, it is also a general ethnography, accountable to the long-standing tradition of historically grounded ethnographic description in anthropology. The global has only recently entered Kurdish life in a readily discernible way, and the proportions of this book's content reflect that. This is mainly a book about social and symbolic life in Iraqi Kurdistan, and it is secondarily a look at global influences there.

The tweet at the beginning of this chapter went out on Tuesday, the 21st of June 2011. At the time, Barham Salih was prime minister of the Kurdistan Region of Iraq. If he was in Kurdistan when he tweeted, it was 1:30 A.M. where he was. I imagine he returned to his home in the regional capital of Hewler after a long day of governing, and, before turning in for the night, decided to let the world know the good news.[2]

Prime ministers tweeting is of course a new and novel thing wherever it may be taking place, but it seems all the more remarkable in this case given Kurdistan's history of isolation, violence, and status as landlocked and surrounded by frenemies. Or is it that unlikely? In this book, I use the rubric of "connecting" to show how local social connections and their logic and maintenance are quite easily adapted to a much larger scale of relating. Tweeting, the new, and socializing over tea, the old, are both connecting. In this case, the prime minister's tweet is the culmination of a long and complicated set of debates. The issues of female genital cutting (FGC; also "female genital multilation" or "female circumcision"), early and forced marriage, and child labor have pitted an old Kurdistan—a Kurdistan in which these practices have taken place probably for thousands of years—against a possible new Kurdistan. In this new Kurdistan, such behaviors are no longer tolerated by a "modern" society that lives in, and is self-consciously accountable to, "global" standards of conduct rooted in "human rights" and other values promoted by international publics and organizations such as the United Nations. That society is knit together by social connections. Connections take place between people belonging to kin and tribal groups, between friends, between patrons and clients, and so on. Some of the logics that animate those connections run contrary to the new laws. As part of a complex of conventions surrounding the patrilineal (agnatic) reckoning of descent, for example, brothers have long had the right to discuss the marriage of one of their daughters to the other one's son, and to take steps toward that outcome if they come to an agreement. The prospective bride and groom have also long had the right to say no, but despite that right, there are still many people in Kurdistan who will later tell you that it was not granted to them, and that they were married off against their will, in many cases at a very young age. How many brothers discussing their children's marriage will now also mention to each other the need to defer to the law? How will the new laws be enforced? Will the laws catch on as new norms, or be seen as an imposition? Today, in a globalizing Iraqi Kurdistan, connecting is going global as the region's leaders and people alike interface with people and institutions located or emanating from distant places potentially representing disparate reference points and value systems. They do so through their own diaspora, through satellite television and the Internet, and person-to person, for example by receiving outsiders like me from abroad. Everyone now knows that a new set of "modern" ideas is in the mix of possibilities. I do not know how many people saw the prime minister's tweet—at least those who can read the global language in which he tweeted it—but the word is out. Kurdistan's old forms of connecting are now juxtaposed with new forms.

Kurdistan, "the land of the Kurds," is a country that might have been and that might yet be. There is no politically recognized independent state called Kurdistan, but Kurdistan is socially recognized by millions of people as their ethnic homeland. Arcing across portions of four countries, it is a mainly contiguous area that includes much of eastern Anatolia, a good portion of northeastern Syria as well as pockets farther west, the mountainous areas of northeastern Iraq as well as some areas in northwestern Iraq, and areas in northwestern Iran. Kurdistan is a nonexclusive homeland in that many people of other ethnic identity categories also live there or claim it as their historic home. In some areas of Kurdistan, the majority belonged to another category until very recently, but today the majority of people living in the area long called "Kurdistan" are ethnolinguistically Kurdish.[3] There may be 20 million Kurds in the world, or there may be 40 million; no government or agency has counted them, but those seem like a reasonable minimum and maximum given the known total populations of the countries where Kurds live, and the approximate proportion of those populations that are Kurdish. The subject of this book, the Kurds of Iraq, now have a recognized enclave in the northeast of Iraq called the Kurdistan Region, an area of approximately 40,000 square kilometers (15,000 square miles). Including those who live elsewhere in Iraq, Iraqi Kurds are said to number about 5 million.[4] Some of the region's internal boundaries with the rest of Iraq are disputed, but its other borders, with Syria, Turkey, and Iran, are well defined, since they also constitute the Iraqi state border.

FIGURE 1.1 "Kurdistan" is the area recognized by ethnic Kurds as their historic homeland. Today it stretches across the modern states of Iran, Iraq, Syria and Turkey. (Reproduced from a public domain source, Robson and Refugee Service Center 1996.)

In Iraq, Charles Tripp writes, "the community is not one of citizens, but of family and clan members, fellow tribesmen, co-sectarians or conspirators" (2007:2), and this is no less the case in the Kurdistan Region. The majority of people in the Kurdistan Region, and most of the people featured in this book, are Sunni Muslim Kurds who follow the Shafi'i madhhab.[5] A minority of Kurds are adherents of Yezidism, a religion that is indigenous to Kurdistan.[6] The Assyrians (who were called "Nestorians" until the turn of the twentieth century) and Chaldeans are members of ancient Christian churches and speak neo-Aramaic. A few Armenians live in Iraqi Kurdistan as well. Kurdistan used to have a significant Jewish population, but after the founding of Israel in 1948, almost all of them left, and the few who stayed converted to Islam. Turkomans live mainly in the southern part of Iraqi Kurdistan and speak a Turkic language. Several other ethnosectarian categories are represented in Iraqi Kurdistan as well.

Kurds constitute the fourth-largest ethnolinguistic group in the Middle East region. Their homeland was partitioned following World War I. In each state in and near the historic Kurdish homeland, people belonging to an ethnic group whose identity is closely linked to the idealized nation-state has mistreated Kurdish people: Arabs in Iraq and Syria, Turks in Turkey, and Persians in Iran. This mistreatment has ranged from marginalizing Kurds to outright attempts to eliminate them through assimilation and/or attempted genocide. The Kurds, it is often said, are "the world's largest nation without their own state," but this might be a less excruciating claim had many Kurds not been at best marginalized and at worst hunted in their homeland states by some people belonging to the three ethnic majorities in those states. Lines of perpetration and victimization never overlap neatly with ethnic categories. Violence and abuse know no ethnic bounds anywhere in the world. However, when members of an ethnic group that has the power of the state in its grip harness that power against outnumbered members of a group without state power, the contest cannot be even. Kurds have, in the vast majority of cases since the modern states of the Middle East came into being in the early twentieth century, been the losers in these uneven contests.

Today millions of Kurds live outside Kurdistan. Istanbul, former seat of empires and the largest city in Turkey, is also the largest Kurdish city in the world. Anna Secor (2003:2211) found in a survey conducted in 2002 that only 34 percent of Istanbul residents had been born in the city. Many are migrants from the rural, Kurdish-majority areas in the east. Small Kurdish populations are found in the Caucasus, Lebanon, and other nearby countries. Following some significant flows of refugees and asylum-seekers starting in the 1970s, large numbers of Kurdish people now live in the West, with at least 1 million in western Europe and perhaps 40,000 in the United States.[7] In a way, in the Kurdistan Region of Iraq the Kurds now "have a state" after all, now that the Iraqi quadrant of Kurdistan is a recognized region in federal Iraq.[8] I will have much more to say about that in the pages to come.

Sociocultural Research in Iraqi Kurdistan and Iraq

Despite the Kurds' rise in prominence in global public consciousness, the sociocultural anthropology of Iraqi Kurdistan was arguably more robust decades ago than presently, even if most of the early researchers stayed for only a short period. The Sorani dialect area has received the most anthropological attention. Martin van Bruinessen's ethnography (1992a) is widely regarded as the leading book on Kurdish social organization. He spent six weeks in the Sorani area in the mid-1970s, as well as traveling to a variety of locations in Iran and Turkey during a two-year period of fieldwork. Two influential twentieth-century anthropologists, Edmund Leach (1940) and Fredrik Barth (1979 [1953]) conducted fieldwork in Iraqi Kurdistan for five weeks in 1938 and five months in 1951, respectively, which in each case was the author's first ethnographic work. Barth later became Leach's student, and both went on to influential careers, contributing to important debates in anthropology in the areas of kinship, sociopolitical organization, and identity. Both authors' ethnographies of the Kurds are enjoying something of a revival in Turkey, their works having recently been translated into Turkish.[9] I mention the work of a few other researchers elsewhere in this book.

Iraq has been called "the most understudied society in the Middle East" (Potter and Sick 2004:136), which is deeply ironic given that it is also "among the most 'mediatized' in the world" (Dawod 2012:89). Ethnographic studies of Iraqi life outside the Kurdish-majority areas are extremely rare. Robert A. Fernea did fieldwork in southern Iraq starting in the 1950s (Fernea 1959, 1970), and, based on her time with him there, his wife Elizabeth wrote what was likely the best-selling book on Iraq before the 2003 war (Fernea 2010 [1965]). Dorothy Van Ess wrote an ethnography of Iraqi women (Van Ess 1961) while working under the direction of Margaret Mead (Van Ess 1974:185). Research by Amal Vinogradov (1974) and Amal Rassam (1977),[10] and by Suad Joseph (1982, 1991) was of shorter duration and also contributed importantly to the sociocultural anthropology of Iraq.[11]

The "Connecting" Rubric

"Connecting" is the main rubric for this book. "Connecting" entails the combining of two aspects of Kurdish social and symbolic life, those that are grounded in the local and may have a long history, and those that are from elsewhere and new. The two aspects form a continuum to bring together two seemingly disparate aspects of social life in Iraqi Kurdistan. At one end are social relations of the "old-fashioned" kind, such as the tracing of patrilines. Both the Kurdish term for patrilineage, *mal* (or *binemal*), and Arabic, *'a'ila*, are used in Kurdistan. An alternative term in English is "house."[12] In the system of patriliny, people recognize lines of male ancestors stretching back into history, and this tracing fosters certain kinds of interactions and resource allocation. Marriage arranging, relating to kin and neighbors, highly specific gender roles, and the limiting of female autonomy are the stuff of these relations. Other locally derived sets of values and practices foster rich sets of small-scale social connections, many of which have been practiced for a long time. These interactions encompass particular logics, and their maintenance fosters specific social conventions. Patriliny is the concept at the "local and long-standing" end of the continuum that I emphasize the most, but I identify both direct and peripheral influences for patriliny within a larger relational frame in Kurdistani life. This book therefore explores other ways in which Kurdish people connect socially, such as through patron-client relationships, and as people belonging to gendered categories. Kurdistan is a very socially rich place, a place in which people invest very deeply in social relations. Most people devote much more time to social interaction than in other parts of the world that I have visited and in which I have lived, especially in advanced economies where most people's time allocation centers around work and the nuclear family.

Some aspects of social life in Kurdistan as recounted by early traveler and missionary accounts and earlier ethnographies ring very familiar based on my fieldwork. From various chroniclers' accounts, such as Badger's (1852), Grant's (Grant and Murre-Van Den Berg 2002 [1841]), and Bird's (2010 [1891]), it is possible to conclude that some of the basic rhythms of social life in Kurdistan that are still observable have been in place for at least hundreds of years and probably much longer. Of course, these relations have been far from static; trends, events, and interventions have come and gone, but it seems clear that some general patterns have prevailed. An account from the mid-nineteenth century, for example, might describe a Kurdish family hosting a traveler in their home and presenting a lavish tray of fruit at the end of the evening, just as a host is likely to do today. (Such an account's *interpretive* frame would likely be different though; many early Western accounts offer a jaundiced view, clearly fitting Edward Said's particular definition of "Orientalism" [1979].) An earlier ethnography might describe village families' system of reciprocity in village labor, with many hands making it light on my plot of land today, and on your plot of land on another day, just as village families still do. Fredrik Barth (1979 [1953]) described the nightly practice of visiting that he encountered during fieldwork in Iraqi Kurdistan in 1951, and noted that the practice he observed differed little from that described by travel writer Claudius Julius Rich in the early nineteenth century (Rich 1836). Barth noted that Rich was "surprised at the regularities of the patterns of visiting, at the large groups that would congregate in the house of some 'nobleman' or out in the open, and spend their time smoking and drinking tea, while talking away into the small hours" (Barth 1979 [1953]:103). I, in turn, also observed intensive patterns of visiting, with which my research interviews and observation often dovetailed.

At the other end of the continuum of Kurdish social and symbolic life is the global, which now encompasses, transforms, and shapes older forms of interpreting and relating. It happens both in shared physical space and in technologically mediated space. Globalization is a broad concept like "modernization" or "postcoloniality" and thus is susceptible to uses that can seem to say a lot without really saying much, but in this book I follow the basic definition offered by Jonathan Xavier Inda and Renato Rosaldo: "the intensification of global interconnectedness, suggesting a world full of movement and mixture, contact and linkages, and persistent cultural interaction and exchange. It speaks, in other words, to the complex mobilities and interconnections that characterize the globe today" (2008:4). Inda and Rosaldo go on to elaborate on several important elements of their definition, including a disconnecting of culture from particular locations and Western/American cultural imperialism, both of which I touch on in this book.

The global in Kurdish life links to events and trends taking place on a very large scale, and is new. The arrival of ideas, goods, and people from the West in the relief effort after the 1991 Gulf War started what has now expanded far beyond relief and development. Especially starting with my two trips to Kurdistan in 2008, it has seemed to me as though new, technologically mediated connections to the rest of the world are everywhere in Iraqi Kurdistan. To get there in 2008, I flew for the first time on a plane that landed in the region rather than in a neighboring country. The airline was Austrian, a member of Star Alliance, which has as its motto, "The Way the Earth Connects." This seemed especially apt as I reflected on past difficulties with arrivals and border crossings. I was connecting, seemingly matter-of-factly, and Austrian indeed made it happen. What a contrast this was to my first two departures from Kurdistan in the 1990s, when carsful of friends and fictive kin escorted me to the riverbank for a parting, a tearful one because we imagined that we might never see each other again, before I crossed a clanky steel bridge to Turkey or climbed into a dinghy that would take me across the water to Syria! Given the tenuous political situation of Iraq and its neighbors, the extreme difficulties almost everyone, from Westerners to local people, faced in getting across the border (which I had requested to cross for over a year before being granted authorization), and my friends' lack of financial means, we told each other we did not know if we would ever be able to meet again. But there I was, flitting in and out with ease a decade later. On the streets of the regional capital Hewler, taking advantage of the large vertical space next to the street afforded by T-walls, in 2008 the Nokia mobile phone company was advertising its phones with a billboard-sized banner reading, "Nokia: Connecting People . . . Presence Beyond Borders." Fittingly, the banner was on a main street by the Ministry

PHOTO 1.1 An advertisement for Nokia mobile phones on a T-wall, a fortified barrier in downtown Hewler, 2008. (Photo by the author.)

of the Interior's passport office, a required stop for anyone from abroad seeking to stay for more than two weeks or anyone with an Iraqi passport seeking to leave. It was seen from thousands of cars each day.

But connecting in new, technologically mediated ways was not merely a slogan used to sell products. It seemed to be happening at every level of social organization. Young people who previously had had no opportunity (or at least few opportunities) to speak to a prospective wife or husband were courting by phone. A boy might take interest in a girl he sees on the street or at school. In the past, he would have had to involve other people if he wanted to sit and speak with her. Her brother, for example, might make such a meeting happen, and would be a part of the meeting. His own family, his father and mother, and perhaps older siblings and his father's brother(s) could, if they were opposed, prevent even a first brief conversation between the two. Now, however, he could see a girl on the street, get her phone number from someone they both know, and from then on have direct conversations with her without any intermediaries involved.

This book necessarily portrays Kurdish life in its present historical context, a particular ethnographic present.[13] Life in Kurdistan is changing at a tremendously fast pace. Like other parts of the world that are being impacted by new technologies, it displays what David Harvey (2004) calls "time-space compression"—in which satellite communication, faster modes of transport, and other means of speeding up the processes of trade and human interaction are accelerated.[14] Clifford Geertz pointed out that it can be difficult for a second anthropologist to sort out what an earlier one asserted about the same group. "Unable to recover the immediacies of fieldwork for empirical reinspection," he wrote, "we listen to some voices and ignore others" (1998:6). In the case of my field site of Kurdistan, I have often thought of this assertion of Geertz's as applying not only to a hypothetical ethnographer who might come along later, but to me as a repeat visitor. I marvel at the pace of changes I see even from one trip to another. You can never step into the same field site twice.

At the same time, many long-standing social and symbolic values and categories persist, even as they absorb the global. Nowhere do people take the "global" and consume it wholesale; they pick and choose and have their own way of taking it in, as has now been argued by many authors such as Fariba Adelkhah for Iran (2000), and Dimitrios Theodossopoulos and Elisabeth Kirtsoglou for a variety of locations (2010). Two early and influential models for the blending of the locally specific and the larger scale and universalizing are Arjun Appadurai's concept of "scapes," such as ethnoscapes and mediascapes, that "are inflected by the historical, linguistic, and political situatedness of different sorts of actors" (1990:7), and Roland Robertson's model of "glocalization" (1995) in which "the problem becomes that of spelling out the ways in which homogenizing and heterogenizing tendencies are mutually implicative" (27). Anna Tsing's metaphor of "friction," for "the grip of worldly encounter" as global and local meet (2005:1), is supported with rich ethnography from Kalimantan, Indonesia. In Kurdistan, as in Kalimantan or anywhere, the local and the global blend, forming the glocal. As Kurdistanis grapple with and appropriate the global, they do so in their own local ways, absorbing what has newly come to them by connecting in ways that are already familiar. What people talk about when they are visiting is one example. In the early years, I would often hear people commiserating about hardship, recounting difficulties stemming from violence and the fear of violence. Later, as the area grew more peaceful, the topics of conversation branched out significantly.

On a visit to my longtime Kurdish friend Hala, [15] a full-time homemaker, in Zakho in 2010, we spent the first few minutes talking about her family, and especially her new grandchild, but then she suddenly changed the subject and asked with excitement in her voice, "What do you think of WikiLeaks?" The WikiLeaks organization had been in the news for its unauthorized leak on the Internet of thousands of United States government documents. In our discussion, it was clear that Hala had been getting the same news I had in the United States. When I started to mention one juicy tidbit relating to the Middle East, the Saudi king saying that he wanted the United States to "cut off the head of the snake" and attack Iran, she finished my sentence for me with a tone of delight, as though recounting a particularly salacious piece of gossip. Whenever I had heard this tone from her before, it was in reference to something or someone highly local. Kurdish women's lives are lived through connections to friends, relatives, and acquaintances, argues Choman Hardi (2011:192), and which Hala's life had seemed to exemplify. This time, however, we were trading gossip of the highly globalized kind.

The advent of the telephone has also influenced people's interactions. By the early to mid-1990s, most urban homes had one landline telephone, and rural homes did not have telephone service, but even when landline phones were becoming increasingly common, there was little need to call. If you wanted to visit someone, you just went and knocked on their gate, and if they were home, there was a very high probability that they would let you in.[16] To contact a business or institution, you went there in person. Now, as in many other places, the landline is passé (although still in use) and the mobile phone is ubiquitous. Kurdistanis joke that even the sheep and goats each have their own mobile phones. Many people have multiple phones to use with different carriers, and they use the one that is least expensive, and that works, for wherever they are calling. Visits are increasingly arranged by telephone. While it is still possible to appear at someone's gate and they will feel an obligation to let you in—and probably do so with great warmth—such unannounced encounters are on the wane. Many people call ahead now.

Social connections and practices of social and economic exchange in the Kurdistan Region, as anywhere, are inextricable. In the rest of this book I emphasize other aspects of social life, such as kinship and descent, over the economic. However, two major economic realms are so important that they must not be overlooked: agriculture, which is ancient, and the extraction of hydrocarbons, which is approximately a century old. Until the mid-twentieth century, Iraq, including the plains areas of Kurdistan, had an agricultural economic system similar to that found throughout the Middle East. It fostered patron-client relationships in which the landowner, the patron, controlled land, money, and protection and left the peasant with few other options (Richards and Waterbury 1996:311). Around the same time that large landowners were losing their power, Iraq was becoming a major extractive economy, a type of economy that fosters patronage networks (Karl 1997; Reyna and Behrends 2008). Kurdistan's political economy is postfeudal, and many people are only one or two generations removed from a strictly defined peasant economy with wealthy landlords ruling and sometimes making small wars, and impoverished tenant farmers being ruled and working the land and sometimes fighting small wars. Iraqi Kurdistan has undergone several phases of land reform by both the national and regional governments, and the population has also been urbanizing. Despite this, there are still a significant number of people living a life similar to that of peasants anywhere, past or present, subject to the rhythms of agricultural labor and household tasks. Even away from the villages, the village lifestyle is still held up by Kurds with pride as archetypal, very similar to the way in which Ted Swedenburg (1990) argues that Palestinians do. On numerous occasions I have heard people who have spent very little time in a rural setting insist that they are, at heart, villagers. My friend Sevi had a story that she delighted in telling: "I used to be very proud of being a villager. I would tell people that I was really a village girl even though I spent most of my growing up years in the city. Then one day, I was in a village and someone persuaded me to milk a goat. I chose a goat and began to try to milk it. But something wasn't right. No milk was coming out. People began to laugh at me. Finally someone blurted out that I was trying to milk a male goat! We all laughed and laughed. So, after that, I had to admit I really belonged to the city."

Many aspects of social life in Kurdistan seem similar to what Eric Wolf (1966) called "manystranded" social relations. Wolf wrote that in peasant society, some types of coalitions can have multiple strands, in which "[e]conomic exchanges imply kinship or friendship or neighborliness; relationships of kinship, friendship or neighborliness imply the existence of social sanctions to govern them; social sanctions imply the existence of symbols which reinforce and represent the other relations" (1966:81). Good community relations must be maintained by every Kurdistani household in order to maintain successful ongoing participation in the community. People spend many hours in the socializing required to maintain these relations, in much the same way as Lale Yalçin-Heckmann has described for a Kurdish village in Hakkari, Turkey (1991:169–175).[17] Exchange relationships are, in the twenty-first century, by no means only associated with rural people, or those living a more "traditional," labor-heavy lifestyle. They are practiced by virtually everyone. Everyday acts of exchange may include bringing a meal to a family that is settling into a new home, or giving someone a ride somewhere. None of these acts are pure gifts (Mauss 2002 [1923–24]); each act has a strong possibility of being reciprocated after some time has passed. People keep track of elaborate tallies as to whom they owe what and vice versa.

Suad Joseph offers a model she calls "patriarchal connectivity" for social relations in the Arab world that I think also applies well to the Kurdish world. "By connectivity I mean relationships in which a person's boundaries are relatively fluid so that persons feel a part of significant others. Persons . . . did not experience themselves as bounded, separate, or autonomous. They answered for each other, anticipated each other's needs, expected their needs to be anticipated by significant others, and often shaped their likes and dislikes in accordance with the likes and dislikes of others. They saw others as extensions of themselves and themselves as extensions of others. Maturity was signaled in part by the successful enactment of a myriad of connective relationships" (1993:452). In Wolf's model, people play a variety of roles in their associates' lives, roles that would likely be played by different individuals in an urban society far removed from peasant social patterns. While Joseph's emphasis is more on the self than on an overarching social pattern, she shows how selves are indelibly shaped by their social connections in a Middle Eastern environment—connections that may be richly multifaceted, just as those that Wolf describes. Joseph goes on in the same article to emphasize the powerful role played by patrilineal kinship relations that foster patriarchy. In Kurdistan, too, individuals belong to patrilineages, successive generations of males traced back in time to an apical ancestor, that strongly influence who they are and become as persons, and how and to whom they relate in a variety of relationships ranging from friendships to professional relationships. There is, as Joseph also emphasizes, a great deal of hierarchy: old over young, member of a prestigious patriline over member of a nonprestigious one, male over female. Self-made men exist, but from each of them issues a new patrilineage that carries collective prestige forward for at least two generations, and more if successive generations of males exist and are successful.

As I use the term in this book, "connecting" is a similar concept to Wolf's manystrandedness or Joseph's patriarchal connectivity. It is people's social and symbolic life, enacted in ways specific to their milieu. What I do in addition, however, is to contextualize Kurdistani connecting within the global. Much of what this book is concerned with could be called "primordial" symbols and social relations, which are now maintained, reformulated, and questioned in globalizing Kurdistan, forming something not local, not global, but glocal.

Globalizing Kurdistan: Antecedents

It is possible to make a case for globalization having begun, in a *longue durée* sense, in and around the territory that is today Kurdistan. A number of theorists ranging from Robert Braidwood and Bruce Howe (1960) to Simcha Lev-Yadun and colleagues (2000) have argued that the first domestication of plants and animals took place in the area now known as Kurdistan. There is much evidence for earlier human activity in Kurdistan as well. Shanidar Cave, made famous by Ralph Solecki's excavation of Neanderthal skeletons from beneath its floor and subsequent theorizing about Neanderthal life (Solecki 1971), is in Kurdistan. I visited the cave in the spring of 1998, and found empty but recently constructed livestock stalls inside it and generous amounts of manure on the floor. No one was present at the time, although a young boy from the nearby village hiked up to it when he saw my friends and me go inside. The state of the cave and the simple trail leading to it belied its significant contributions to the global paleoanthropological record.

The ruins of the world's first known aqueduct are in Kurdistan. It was built by the Assyrian king Sennacherib in 690 BCE and excavated and

PHOTO 1.2 The view from inside Shanidar Cave, spring 1998. (Photo by the author.)

described by Thorkild Jacobsen and Seton Lloyd (1935). At Göbekli Tepe, an archaeological site on the western edge of the Kurdish area in Turkey, Klaus Schmidt (2008) and colleagues have uncovered unique stone monuments that they assert were erected around the same time as humans first left a nomadic lifestyle centered around gathering and hunting seasons, and began to settle. As a mountain refuge zone adjacent to the plains civilizations of Mesopotamia and Anatolia that arose after domestication, the area that later became Kurdistan can be said to have had a "front-row seat" at the very origins of settled and urban life, without which there would be no globalization. Emphasizing the accumulation of capital made possible by early practitioners of agriculture, André Gunder Frank and Barry Gills (1996) have argued for continuity between the Mesopotamian civilization of approximately five thousand years ago and the modern world system.

More recently, some important regional events that reverberated throughout the Middle East and beyond emerged from or took place in Kurdistan. Ṣalāh ad-Dīn Yūsuf ibn Ayyūb (Saladin), one of the main leaders of the Muslim defense during the Crusades, was a Kurd, and there were many encounters between Kurds and people from beyond the Middle Eastern region, especially Europeans, around the time of the Crusades. Near the Syrian coast, the castle Crak des Chevaliers is still known locally by its old name, *Hisn al Akrad* (Castle of the Kurds), and the nearby Afrin area is still dotted with Kurdish villages. These encounters occurred outside Kurdistan proper, while Kurdistan itself was more isolated. However, with the Silk Road not far away, during its heaviest centuries of use there must have been many encounters between Kurds and people from far places both Eastern and Western.

Kurdistan suffered under the Mongol invasion and ensuing devastation of much of Southwest Asia in the thirteenth century. The Battle of Chaldiran in 1514 decided the borders between the Ottoman and Safavid territories and resulted in the majority of Kurds living under the Ottomans thereafter. Historian David McDowall (2004) argues that the battle ushered in "a period of relative stability" (26). It might have been more appropriate for McDowall to italicize his use of the word "relative," since he goes on in the pages to follow to describe a number of contests and conquests within Kurdistan. Still, there was *relative* stasis until a period of tremendous violence and shifting political control began in the first half of the nineteenth century, when the declining Ottoman Empire instituted reforms and sought to introduce more direct rule.[18] This ultimately led to the fall of all of the Kurdish principalities that had been nearly sovereign, under only loose Turkish control, for hundreds of years.

Despite Kurdistan's important role in human prehistory and occasionally in history, it can be argued, if one is looking only at the period since the Industrial Revolution, that globalization came late to Kurdistan, or at least that it has come in fits and starts. Jean-Baptiste Tavernier, who died in 1689, was the first Westerner to enter the Kurdish mountains in recorded history (J. Joseph 2000:73). By the 1830s, Kurdistan was receiving Western travelers on a regular basis, and at least a few people had a sophisticated understanding of global geopolitics. American missionary Asahel Grant described an encounter with one of the Bahdinan princes of Amadiya (probably Ismael Pasha) on 1 July 1836: "[W]hile speaking of the English, as we are called, he remarked that people say that the English visit every country and write what they see, and then send and take it. Upon my observing, that he certainly could have nothing to fear from the Americans who live eight thousand miles distant, he very shrewdly inquired whether America was not very far from England, and if the English did not first learn what that country was, and then take possession of it" (American Board of Commissioners for Foreign Missions 1837:58).

Kurdistan has had ties to its east for many centuries. For example, in the seventh century the Nestorian church, forebear of today's Assyrians, sent missionaries all the way to East Asia from what is today Kurdistan. Much later, important Naqshbandi leader Shaikh Khalid al-Baghdadi of Silemani studied under a sufi master in India and returned to have a major influence on sufism in Kurdistan in the mid-nineteenth century. As C. A. Bayly and Leila Fawaz have noted, "[T]he Mediterranean–Middle East and Indian Ocean–South Asia zone was, in fact, a unity constructed by a myriad of long-range connections of migrant communities, trade links, and religious doctrines" (2002:7).

For the most part, however, Kurdistan's recent relationship to the broader world emerged slowly before Iraqi Kurds' dramatic introduction to the world, and the world's introduction to Kurds, in 1991. British explorer Austen Henry Layard wrote during a mid-nineteenth-century visit to the Armenian and Kurdish town of Bitlis that "[t]here was a fair show of Manchester goods and coarse English cutlery in the shops. . . . The trade is chiefly in the hands of merchants from Mosul and Erzeroom, who come to Bitlis for galls, at present almost the only article of export from Kurdistan to the European markets" (Layard 1853:36). Centuries of contact and trade had come down to Kurdistan exporting only an unprocessed commodity gathered from its hillsides to the neighboring continent flush with activity from the Industrial Revolution. A few decades later, oil, a commodity of vastly greater significance, would be discovered just outside Kurdistan, affecting its fortunes for a century and beyond.

Basic infrastructure would arrive in the late twentieth century. In 1956, author "W.L.E." asserted, "As more motor roads are built connecting with the Ruwanduz frontier route, it will be only a matter of time until most of the valleys and their products are accessible to civilization and markets" (1956:422).[19] Linguist Margaret Kahn wrote of her time in Iranian Kurdistan that in 1974–1975 she "saw the first paved roads connecting Rezaiyeh [Urmia] to nearby cities, the first inter-city telephone service, and the first all-free public school system" (1976:6). Today there are still a few villages in Kurdistan that are accessible only on foot, but the trek between the village and the nearest road is no longer a long one, and/or the village is not inhabited year-round. Roads through Kurdistan's mountain valleys and canyons are still important, but they are unlikely to be the first thing to come to mind when one thinks of accessibility to "civilization" or "the outside." In that contest, they have been resoundingly trumped by the jet airplane and the satellite downlink.

British Colonization as Prelude to Globalization

Prior to the current era that began in 1991, Kurdistan was last in the global spotlight in the 1920s, the decade during which it ceased to be identified on most maps. By the end of World War I, the British had solidified their hold on most of present-day Iraq with the exception of the mountainous Kurdish areas, where they met fierce resistance in some locations. Oil was fast becoming the world's most vital energy product. It was discovered by the mainly European-owned Turkish Petroleum Company in impressive quantities below the plains areas near the Kurdish mountains. The Ottoman Empire had fallen. The European winners of World War I and the Young Turks haggled over how to partition the former Ottoman territories, including Kurdistan. Should Kurdistan become an independent state? The Treaty of Sèvres in 1920 had provided a pathway to such an outcome, but it was never ratified and was replaced by the Treaty of Lausanne in 1923, the same year that Mustafa Kemal founded the Turkish Republic. In a few short years, the Kurdish Question went from debating exactly where a new ethnologically defined state's borders would be, to the completely differ-ent question of the location of the border between the new states of Turkey and Iraq, contentious because of the discovery of oil. Various ideas were floated. In 1925 Sir Ronald Lindsay, British ambassador to Turkey, sug-gested that some territory between the small Kurdish towns of Amadiya and Rowanduz be ceded to Iran (Olson 1989:141). Another proposal had the border at the Great Zab River, which is also a dialect border between the southern Sorani Kurdish dialect and northern Kurmanji Kurdish, the local variant of which is referred to as "Behdini" after the Bahdinan Principality that formerly ruled the same area. However, the British, desirous of includ-ing the oil-rich Mosul *vilayet* in Iraq, won out. Ethnolinguistic logic, logic more in line with the idealizing of "nation" and "state" as hand and glove, was outdone by petroleum-seeking, capitalist logic. The Kurmanji-speaking area long at the heart of the Middle East has had the Iraq-Turkey border running across it ever since.

Globalization's impact on Kurdistan in the twentieth century was somewhat paradoxical. The British Empire, the largest empire in the history of the world and a major force in the process of globalization by any measure, had a significant presence in Iraq when it was still under the Ottomans, and was even more involved as a direct colonizer and state-builder after it was awarded the Iraq Mandate by the League of Nations in 1920. The British faced rebellion in the Kurdish areas, and it was costly. Rupert Hay and John Paul Rich (2008:255) list a series of killings of British colonial officers in 1919 that makes it very clear that the British were not welcome in Kurdistan at that time. But Iraq was clearly a priority for the crown despite its considerable holdings elsewhere in the world. "In the Royal Air Force there are thirty-three fully formed squadrons—21 overseas, as follows:" notes the Aircraft Year Book of 1923, "1 on the Rhine, 1 on the Mediterranean, eight in Iraq, 6 in India, 5 in the Middle East. Twelve squadrons are maintained in the British Isles" (Faurote et al. 1923:168). Superior weaponry helped it to hang onto restive Iraq in the short run, but could not prevent Britain from losing Iraq to revolution in 1958.

The British put a great deal of energy in Iraq into trying to bring the Kurds under their control. Thousands died in the process. Some parts of Kurdistan were friendly to British administrators, and some were not, but throughout the country, the British presence in Iraq laid a foundation for Kurds' and Iraqis' connections to the wider world. English was well on its way to becoming the language of globalization, and it was the second language (or third, in those few areas in and around Silemani with Kurdish-language classrooms) studied by educated Iraqis. Even when I arrived in 1995, nearly four decades after the British had been expelled, English speakers were very easy to find in Iraqi Kurdistan, whereas just across the border in Turkish Kurdistan, there were very few (this has changed since then and English is now in much wider use across Turkey). The educational model that I found used at all levels of Iraqi education, and to some extent had to use myself, when I taught at the University of Dohuk for one term in 1998, was a mix of midcentury British and Ba'thist authoritarian educational styles leavened with pan-Arabist and socialist ideology. Although changes are taking place, this educational style is still to a great deal operative in

Iraq. It transmitted a nationalism that, for all of its insularity, also had a cosmopolitan side to it. In secondary-school English-language textbooks that were published while Saddam Hussein's Ba'thist regime was in power, role players travel to England, praise the Iraqi military, and recite their goals for Iraq to take its place among the great nations of the earth (Al-Hamash et al. 1993; Al-Hamash et al. 1998). A set of cosmopolitan ideas was handed down by the regime, but on its own terms. The regime wanted to show off its worldliness, and it wanted the population it ruled to assist in that endeavor, but only in the limited ways it saw as serving its interests.

The concept of genocide, an idea that is closely associated with the rise of the modern state and globalization, and clearly needed a neologism in the twentieth century due to its ubiquity, has its roots in the British relationship with Iraq. Simel is a small town that lies just off the main road between the larger towns of Dohuk and Zakho, the area where I have done the majority of my fieldwork. Simel is such an unassuming place that it might be difficult at first to see it as globally significant. But in 1933, the Iraqi army carried out a heinous attack there that was an outgrowth of a complex web of political contests involving the British, the Ottoman Empire, and later Turkish nationalists, Americans, Arab nationalists, and local ethnic leaders such as Kurdish chiefs. As R. S. Stafford writes, "In August 1933 the Iraqi Army—or at any rate, that portion of it in the north— was intensely anti-British, and a special flavor was given to the slaughter of the Assyrians because they claimed to be the friends of the British and had loyally served them" (2006 [1935]:152). Army personnel then killed several hundred Assyrian men (164) and raped the surviving women (162). Bakr Sidqi, the Iraqi military officer who staged the Simel massacre, was Kurdish, commanding a mainly Arab force. Despite his own ethnic identity, Sidqi had Arab nationalist sentiments and later staged a coup in Baghdad. Later in the twentieth century, the term "genocide" was coined by Polish lawyer Raphael Lemkin, who was inspired to use the term to refer to what occurred in Simel (Cooper 2008:18).

Economic Connections

The Iraqi Kurds' state of being cut off from the rest of the world in the years prior to 1991 carries with it a bit of irony. During the course of the Iran-Iraq

War, despite its abundant farmland and water for irrigation, Iraq gradually lost the ability to feed itself as it put its energies into waging conflict. By the 1991 Gulf War, the vast majority of foodstuffs were imported. Virtually all complex technological items such as cars were imported. Oil continued to be exported. So, even though most of Iraq's *people* were not engaging with the outside world, *goods* were coming and going on an expanding basis. Iraq had an increasingly robust material reliance on the global economy even as its population remained relatively cut off from global influences and cultural flows. That has now changed dramatically. The 2003 war by the United States and Britain against the Saddam Hussein regime had important outcomes for Iraq and Iraqi Kurdistan. Most significantly, the war meant the removal of the threat posed by the regime, and the reinclusion of the region in a recognized state which allowed for activities that required international legitimacy such as landing commercial aircraft. However, I noticed that Kurdistan was starting to feel much less cut off from the outside world earlier than that, around the turn of the millennium. Mostly this sense stemmed from the number of diasporans who were returning from abroad and bringing new ideas, and also from an increase in business ventures clearly funded by outside money. The region was much more peaceful due to a tapering off of hostilities between the KDP and the PUK, whose peshmerga fighters had been engaged in a civil war from 1994 to 1998. The PKK (Partiya Karkerên Kurdistanê, Kurdistan Workers' Party) was temporarily dormant following the capture and incarceration of its leader, Abdullah Öcalan, in 1999. The economy had improved due to a combination of the United Nations' Oil-for-Food program, a scheme that diverted income from Iraq's oil to buy food for its sanctions-squeezed population, as well as increases in embargo-breaking smuggling. The KDP and PUK had intensified their efforts to improve the general welfare through activities such as the coordination of village reconstruction and development efforts, the use of the Kurdish language in education, and improvements in infrastructure. A few people told me that these improvements had tempered their wishes to out-migrate, although Kurdish people continued to pour into Europe from Iraqi Kurdistan, thus frustrating public officials at both ends and providing endless discussion fodder for government representatives, aid workers, and journalists. The flow would be reduced to a trickle by 2003. In addition to the improved conditions in Iraqi Kurdistan, this was because it became much more difficult to cross the necessary borders without getting caught, and more difficult to get asylum once one was there. People who might otherwise have out-migrated thus stayed home and sought jobs and futures. Then came the 2003 invasion of Iraq by the United States and Britain. While the rest of Iraq was an active war zone in which thousands were dying, Kurdistan was mostly calm. The war led to a provisional government in Baghdad, which led to the recognition of Kurdistan as an officially autonomous region in the state of Iraq. Legitimacy in the eyes of the world's other sovereign states suddenly allowed for economic activity that had previously been impossible or necessarily clandestine. The stage had been set before the war for Kurdistan to open its economy to the world; the war inserted additional momentum into that process. Kurdistan became a peaceful staging zone, which boosted the economy, and it also attracted war tourists as a place where soldiers and contractors came during breaks and weekends to get away.

PHOTO 1.3 Nashwan Said Saib takes orders while Dildar Salih AbuBaker works in the background. Each of Kurdistan's bazaars has several juice bars, which are very popular with shoppers, especially in the summer. This is Kara Juice Shop, in the main bazaar of Dohuk, Iraqi Kurdistan, Iraq, on 6 June 2008. (Copyright 2009 American Anthropological Association. Photo by the author.)

When the United States invaded Iraq and deposed the Saddam Hussein regime in 2003, then, a period of dramatic change was already under way in Kurdistan. The pace of this change is still increasing. Local people are able to come and go with greater ease, and now a large foreign population ranging from Western professionals to South Asian laborers is resident and bringing with them new ideas and ways. Funded by taxes and tariffs from trade, oil, agriculture, remittances, as well as the war economy until the departure of the United States in 2011, Kurdistan is comparatively awash in capital.

On my last three field trips, two in 2008 and one in late 2010, I entered and departed the region by plane on Austrian Airlines and Lufthansa. The first time the plane was landing in Hewler, prerecorded landing instructions came on in three languages: German, English, and Sorani Kurdish. I looked around and saw several people who were visibly affected emotionally. As a recorded voice told us in Kurdish to bring our seatbacks to an upright position and fasten our seatbelts in preparation for landing, I, too, found the experience deeply touching and felt a bit of disbelief. A plane landing, instructions coming over the address system in the local language—these are very ordinary things in many parts of the world. But in Kurdistan, a former killing field full of people despised by many of their neighbors and lacking status as an independent state, such "ordinary" things had been a mere dream for a long time. The coming of such markers of participation in the global economy seemed all the more unlikely because much of the rest of Iraq remained unstable and dangerous.[20] Moreover, Kurdistan was just a short while ago considered by many Middle Easterners to be the backwater of Iraq. "Is it true?" people would ask me in Beirut when I was there between 2000 and 2006. "Is it true that the Kurds are really making something for themselves over there?" By this people usually meant that they heard that Kurdistan was peaceful, that it was relatively well governed, that it was becoming materially more prosperous and more technologically advanced. I would answer that indeed things were looking up in many ways.

Profound economic and social changes are taking place in the Kurdistan Region as it connects to the world beyond. Is this the same place of which historian Stephen Longrigg wrote that "[i]n appearance and amenities the 'Iraqi towns had by 1900 changed little for centuries" (1956:18)? It seems hard to believe. My sense is that this particular ethnographic present is a time of greater change in the Kurdistan Region's "appearance and amenities" than perhaps the previous 10,000 years. News of material, technological and economic "progress" now comes rapid-fire: A five-star Marriott Hotel is under construction! Oil is flowing! A huge mall, the largest in Iraq, is opening! A U.S. Consulate is opening! People say McDonald's is coming to Hewler! Yet another English-language private school has been founded! It is clear to any visitor to the area that in the past several years there has been a major infusion of capital. Vigorous construction is taking place in every city and in many towns, and ostentatious new products are for sale and expensive vehicles crowd the streets. A side of Iraqi Kurdistan that no one has seen before, an urban sophisticate side, is emerging. People talk of the region—at times disparagingly and at other times admiringly—as a place undergoing "Dubaification." The most obvious precedents for what is happening in Kurdistan are indeed in the Gulf, where a similar rise in fortunes has brought profound changes to everyday life (Kanna 2011; Limbert 2010). In 2010, at a conference on higher education convened by the regional Ministry of Higher Education, I spoke with a professor just in from England who could not seem to stop gushing about what he had seen in his stay of fewer than twenty-four hours. "They put me in the Rotana Hotel," he said. "[T]hat is the nicest hotel I have ever *seen*, much less stayed in!" Rotana is a Gulf brand, from Abu Dhabi.

The money being injected into Iraqi Kurdistan comes from a variety of sources. Trade, especially in goods crossing the borders with Turkey and Iran, has long been a major source of revenue both for the traders themselves and the government in the form of duties. The oil industry is the newest major source. The Norwegian company DNO began constructing exploratory drills just outside the town of Zakho in 2004, and struck oil on its very first try in 2006. Oil had previously been extracted in the area around Kirkuk. Kirkuk's status as a part of the Kurdistan Region is disputed, so its oil is controversial. Zakho's, however, is not, so the news of oil being discovered there nearly a century after it was found elsewhere in Iraq felt momentous. People in Kurdistan were so used to the idea that "Arabs have oil, and we Kurds do not" that my sense is that the news still has not sunk in yet for many people, especially those who have not yet benefited. The fact is that if the Kurdistan Region is able to avoid major conflicts and disasters and to improve its governance (and Iraq is able to do the same), within a few years it will become very, very wealthy in a per capita sense, even if the question of who will benefit remains open. The DNO discovery was followed by many more, and since then the Kurdistan Regional Government (KRG) has signed over forty new Production Sharing Contracts (PSCs) with foreign oil firms, and drilling infrastructure is being installed all over Kurdistan. A PSC typically includes a signature bonus and ongoing minority ownership dividends paid to the KRG, as well as the requirement to complete specific infrastructure projects.[21] The signings have continued even though Iraq has yet to approve a comprehensive hydrocarbons law, which would spell out the details of revenue-sharing between the region and the central government.

Construction is another major industry. The skyline of Hewler, a city that claims to be the world's oldest inhabited city (a claim also made about Damascus and several other cities), is now crowded with construction cranes and new and partially completed high-rises while international passenger flights land nearby. Flying into the ancient city of Hewler, one can see the old city clearly defined by its iconic citadel and the adjacent older parts of the city. Surrounding that, however, is a much larger area that is strikingly modern, much of it still under construction. Just a few years ago a building boom of this magnitude was unimaginable.

PHOTO 1.4 A new park and buildings in Hewler's city center, taken from the ancient citadel. 2010. (Photo by the author.)

This scene from my field notes illustrates how Iraqi Kurdistan has caught the attention of international business:

Field Note, 20 June 2008:

I'm writing this on the plane from Hewler to Vienna. . . . The plane is mainly populated by 50- and 60-something white males, both Europeans and Americans. . . . They seem out of place somehow. This plane took off from Kurdistan, so it seems to me like the people on it should be, in some way, representative of the Kurdistan population, but clearly they are not. The middle-aged white American man in front of me is reading *Fever & Thirst*. . . .[22] Now and then he carries on loud conversation with the man across the aisle. He's conspicuously chewing gum. He, like most of the other men on this plane, is wearing a hyper-functional wristwatch that probably has a GPS, altimeter, the works. . . . The middle-aged man next to me appears to be German . . . he flips through a manual entitled, "Qualitätsmanagement und Prozessmanagement Grundlagen [Quality Management and Process Management Principles]," Version 2008.

Much of the capital being injected into the Kurdistan economy consists of investment on which a return has not yet been realized. Its effect, however, is felt in many households and has changed many people's standard of living, in some cases profoundly. Even the credit crisis of recent years seems to have done little to curtail economic growth. This may be because there is very little lending by banks in Iraqi Kurdistan and Iraq. "The credit crisis that is going on in most of the world is not affecting us because everything runs on cash here," a businessperson told me in 2008. "It is good for us, actually. We are insulated because there is hardly any credit here." Another way to look at Kurdistan's economic growth despite the crisis is that the investors from outside the area are so optimistic following the discovery of tremendous oil reserves in Iraqi Kurdistan that they have pushed through any difficulties and found a way to generate the capital.

In 2010 I saw evidence of significant material improvements in the lifestyles of some people I knew, improvements that had taken place since my last visit in 2008. One nuclear family, members (except for the wife/mother) of the Haweri lineage with whom I have periodically stayed since the late 1990s,[23] had struggled economically to the point that they were involuntarily living with another family in the lineage just a few years earlier. In 2010, I found them newly wealthy from trade, and living in a luxurious new villa. My friend gave me a tour of the house and emphasized her new double kitchen, excitedly showing me how it has a "back stage" food preparation area that is not to be seen by guests, and another area intended to be seen. It was clear that she used the former every day, but the latter she kept spotless. In another household, three young Haweri men who had been out of work on my previous trips were employed as couriers with oil companies and their subcontractors. Their salaries were not high; another employee in the oil industry told me that unskilled workers are paid about $25 per day, but it was enough for them to afford payments on a newish SUV, which they proudly showed off. Since then, I have seen photos on Facebook of one of them visiting Istanbul with friends, his first time to fly on a plane and travel abroad. Yes, all three men are on Facebook.

Iraqi Kurdistan remains a place of tremendous political uncertainty. Will Sunni Arabs rise again in Iraq and try again to crush the Kurds? Will Shi'i Arabs, who now dominate the Iraqi government, try to do the same? What about Iran? What about Turkey? What if Israel and Iran went to war? What about the border dispute between the region and Baghdad over Kirkuk and the undefined areas near Mosul, and smaller-scale disputes within Kurdistan, some of which go back decades? There has been a new uprising, as well. Inspired by the "Arab Spring" taking place in Tunisia, Egypt, and elsewhere, for sixty-two days beginning in mid-February 2011 protesters gathered in Silemani to challenge the KRG, demanding more transparency and accountability. In clashes between the protesters and KRG security forces, ten people were killed and many more on both sides injured. The economic changes taking place in Kurdistan have negative aspects, of course. One is that little attention is being paid to heritage preservation, and bulldozers are busy removing those old houses and buildings that had not changed in a long time, those few that were left after the destructive twentieth century. There are many urgent environmental problems. Poverty persists. Perceptions of corruption are high. The economy is not diverse enough, which leaves people especially vulnerable to the swings of the global market. Some of the economic growth is attributable to the Iraq War and occupation.

In short, the new era has its downsides, and there remains plenty to worry about if one wants to. What is indisputable at present is that for being a place purportedly on the margins of the system of global states and economies, Iraqi Kurdistan begins to feel as though it is transitioning to a position closer to the center. It is not yet connected in the sense that it is a full participant in the world of global knowledge dissemination, consumption, capital flows, freedom of movement, and so on. A considerable portion of the flow of goods in and out has been illicit, a practice perfected during the sanctions years but one that in all likelihood still comprises a large portion of Kurdistan's GDP (as Nordstrom [(2005)] argues, such flows are everywhere). It is connecting, however, at a dizzying rate. It is, in the process, a place where some of the "big questions" of connecting to the global economy, state-building, and civil liberties are being voiced and reckoned with. It is also quite clear that connecting to the world is dignity inducing for people in Kurdistan. While I feel wistful at witnessing my beloved field site becoming less "itself" and more like "the world"—at least the "developed" world—at times such as when the plane was landing in 2008, I cannot help but feel happy for the people around me, since so many have expressed positive feelings toward the changes. Kurdistan as a place that is fully connected to the rest of the world may be only in process, but the process continues.

Connections of Ideas, Labor, and People

To ask many people in Kurdistan about their knowledge of the world in the past is to hear a chronology of significantly increasing awareness. It is one thing to eat a banana that has been imported from Lebanon or to drive a car that has been imported from Brazil as people did in the 1980s, but it is another thing to know about and be able to travel to Lebanon or Brazil. It is one thing to know that your son, who had been fighting in the Kurdish resistance in the 1970s, had been accepted as a refugee to the United States after a few years in a refugee camp. It is quite another to know which American state he is living in and to be able to telephone him or write him a letter or speak with him by Skype. In the years prior to 1991, people's access to and knowledge of the outside world was characterized by the former in each of these cases.

The Kurdistan Region of Iraq is not only a site for global flows of capital, but of ideas, labor, and people too. Mobile telephones connect residents easily and cheaply to the outside world. Migrants returning from abroad to the homes of kin and friends bring ideas and goods that transform the way people think about themselves and their place in the world. A great deal of Kurdish connecting happens long-distance now. Starting in the 1970s but with massive increases in numbers in the 1990s, thousands of Kurds settled in the West, where they began to learn a new way of life. Those in the workforce learned to balance longer work hours in the West with their ongoing social obligations within the Kurdish community. Women adapted to different food preparation techniques, for example, learning to chop vegetables on the counter rather than on a plastic cloth spread on the floor. Children learned what it meant to be "American" from their peers and teachers. However, none of these people, at least none I know, ceased to identify as "Kurdish" or ceased to be concerned with life and people in their homeland of Kurdistan. Rather, they settled into becoming diasporans, people who maintained their ethnic and homeland identity and social life like the people described by Linda Basch, Nina Glick Schiller, and Cristina Szanton Blanc (1994) and others. As "transnationalists," Kurds resident in the West maintained their connections to Kurdistan. By now, it seems that the majority of Kurdish adults whom I know in the United States have returned "home" to Kurdistan for at least one visit. "Who returned?" "Who is planning to return?" (from the diaspora). "Who went out?" "Who is planning to go out?" (from the homeland) are frequently addressed questions wherever Kurds live on the globe. Some people come and go regularly. All in the diaspora, and many in the homeland, use technology to keep in touch. Phones with discounted calling plans or cards are still common, but many people now make extensive use of the Internet as well.

My own engagement with Kurdistan has been greatly facilitated by communication technology, and in recent years Kurdistan has become a place where cultural hybridity and going back and forth have become increasingly normalized. By my trips in 2001 and 2002, I noticed that most strangers had ceased to automatically treat me as though I were "foreign," and they would frame a question tentatively as to who I was. No longer did they necessarily ask if I was an American, or where I was from, but oftentimes someone would ask, "Are you Kurdish?" They recognized a Western-ness about me, but thought I might be a Kurd from the West. I was usually traveling alone, and the idea of a Kurdish woman traveling alone had previously been unimaginable but was starting to be engaged in by a few female diasporans, so my alone-ness was no longer a clear signifier of difference. It also had to do with dress, since many Kurdish diasporans entered Kurdistan clad completely in "Western" clothing and lacking head coverings, so the fact that I did as well ceased to stand out so much. I, like those who are Kurds from the West, supplement my intermittent physical presence in Kurdistan with Skype, Yahoo Messenger, email, and Facebook, and I am sure my Kurdish interlocutors and I will also adopt whatever new technological tool is coming next.

Meanwhile, other diasporas now have contingents in Iraqi Kurdistan. Most foreign laborers, who never had a significant presence in Kurdistan but were once common in other parts of Iraq, left during the 1980s due to the Iran-Iraq War, and all but a hardy few had departed by the end of the 1991 Gulf War. They are back now in force, however, this time in much greater proportion in the Kurdistan Region than in the rest of Iraq, where some conflict that began with the invasion by the United States and Britain in 2003 still continues. On my trips since 2000 I have seen increasing numbers of people who appear to be from elsewhere performing the tasks of daily life—from a woman seen on the street assisting an elderly local woman into the back seat of an SUV whose appearance suggests she is from sub-Saharan Africa, to women who appear to be from South Asia buying large amounts of food in the market, to Ethiopian men working as baggage handlers in the airport.

Domestic laborers from countries already known for sending laborers abroad, such as Ethiopia and Indonesia, now do the main physical labor in many Kurdistani households. Men from South Asia, Georgia, Ethiopia, and elsewhere work as laborers in a variety of sectors, such as construction and the oil industry. As for skilled laborers and businesspeople, Michael Gunter has written that "15,000 Turks are working in Arbil and other parts of the Kurdish region, and Turkish companies make up two-thirds of all foreign firms there" (2011:105). In 2008, a KDP official told me that 5,000 Lebanese live in the region, and that they are very active in business, exceeded only by Turkish people in terms of their presence and investment level.[24] Turkish products, and signs of Turkish economic presence in the region, are not new, since businesses in Turkey began trading heavily with Iraq, including Kurdistan, in the 1990s. Some of the trade was licit, but much was illicit, illegal under international law, specifically the sanctions imposed on Iraq by the United Nations Security Council. A significant Lebanese presence, however, is new and now visible everywhere, from brands of products in the stores to restaurants and construction projects.[25]

Everything Has Changed Now!

"Everything has changed now" is a phrase I have heard on an increasing basis in Iraqi Kurdistan. To illustrate just how quickly things have changed, I present three vignettes.

1. In a conversation in Dohuk in the late 1990s, someone pointed to a certain house and told me in an envious tone, "That family has the first Western toilet in town!" A Western toilet, while to my thinking no better than a local-style toilet, clearly was cosmopolitan and superior, judging by her tone and further comments, to the person who volunteered this information to me. Then, there were still a few people in Kurdistan who apparently did not know that Western toilets existed, or if they had seen them on television, they did not fully understand how they worked. I remember explaining the differences to people on several occasions, telling them how in the West, people sit on toilets rather than squatting over a floor-level bowl as is done in Kurdistan (and across Asia). Today there are perhaps thousands of Western toilets in Kurdistan's homes and businesses (although they are still uncommon and far from preferred by most people) and it would probably be difficult to find anyone living in a city who had not seen one in Kurdistan itself. To many young people, the idea that until recently someone in Kurdistan might not have known about the two types of toilets would be a big surprise.

2. The Ba'th regime prohibited satellite dishes as part of its overall campaign to control information, in particular because it did not want information coming into Iraq from the "outside world." Once Kurdistanis broke away from Baghdad in 1991, having a satellite dish became possible since they were becoming widely available worldwide, and they also

became highly desirable. Now they can be seen atop virtually every house in urban areas, and many houses in rural areas; the programming beamed in promotes a materialistic, technology-rich life which many people have come to covet. People living on the other side of the boundary between the Kurdish and Baghdad-controlled areas, however, continued to be deprived until 2003. The government was clearly very committed to its policy of denying Iraqis access to the media aspects of globalization. A Kurdish woman from Baghdad related the following to me during a visit to the Kurdistan Region while the Saddam Hussein regime was still in power: "Did you know that in the government-controlled area it is forbidden to have a satellite dish? The penalty is six months in jail. They don't want us to have any contact with the outside world, to know what is going on out there, about the Internet, things like that. One of our relatives had a dish hidden on their roof, and the government found out and has been harassing them for months. They put one son in jail, and then they let him out and put another one in. One of them had exams, so they took him every day to the school and then back to jail again after the exam. All for having a satellite dish!!" Before 1991, Kurdistan, too, was under such restrictions. Afterward, people made very clear their desire to make up for lost time. A whole generation has now come of age on satellite television. Of the many available channels, some originate in the West and in regional countries such as Turkey and the UAE, and there are also several Kurdish satellite channels that are watched both in the homeland and the diaspora. Local television is also still important and has played a major role in promoting a distinctly Kurdish vision of the body politic in a media space that was previously dominated by the Iraqi government.[26]

3. "I have been working very very hard on this Internet system. It is my project," a man with a high-level position in the Kurdistan government told me in the city of Hewler in 2002. The project he was working on was large scale, potentially involving millions of households, but it was also highly covert. "I have had to be very creative with smuggling. I smuggled one part of it from China, another from somewhere else, another from somewhere else. . . . It involves using satellite link-ups, and people will connect through their home phone lines. It's going to be big, and we are very excited about it. You know, one of our biggest problems here is access. We can't land planes here. We have trouble getting people in and

out. But the Internet is a way for us to connect to the outside world, and the surrounding states can't do anything about it! We are creating a free enclave here even though we are surrounded by states that think differently." The project succeeded, and the Kurdistan Region now has many Internet users. Like many parts of the world, speeds are slow and upgrades are needed. But because of satellite technology, Kurdistanis did not need to wait for the Baghdad regime to change its ways, or for neighboring countries to allow cables into Kurdistan. They could connect to the rest of the world directly, through the sky.

Paradoxes

Although Iraqi Kurdistan has undergone tremendous change in the past twenty years and especially in the past decade, many people's daily lives remain much as they were before. While some people in Kurdistan are extremely "plugged in" to the outside world, spending significant amounts of time online or watching satellite television, others are much more isolated, or were until recently. Here is a field note that I wrote after a trip to a village high in the mountains, in the Barwari tribal area, which I visited as part of a convoy of picnickers on a beautiful day early in the picnicking season:

Field Note, 8 March 2002:

After we got out of our vehicles and were walking toward the village houses, a group of children came running up to us, with a few adults just behind them. The children were talkative and giddy and very cute. One small boy came up to us next to his mother. As they got close to us, he suddenly started to cry and clutch his mother's *dis-das* (house dress). "What's wrong?" someone in our party asked him. He wouldn't answer us, so his mother quietly asked him to tell her. He whispered the answer to her. She spoke gently back to him. Then she turned to us, laughing. "He has never seen eyeglasses before. He told me he is very afraid of you because of that." Two people in our group were wearing glasses. We all found this amusing and the boy gradually calmed down as his mother comforted him.

On another occasion, in 2008, I was in a different village in the same area of the Barwari territory. I was with a group of people, and a man in our party was named "Osama." He was Kurdish, from the Arab-majority city of Mosul. Osama is a common Arabic name, and many Kurds, especially those from ethnically mixed areas, also have Arab/Muslim names. We were visiting a family I knew.

Field Note, 15 October 2008:

I introduced Osama and the rest of our party to a woman in the village who appeared to be in her late thirties. When she heard Osama's name, she turned in my direction and I suddenly realized she was shaking with laughter. I asked her what was so funny. Continuing to chuckle, she said quietly so Osama would not hear her, "Just like Osama bin Ladin!" She kept her face turned away from Osama a bit longer. "Osama! Osama!" she continued to snicker, as though she had never met someone with that name and found it hilarious that it was a real individual's name.

I found the encounter noteworthy since it spoke to the woman's isolation. I do not believe someone from a more ethnically mixed area in Iraq, or an older person who had come of age in a town or city prior to 1991, would react that way. Everyone had heard of Osama bin Ladin, but then again everyone knew other people named Osama, so the name would not necessarily bring Osama *bin Ladin* to mind. This woman demonstrated with her reaction that she certainly knew who the famous Al-Qaeda leader was, but her access to that knowledge of global significance was direct and not mediated through personal exposure to Arab people and Arabic names. I thought her reaction spoke to the way in which Kurdistan is coming into its own in the world as an unmediated place, one that interfaces with the global on its own terms, and no longer through Arab, Turkish, or Persian intermediaries. It connects directly to a satellite without waiting for a fiber optic cable across Syria that never comes.

On another occasion that same week, Osama told me and several others that in 2004, he was driving in Mosul when he came to a U.S. military checkpoint. The Americans checked his ID, and when they saw the name "Osama" they reacted with alarm. "Because my first name is the same as

Osama bin Ladin's, they called for help, and six military vehicles came!" he said with a tone that indicated his amazement. After an intense interrogation, they let him go. Telling the story four years later, Osama was jovial, and we laughed with him as he told it, although it sounded as though the experience had been somewhat traumatic at the time. The reactions of the woman in the village, and those of the U.S. government and military, stood in tremendous contrast. For each, Osama bin Ladin was a referent, but for one, it was absurd and humorous, while for the other, he represented a *casus belli*. The Osama before us looked absolutely nothing like Osama bin Ladin. He was at least twenty-five years younger and significantly shorter, to list the two most obvious differences. A feeling of embarrassment at the apparent naiveté of some members of my country's military washed over me as Osama told his story. Did they actually think they might have Osama bin Ladin on their hands? Or did they think that perhaps Osama's parents had chosen his name because they admired bin Ladin, which might imply that this Osama, if he shared the same loyalties, was a danger to them? I admired the way Osama seemed to have taken the experience in stride.

"The future is already here—it's just unevenly distributed," joked science fiction writer William Gibson (Economist 2001). Indeed, each time I visit Iraqi Kurdistan, I see its contrasting levels of prosperity in sharp relief. My observations during a two-day period in December 2010 exemplify some of the contrasts. On the first day, I was in a village among an extended family of Yezidi Kurds who had fled a terrible blood feud that had resulted in several deaths and threatened to cause more bloodshed (I tell their story in more detail in chapter 6). They and their enemies were now separated by Kurdistan's internal boundary with the rest of Iraq, and their leader told me they felt reasonably safe. Upon touring some of their living quarters, however, I saw that they were short of comfortable in my own judgment, with overcrowding, sanitation problems, reduced access to food (since they had previously grown much of their own food), limited electricity, and no local access to schooling. Although their leader told me that they had left behind a relatively prosperous agricultural enterprise, it did not appear that they had been very well off to begin with. When I asked him how much income his business had provided, he said in a tone as if to emphasize its productivity, "My brother and I, we might get maybe 9 or 10 million dinars every year!" Ten million dinars is approximately US$8,500. That my interviewee, who had a very large family to feed, seemed in his tone to regard an annual income of half that as abundant, was perhaps his attempt to put a brave face on the situation, but it also suggested that he was a part of Kurdistan's (and Iraq's) large and, despite a significant upturn in the overall prosperity of people in the region, still somewhat desperate underclass. To lease, for a year, a very modest house in town would cost more than his annual income, and he was supporting a large family. I also gathered from a number of indicators that the family's over-all education level was low. One young woman revealed that she did not know how to read. A number of the young married women appeared to be no older than their mid-teens.

The second day, I was in Dohuk for a round-table discussion at the university there. We were in the university's beautiful and relatively new facilities, which had all of the infrastructure one would expect of a modern university, with constant electricity, climate-controlled comfort, clean facilities, computer labs, and so on. The event was sponsored by the British Council. A number of colleagues and I carried on a stimulating academic conversation. The shock of the contrast from one day to the next was already in the back of my mind when one of the colleagues, an Arab woman who had moved to Kurdistan from Baghdad and was teaching at the university said to me (in English, the language of the event), "I think by now every home in Kurdistan has a computer. People are on the Internet, they are completely connected to the outside world, and there is very little they don't know or have access to." Based on what I had seen the previous day as well as on many other occasions, I vehemently disagreed with her, citing as many examples as I could think of in the limited time we had to talk. I realized as we spoke that she lived in a bubble of people living a middle- or upper-class lifestyle. To have never been in the home of some-one who did not have a computer or Internet connection was to be unex-posed to thousands of local homes. They were visible everywhere, but apparently she had never been inside them. During the same trip, I came to understand her as living a busy professional life very similar, in terms of time allocation, to my own in the West, mainly focused on work and an already-established circle of family and friends. It seemed to me that whether she wanted to or not (and I did not ask), she did not have a lot of time to get to know the people around her who were not a part of the university-connected community. Moreover, she was part of a global academic enterprise, in Iraqi Kurdistan. I thought back to my own stint of teaching at Dohuk University in 1998, and remembered how cut off from the rest of academia I felt at the time. Those days are over. Kurdish academia is part of the global academic community.

The Remaining Chapters

In chapter 2, I document some of the challenges I faced in getting to and working in the field, and in so doing illustrate the challenges and dangers faced by Kurdistanis themselves in a zone of limited sovereignty and periodic outbreaks of horrific violence. I recount some stories from other parts of the Kurdish homeland, those in Turkey and Syria, to illustrate the kinds of social and political forces faced by people in the rest of Kurdistan. A modernizing mid-twentieth-century Iraq became increasingly closed to the world, and with the rise of Saddam Hussein it became a zone of intense totalitarianism. I describe how the Iraqi government went on a killing spree, using chemical weapons and bombs on Kurdish villages, resulting in around two hundred thousand dead and hundreds of thousands displaced. I describe some of the threats and fears I encountered in the years after these attacks.

Patriliny consists of a set of ideas about ancestry, kinship, and gender roles that center on lines of fathers and sons traced through time. In Iraqi Kurdistan, patriliny is coupled with the idea of patrogenesis, the idea that an infant is not constituted by mutual contributions from each parent, but that the father supplies the constitutive element and the mother is simply a vessel. Patriliny and patrogenesis are found throughout Kurdistan and provide a powerful set of symbols and practices with which people make their world (Goodman 2001). In chapter 3 I elaborate on these symbols and show how patrilines are connected to claims of origin in specific places, which lend identity to the members of the patriline. In globally connecting Kurdistan, it might be logical to expect patriliny to wane in importance, but that is not what I observe in the field. On the contrary, it continues to be the case that each "legitimate" member of society is a member of an identifiable patriline, descended from a particular man, who is associated with a particular location. Chapter 3 elaborates on this.

In chapter 4, I focus on the difficult balance many women are called upon to maintain in a Kurdistan that is connecting to the world. The logic of patriliny impels women to cloister themselves and their male kin to enforce their cloistering, and yet the new and globalized world invites them to exercise their "freedom" as "modern" women. Female education rates have skyrocketed in Kurdistan, creating some of the most dramatic intergenerational contrasts in the world as both nonliterate older women and highly educated younger women are now found within many families. Honor killings, which are sometimes portrayed in the West and in Middle Eastern nationalist and modernist narratives as symbolizing backwardness, seem to be on the increase in Kurdistan, and they are a major topic of conversation in both the public and private spheres. I have argued that honor killings are an outgrowth of patriliny and are only found in those parts of the world where kinship is understood patrilineally (King 2010). In some ways, Kurdistan's connection to the world seems to be shoring up the system of patriliny and patrogenesis rather than diminishing it as some might have predicted.

The Kurdistan Region is abuzz with politicking, a form of, and impetus for, connecting. As an "official" region within a state rather than a separatist region governed by authorities not fully recognized by the central state government in Baghdad, Kurdistan has held elections since 1992 and has many of the features of a democracy. It also has many of the features of an oligarchy, since two families dominate its politics. Its government has excellent relations with most Western countries, and has, in recent decades, been highly dependent on the United States for security and advocacy on the international stage. In chapter 5, I explore political jockeying in Kurdistan. Such jockeying has long taken place between (prospective or actual) patrons and clients, and in the new global milieu this is more complex than in the past. Everyone, even a very powerful person, is a client of someone. A politician, or aspiring politician, tries to amass clients by behaving like a patron. Patrons must have something before they can give it away to others to gain their loyalty, so they busily cultivate their own patrons higher up the ladder. Rich, varied, and creative connecting is the result.

Chapter 6 is about people who seek refuge within and from Iraqi Kurdistan. I argue that contemporary Kurdish migrations complicate both primordial/local, and modern/global refuge and asylum regimes. Refuge seeking is connected to the global, but also contextualized patrilineally. How a refuge seeker is understood by the broader community and state, and what happens to that refuge seeker, is connected to the specific territory within the state from which everyone in their patriline is understood to hail, and ultimately is a concern of the state and the international refugee regime. I tell two stories. The first is of a group of Yezidi Kurds from outside the Kurdistan Region who fled a blood feud with relatives in which several people were killed. Following intervention by regional authorities and a tribal chief, they came to live in a village. The second account is of the experience of a man recently released from being held as a prisoner of war in Iran. Finding that "home" was not what he hoped it would be, he ultimately chose to out-migrate to Europe.

In chapter 7 I show how the Kurdistan Region of Iraq is a participant in the world's system of states, even though it is, technically, only a "region" within a state. It has offices in Western capitals that function like embassies. It conducts its own foreign policy business without going through Baghdad. Iraqi Kurdistan has long been called "autonomous" within Iraq, but in many ways it now exercises autonomy in the world, too. At the same time, it has become a center for Kurdish nationalism generally, a place where dissidents taking refuge from neighboring governments meet, and where linguists are refining the Kurdish language and authors are producing copious amounts of literature in it. Largely at peace after decades of war and suffering, it serves as a kind of "homeland" even for Kurds who are from the rest of Kurdistan and now belong to the Kurdish diaspora outside the Middle East. The Kurdistan Region is a connector of Kurds worldwide, and the new heart of what it means to be Kurdish. Without it, Kurdish identity in the world would be going in the direction of extinction as Michael Chyet (2003) predicted. With it, Kurds connect in Kurdistan, and in turn, to the world.

2

Fieldwork in a Danger Zone

The free world has listened for so long
To the pulse of oil deep in the heart of things
It has become humpbacked,
Stone deaf.
It doesn't hear the mountains burning.

–Abdulla Pashew (2004; used with permission)

In 1991, the Cable News Network (CNN) and other television channels broadcast the plight of the Kurds to the world. Thousands of people fled Saddam Hussein's military, up muddy, inhospitable slopes, afraid they would be attacked as they had been in previous years, when hundreds of thousands died. Millions of people around the world, including me, started following the developments in Kurdistan. Refuge seekers fled toward Turkey and Iran (United Nations High Commissioner for Refugees 1992), and reporters had assembled at the Turkish border to document their plight. "The Kurds" became a household phrase, and the refuge seekers' desperate state prompted a global outpouring of compassion and aid donations. The United States and its European allies sent troops in to start a relief effort beginning with airdrops of food and water, and this expanded into a full-scale relief program coordinated by the United Nations High Commissioner for Refugees (UNHCR). The military and relief effort coupled with a pullout by Iraqi troops resulted in the majority of those displaced returning to their homes by September 1991. With the assistance of an American military presence on the ground that lasted in a small way until 1996, ongoing relief and development programs by NGOs (nongovernmental organizations) and UN agencies, and a no-fly zone that prevented the Iraqi government from further attacks, most of the

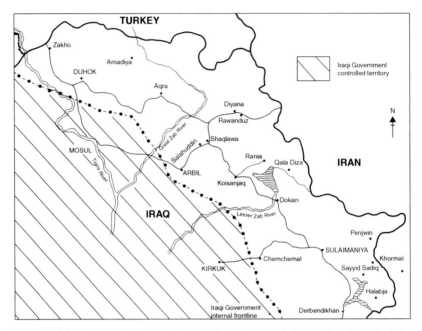

FIGURE 2.1 A map given to the author by an NGO staff member in Dohuk in 1998, showing the face-off line between the Iraqi military and the peshmerga. It was orally attributed to a local United Nations office. Many maps of Iraqi Kurdistan were circulating in the 1990s. Some NGO staff said that the maps lacked written attribution because their authors did not want to be perceived as endorsing territorial boundaries. (UN publicly released documents are in the public domain.)

Kurdish-majority area of Iraq became a rebel zone under Kurdish control, beyond the reach of the Baghdad government. The zone approximated the area of three of Iraq's eighteen governorates. Aided by the West, mainly the United States, the 1991 Kurdish uprising, one of many in the past century, held its ground, and Iraqi Kurdistan has been a "de-facto state" (Prados 1994) or a "quasi-state" (Natali 2010) since then.[1]

The Kurdish rebel zone became a globalized zone seemingly overnight that spring of 1991. Members of Western institutions—the press, militaries, government aid apparatuses, and NGOs—were there documenting and rescuing and inserting into the global record the story of what was happening, such as in UN meeting minutes, Agence France-Presse articles, and BBC radio broadcasts. As local people later told me, seeing representatives of "the outside," which people in Kurdistan call the world beyond Iraq and its immediate neighbors, was a completely new experience. Some of these representatives, such as American Robert Brenneman (2007), stayed for several years and became familiar faces to many local people. But for Iraqi Kurdistan to assume a globalness itself would take longer. Kurdistanis would have to find their own way to connect to the world, and go about inviting and allowing the world to connect to them. As I write this in the second decade of the next century, that is what is now happening, and vigorously. The inhabitants of Kurdistan are what Hannerz (1987:547) calls "involved in an intercontinental traffic in meaning."

I took more specific interest in the Kurds in 1994, when I was about to enter a Ph.D. program in anthropology and was searching for a research site. I was interested in a rural setting in the Muslim swathe of Asia. In early 1995, through volunteer organizations and churches that had been assisting Kurdish refugees, I met Kurds in the United States who had arrived as refugees a few years prior. They enthusiastically encouraged me to do research in their homeland.

The following summer, 1995, I entered Kurdistan on an exploratory five-week trip to investigate possibilities for a longer stay for Ph.D. dissertation research in sociocultural anthropology (King 2000), intended to begin the following year. Little did I know that multiple challenges and dangers would lie ahead. My main point in documenting them here is to illustrate the challenges and dangers faced by Kurdistanis in a zone of limited sovereignty and periodic outbreaks of horrific violence. I also present it to make the point that logistics and epistemology cannot be separated. What I present in this book mainly comes from "being there" (Geertz 1998) in Iraqi Kurdistan.

Getting to Iraqi Kurdistan from abroad in the mid-1990s was not simple. The border between Turkey and Iraq was crossable only by those people who had local citizenship or family history, which did not apply to me as an American with no local ties, or by affiliates of NGOs and UN agencies. Turkey and the United States controlled the border. My first step before traveling to the area was to find an NGO to take me on as a research affiliate, which involved a great deal of networking by phone, fax, and in some cases email. A few people and agencies working in Iraq were just beginning to use email in 1995. Satellite phone connections were the only medium for international calls, faxes and email to NGO offices in Kurdistan, so each communiqué was very expensive. After a number of rejections, I was able to secure NGO affiliation in early summer 1995 with a nonprofit agency based in the United States, Medical Assistants International.[2] Each of us hoped to forge a collaboration that would result in improved service to the NGO's constituents once my research was written up. The staff directed me through the steps of sending my passport to the State Department for a stamp that would allow me to cross into Iraq from Turkey. The Turkish Foreign Ministry apparently took cues from the U.S. Embassy, verifying my possession of the requisite passport stamp. I found it strange that Turkey required a stamp from another government to allow one of that government's citizens to cross out of its own territory.

I then flew to Turkey and went through an additional process of securing border-crossing permission from the Ministry of Foreign Affairs, which took several days. With permission secured from American and Turkish authorities, I was allowed to cross into Iraqi Kurdish territory from the area of Turkey that is mainly populated by ethnic Kurds, and began a five-week stay in June 1995. One of the Medical Assistants International staff members met me at the border and arranged for me to stay with a Kurdish host household in the city of Dohuk. It was headed by "Layla," a widow with twelve children ranging from teenagers to midlife adults, five of whom still

PHOTO 2.1 Passport stamp issued to the author in 1996 granting authorization to travel to Iraq. A similar one had been issued in 1995. (Photo by the author.)

lived with her. Several of Layla's children worked for a different American NGO and spoke some English. Layla also hosted an American nurse who worked for the same NGO. I was thrilled to have a place to live in which I was surrounded by the regular rhythms of household life, rather than in a separate dwelling and with a bodyguard like most foreigners.

On that first visit to Iraqi Kurdistan I experienced a variety of difficulties. The regime in Baghdad remained hostile toward Kurdistan, even though it was not currently attacking, but there were hardships that had lingered since open conflict, such as electricity turned off during the sweltering summer, and land mines posing a danger. A new war had broken out, a civil conflict between the KDP and PUK that had started the year before, and a conflict between the Turkish military and the guerrillas of the PKK was taking place partly on Iraqi Kurdish soil. The UN Security Council had responded to Iraq's invasion of Kuwait in 1991 and its refusal to fully abandon its WMD (Weapons of Mass Destruction) programs by imposing economic sanctions on the whole country, which included Kurdistan. As a result, many products, such as parts to fix a broken vehicle or appliance, were unavailable. I also caught malaria just as I was leaving, and fell extremely ill shortly after returning to the United States. Still, I had a productive and thoroughly enjoyable time, carrying out pilot research and making side trips to villages and other cities throughout the Kurdistan Region. People were overwhelmingly receptive of me and the idea of my research, and my host family and I seemed to click instantly. I was a few years older than the median age of Layla's twelve children. In addition to five of them still living at home, the others, except for one who lived abroad in Europe, visited often. Several spoke English, having learned it in school and by working for an American NGO. We often stayed up late jovially telling stories, and sometimes when I hired one or two of Layla's children to guide me on a side trip, more came along just for fun.

I returned to the United States with a plan to begin in-depth research the following year, 1996, on villagers' perceptions of Western relief and development efforts. The items in my luggage that I prized the most were letters endorsing my research plans: one from the governor of the Dohuk Governorate; another from the *muxtar* (mayor) of the picturesque mountain village where my host family had previously lived and where I planned to base my research; and another from the president of Dohuk University

inviting me to teach there and be tutored in the Behdini Kurmanji dialect
of Kurdish when I returned to the region.

The Kurdistan Region of Iraq is now a place where the global is
potently on display, a place to and from which ideas, goods, and people
flow in great numbers and with relative ease. It has not always been so. The
first time I crossed into Iraqi Kurdistan, on foot after being dropped off by
a shared long-distance taxi on the Turkish side of the bridge on the
Khabur River at the Ibrahim Khaleel border crossing, my feeling of being
an "other" entering a place where I was an utter outsider could hardly have
been more intense. I was not alone there as an American; in addition to
NGO staff from the United States, USAID (United States Agency for International Development) had a visible presence, as did the U.S. military (out
of a small outpost in the border town of Zakho), but it seemed to me that
there was a very strong division between "we" Westerners, people from
Europe and its settler states such as the United States, and "they," the local
population. On that trip I stood out clearly as a "foreigner," and the
Westerners and locals seemed to observe each other, not as coparticipants
in a globalized social field, as can be argued is now the case, but as two
populations on contrasting sides of a great cultural, material, and experi-
ential divide.

I could not know during my first research stint in Iraqi Kurdistan in
1995 that the Westerners' significant presence there was to abruptly come
to an end with the sudden evacuation of USAID, the U.S. military, and
many relief agencies the following year. In late August 1996, Iraqi troops
entered Hewler, Iraqi Kurdistan's largest city, and carried out targeted
assassinations, going door to door and killing those on their list on the
spot. In conjunction with this, President Saddam Hussein issued a death
threat to all Westerners and Iraqis who associated with them. Most Westerners, almost all of those I had met on my previous trip, fled, and their
agencies closed or sharply cut back their programs. When these events
took place, I had just arrived in Istanbul and was about to make my way to
eastern Turkey in preparation to again cross the Habur border bridge into
Iraqi Kurdistan for an eighteen-month stay. Instead, I was delayed in crossing the country for two and a half weeks by an illness in Istanbul that was
probably food poisoning and that resulted in three hospital stays. Kind
American strangers who were living in Istanbul took me in after learning

about my situation. While I was still recovering, I got the terrible news about the events in Iraqi Kurdistan. As soon as I felt well enough to fly, I flew across Turkey to the eastern city of Diyarbakir, the unofficial capital of Turkey's Kurdistan region, to join the Medical Assistants International staff who had evacuated. Arriving on 12 September, I found an assortment of Westerners and local people, mostly elites whose connections or money allowed them to flee across the border. Nechirvan Barzani, who later became prime minister of the Kurdistan Region, was among those staying at the Hotel Grand Kervansaray, an iconic hotel that has long been an important meeting point in the area and which became an informal hub for the exiles. I also stayed there during the first few days, and first met Barzani in the Kervansaray's courtyard. Such was the heatedness of the situation in Iraq, that an up-and-coming leader in the Barzani lineage was temporarily sequestered outside the country.

During those difficult days in Diyarbakir, made more difficult by the local war between the Turkish military and the PKK, my goal oscillated between achieving my original objective of crossing the border to resume my research and preserving my own life and those of Iraqi Kurdish friends I had made the year before who pleaded with me by phone to help them flee. In one case, the pleading took place in person, when Layla sent one of her young adult sons to Turkey to ask me to use my power, power I deject-edly told him I did not have, to get them out of there.

The weeks dragged on, and summer 1996 turned into fall. Initially, the situation across the border in Iraq seemed to be calming, and I had turned my attention to trying to cross the border to carry on with my fieldwork. However, neither the Turkish Ministry of Foreign Affairs nor the U.S. Embassy would allow me to cross. I placed phone calls to the embassy again and again, but its representatives resolutely told me that they and the Foreign Ministry were in agreement that the only Americans allowed to cross would be those who needed to briefly enter to retrieve their belongings before leaving for good. Out of alternatives and running out of funds that could be spent anywhere other than my field site, I returned to the United States on 29 October and began an unplanned year among Kurdish refugees.

First, I went to a West Coast city and visited a classroom for female refugee learners of English. I asked the Kurdish students if any of them would be willing to let me live with them and study the Kurdish language, and one woman, "Asiya," enthusiastically invited me to move in with her family. Her husband was temporarily away, working in another city, and she was struggling to raise their five children alone. She welcomed having another adult in the household. I stayed with them for several months, developing some understanding of their lives as well as the language. I also had the privilege of developing close friendships in the local Kurdish community that continue to the present.

Then, in late fall 1996, the United States government decided, belatedly I thought, but at least it had decided, to evacuate 6,500 people from Kurdistan who had worked for USAID and U.S.-based NGOs. It considered them to be in danger due to the same events that had displaced me. Some had also been on the payroll of U.S. intelligence agencies, tasked by the Clinton administration with overthrowing the Iraqi regime. Then I was offered a job coordinating a resettlement program in another West Coast American city for some members of the NGO group, employees from my sponsoring NGO Medical Assistants International from Zakho, a town of approximately 50,000 located near the Turkish and Syrian borders. I had not previously met most people in the group because I had been based in Dohuk, a city of approximately 200,000 people located one hour by car to the south, but there were a few "small world" experiences anyway. I started work on 27 February 1997, and the asylees began arriving the next day. Once when I went to the airport to welcome some of the new asylees in my resettlement caseload, one young man and I recognized each other from the very brief time I had spent in Zakho in 1995. We marveled at the strange series of events, which we agreed neither of us could have anticipated in our wildest imaginations, that had led to our being on the other side of the world together a year and a half later. Five members of my old host family also came to the United States and were resettled in a large city in the middle of the country. I flew out to visit them a few months after they arrived. We played tourist together, and we marveled, too. I was incredulous that thousands of people from my field site had suddenly come to my country when I was scheduled to be living in theirs, and the novelty of this made my involuntary detachment from my intended field site a bit easier to bear. That whole year, however, I hoped for and investigated possibilities that could lead to my return to Iraqi Kurdistan so I could resume my research there.

After more than a year of uncertainty, I finally was able to return in November 1997. The KDP, one of the two main rebel groups that had come to comprise Iraqi Kurdistan's government and that later came to be known as the KRG, had an office in Damascus. Unlike with Turkey, there was no cooperation between the United States and Syria vis-à-vis the border. Rather, the Damascus KDP office liaised directly with the Syrian authorities on my behalf, requesting that I be allowed to cross a makeshift border on the tiny strip of the Tigris River that was shared by Syria and the Kurdish autonomous area in Iraq. I had regularly telephoned the KDP offices in Washington and Damascus during the year, begging to be allowed across the river so I could resume my research. Although the officials I had talked to had uttered affirming words, they were moving slowly. So, in the fall of 1997 I flew to Damascus to request the permission in person, much to the surprise of the man behind the desk in the KDP office who had been receiving my calls from America. After a few more days of waiting, during which my request was, the KDP staff told me, under review by the Syrian *mukhabarat* (secret police), I was given an eight-digit border-crossing number. I was to present this number at the riverside kiosk on the Tigris. If it matched the number on file there, then I would be allowed to cross. The KDP operated a van service between its office in Qamishli, a Kurdish-majority city in the northeast, and the riverside. The area was a military zone open only to those vehicles that the government approved. Along the way was plenty of evidence of Syria's status as a police state. Children walked to school wearing uniforms that looked more appropriate for a military than a school. Guards recognized the van and waved us through an area fortified with fences and razor wire. Finally we were at the river and thus the border. The several buildings on the Syrian side of the river were small and unassuming, and I could see across the river to an even more makeshift-looking complex to which I was headed on the other side.

As I opened the small notebook in which I had written my number and showed it to the man in the kiosk, I was nervous. Had I come all this way only to be played by the Syrian regime? But the number matched the one next to my name in a dog-eared log full of months' worth of names and numbers. Ecstatic, I was motioned down to the shore of the Tigris to make the crossing in the small boat with an outboard motor that served as a ferry for those fortunate enough to have been granted border-crossing permission. As I looked at the swift flow of the river, I remember thinking that if the boat motor failed, we would be swept downstream into Iraqi government controlled territory, where President Saddam Hussein's price on the head of Westerners like me, reportedly $10,000, was still in effect since its announcement in 1996. But the motor was a match for the current, and, feeling a rush of excitement sweep through my very being, I stepped out onto the soil of Iraqi Kurdistan for the second time. I was finally beginning the extended research period in Kurdistan that had been eluding me. I caught a taxi and headed to the home of the family that had hosted me in 1995, where I had the first in a series of heartfelt reunions.

Thus began a stay that was originally intended to be eighteen months, but that became eleven in large part due to a desire to preserve my safety. But there was an unanticipated dividend yielded by the traumatizing experience of the previous year: I entered Iraqi Kurdistan as an individual who now had to interface with the local population alone, without the help of a significant Western community. The NGO with which I remained affiliated on paper had virtually nothing to do with my research from that point on, since it had evacuated its entire foreign staff (and the U.S. government had evacuated the local staff) from the part of Kurdistan where I was working. Many other agencies had as well. Most of the foreign NGO staff I had met on my first trip were gone.

All along, I had expected to reconnect with people in Dohuk whom I had met in 1995, and I planned to stay briefly with Layla before settling in the picturesque mountain village. But Layla had lost five children to the evacuation, and I had wondered how well I would fit in now that the family was so radically reconfigured. Moreover, when I arrived I found that one of her children, her teenaged daughter Viyan to whom I had become close in 1995, had died suddenly in the intervening year. Of Layla's children who still lived under her roof, only two daughters had declined to go to America, and now one, Viyan, was dead. Layla and her remaining daughter were in a terrible state of grief, and now I was, too. My first few days with them were numbing. I also found that my intended research village had evacuated in the face of threats from the PKK, which was using it and other Iraqi Kurdish villages as bases from which to attack Turkish military and civilian targets.[3] The PKK had begun to attack Iraqi Kurds, too. Shaken by this bad news, I thought back to the time I and others from the village had been hiking up the mountain from it in 1995, and we had encountered a young man dressed in the type of clothing the PKK wears and carrying a Kalashnikov. The area was remote. What was most eerie was that the man had not greeted us in the usual manner, but had simply stared at us and then disappeared behind some trees. One old woman had stayed on in the village, and I feared for her safety.

However, there were some consolation prizes. Layla and her youngest daughter may have been under severe stress along with their grief, and they ended up leaving for Syria to become refugees later in my stay, eventually joining their family members in the United States. But the extra time I had with them before their departure provided wonderful immersion in the world of their household and social connections. Besides, I had missed them very much. We all agreed that in 1995, we had truly felt like a family. Now, five members were in the United States, and I had visited them there. It seemed that they viewed me as a thread running through their broken family, and I did my best to play that role for them in our time together before they left.

Moreover, I gained a whole new set of relationships in the town of Zakho that were a result of the evacuation the previous year. The asylees I had worked with and met in the United States had urged me to visit their families in Zakho when I returned, and I was also couriering letters, small gifts, and money for them. Returning to Kurdistan in 1997 and leaving the asylees, now immigrants, behind in America had felt deeply ironic and even sad, but to say that their relatives warmly welcomed me back to Iraqi Kurdistan would be an understatement. Within the first few days Layla, her youngest daughter Zozan, and I traveled to Zakho, where they visited relatives and I went down my list of families to visit and deliver the couriered items, usually arriving at the next house driven by one of the earlier families on my list. Although I was meeting most of the Zakho families for the first time, due to my status as a person who had helped their relatives in America, they greeted me as though I were a long-lost daughter. Several families vigorously invited me to live with them. One family even quarreled with another over who would host me. I went on to spend the next eleven months splitting my time between Zakho and Dohuk, usually spending half the week in each. I was based in one Zakho household with a family in the Haweri lineage, whom I describe later in this book. In Dohuk, I stayed with

Layla and her daughter for a few months, but then moved on to the household of a young woman from another area of Kurdistan who was in Dohuk working for the UN and wanted a housemate. In both cities, I frequently stayed in several other households. I periodically stayed in villages as well. All of this moving around helped me to get a broad sense of what household life is like in Kurdistan. I saw the daily lives of, and developed deep bonds with, a diverse set of individuals and families. With the relatives of the evacuees, I especially had a feeling of connectedness due to all that we had experienced and because of my own role as a person whose job it had been to help their beloved sons, daughters, siblings, and other kin get settled after they had been whisked off to a far continent.

As of this writing in 2012, I have spent ten research stints in the Kurdistan Region of Iraq, most recently in December 2010. I have continued to stay in households and avoid less socially immersive forms of accommodation such as hotels (except when on a trip for business other than research, such as in 2008 and 2010, when I was invited by the regional government and universities to give presentations). I have also carried out periodic fieldwork among Kurdish communities in the United States (mainly in two West Coast cities), in Lebanon, and online. I went on to build much of my research around the relatives of the evacuees, and, aided by their hospitality, to carry out a research method I came to call "embodied" research. Such research involves the greatest immersion that is practical in local daily life and the deliberate avoidance of creature comforts that might put social distance between me and the people around me. In the early years especially, eating the same food, sleeping on the same floor cushions (*dosek*), and huddling by the same space heaters (*sope*) in winter meant living quite differently from what I was used to, and differently from many of the foreign professionals working in Kurdistan for development agencies, and now for the many foreign firms that are setting up businesses there. But it allowed for very rich relating.[4]

Even on some of my shorter trips, when research in a relatively hurried fashion has been necessary (a kind of research Mary Hegland [2004] calls "zip in and zip out" fieldwork), by returning to some of the same households year after year and slipping into the rhythms of household life shortly after arriving, my research has had a continuity to it that would not otherwise have been possible.

From the very beginning of my research in the mid-1990s, Kurdish families took me in and treated me as one of their own. At first I was taken aback by their warmth. Was it genuine? What did they want from me? I found that Kurdistan is indeed a rich site of complex social exchange, and many more interactions than I was used to involved, it later came to light, jockeying in the service of particular interests. And yet even if all of that were subtracted, Kurdistan was still a genuinely warm place. On the whole, people are very kind to outsiders, at least outsiders belonging to many identity categories, including my own. My daily experience on most research visits has had a very ordinary quality to it, with research activities such as observation and interviewing being subject to the regular rhythms of household activities—children going off to school in the morning, meals being served at their customary times depending on the season, and so on. In recent years, however, I have had more contact with high-level public officials than I did previously. As a professor working in the West who studies the region, politicians sometimes request meetings with me, and occasionally I have requested meetings and interviews with them.

As one of the places in the world where more people died violently in the last few decades of the twentieth century than anywhere else, social research in Iraqi Kurdistan has also been a casualty. Hamit Bozarslan (2000) listed "the difficult conditions of conducting research in the field" as one of the obstacles affecting research in Kurdish studies: "Kurdish scholars can return to their home countries and conduct field work only if they pay a very high cost that can include imprisonment and death. But for non-Kurdish scholars the work conditions are also hard. Many of them are refused a visa and almost none of them can have access to the field. They must worry about compromising the security of the people interviewed for academic purposes."

While I faced a set of serious dangers in my early fieldwork and experienced distress over the suffering of people I knew, in recent years Kurdistan has felt comparatively very safe, even as the rest of Iraq has contained zones of intense conflict. Connectedness to Kurdistan for an outsider like me is relatively easy now. I have many fictive family members and even a fictive 'eşîret (tribe), and have grieved the loss of several fictive relatives in addition to Viyan. Kurdistan is also becoming a place where a "foreign" person fitting any description, including a tall,

PHOTO 2.2 Rubble from the Iraqi government's attacks against the Kurds, Barushki neighborhood, Dohuk, 1995. (Photo by the author.)

light-skinned American like me, is not much of a novelty.[5] This is especially the case in Hewler and Silemani, where there are now thousands of people from abroad. Iraqi Kurdistan, the place that was once full of rubble and one-story structures, is now mostly peaceful and rubble free, and it has high-rise buildings; the bereft, out-of-the-way place that was under a no-fly zone patrolled by Western military aircraft now has multiple civilian airports with many commercial flights coming and going per day (the airport in the regional capital alone served 500,000 passengers in 2010 [Rudaw 2011]); the place that was once objectionable to Baghdad now has legitimacy as a region in the eyes of the Iraqi state, and a Kurdish leader, Jalal Talabani, is president of Iraq.

As of 2003, Iraq has no longer been ruled by a dictator who often turned on the Kurds, but it does have serious ongoing problems of violence. Until late 2011 it played host to the main military that occupied it and changed its government in 2003, that of the United States. Violent insurgents, most of them Islamists, still attack regularly in certain parts of the country. In the United States, the 2003 Iraq War was highly controversial from the start, and as an insurgency refused to bow and other violent actors kidnapped, terrorized, and killed at will, even its staunchest supporters, which included many in the American Kurdish community,

PHOTO 2.3 Signs of industry, a plane landing, and a billboard trumpeting a new lifestyle in Hewler, June 2008. (Photo by the author.)

were forced to admit by the very bloody year 2007 that it was not going well. With few exceptions, violence related to the U.S. invasion and occupation did not materialize in Kurdistan. A suicide bomb in 2004 targeted high-level KDP leaders and killed Deputy Prime Minister Sami Abdul Rahman and his son along with more than one hundred other people. A second major attack in May 2005 killed around sixty people. Both attacks left many wounded. On the whole, however, Kurdistan has become steadily more peaceful and secure during the past decade. As a "stable" enclave in an otherwise-volatile country, it has received many refugees, both individual and institutional. Kurdistan officials now tout it as a "gateway to Iraq" for international business. Thousands of people of every Iraqi ethnicity have taken refuge there. Even Baghdad's famous confectioner Abu Afif opened a branch in Hewler in 2007; I was told that the company was moving its main operations there until the violence in Baghdad abated.

Surrounded: The Kurdistan Region of Iraq as Unlikely Haven

Iraqi Kurdistan is surrounded. In this book, I portray a Kurdistan that is, in many ways, thriving. The era of its current prosperity, relative to its own past and the rest of Iraq in the present, began in 1991. However, I want to emphasize that for the rest of Kurdistan, a longed-for era of prosperity has yet to begin. From the early twentieth century to the early twenty-first century, many ethnic Kurdish people were severely abused by people belonging to the dominant ethnic group in each of the four main states where they live. This abuse continues outside the Kurdistan Region of Iraq. Given its history, I think the odds were slim that Iraqi Kurdistan would become a zone of relative peace and stability, a place many more people are now migrating to than from, and yet that is what has happened. The rest of this book is about the Iraqi part of Kurdistan and its people, but here I recount some stories from the other parts of the Kurdish homeland to illustrate the kinds of social and political forces that Kurdistan writ large has been up against.

Turkey and Syria were my transit countries until commercial air travel was restored to Iraq in 2005, and I came to see my time in each of them as valuable windows into Kurdish experiences there. Turkey, especially, was tense as the scene of a brutal civil war between Kurdish separatists, the PKK, and the state. My travels to Kurdistan originated in the United States, as well as Lebanon, where I lived and worked while teaching at the American University of Beirut between 2000 and 2006. On my trips through Syria and Turkey from 1995 until I flew directly to the Kurdistan Region for the first time in 2008, I sensed the severe oppression of the Kurds there. To reach Iraqi Kurdistan, I traversed Syria, either crossing directly from its northeast corner into Iraqi Kurdistan, or traveling from there up into Turkey and through its Kurdish-majority area and into Iraqi Kurdistan. Meeting Kurds and using the Kurdish language along the way, I saw and experienced firsthand the everyday realities of Turkish and Syrian Kurds' low estate. Once I crossed the border into Iraqi Kurdistan, there was an entirely different feeling. Kurdishness was openly celebrated. A large sign reading "Welcome to Kurdistan" in several languages graces both of the main entry points from Turkey and Syria, and when you see those you are only getting started with the celebration of Kurdishness that Iraqi Kurdistan represents. But the Kurdish zones of Turkey and Syria stand as reminders of how unlikely this celebration is, and how tenuous it may yet be. Globalization is certainly affecting Turkey in profound ways. Its economy is one of the world's fastest growing. Syria too had, despite the obvious reluctance of its dictatorship, begun to open up to the outside world before much of its populace began an open rebellion in March 2011. As I write this in late 2012, the rebellion that was inspired by similar rebellions elsewhere in the Middle East and North Africa has become a revolution, and the Syrian Ba'th regime's days seem numbered.

During my years of travel through Turkey and Syria to Iraqi Kurdistan, I have had a strong sense that conflict and suppression have served to delay the opening up of Kurdistan to the outside world. Even now, Kurdistan of Iraq could be cut off if all of its neighbors were to work in concert, which, given their various rivalries and differences, is fortunately unlikely. Iraqi Kurdistan's best neighbor at the moment is Turkey, even though the relationship of the government to its large Kurdish population remains very tense and oppressive.

Local people I met during my weeks of waiting in 1996 in the mainly Kurdish city of Diyarbakir,[6] Turkey, told of horrific experiences in Turkish prisons and of being caught up in the conflict between the army and the guerrillas of the PKK. Traveling a bit around the area, I saw razed villages along seemingly every rural road. Signs of civil war were everywhere. One of the main routes into the city was lined with tanks on one side of the road whose turrets were pointed across the road; traveling along that road meant running the gauntlet of one of the war's fronts. Drivers of public buses and minibuses communicated by radio to learn the safest routes, and often took alternative routes that rendered a short trip long. On one occasion, other alarmed passengers and I witnessed a man riding in the passenger seat of a public minibus repeatedly fire a pistol out the window as we rode through a remote area, apparently to ward off would-be attackers. On another occasion, our bus was first delayed, then took a highly inconvenient detour as the driver made routing decisions based on the reports coming to him by two-way radio. I had experienced similar navigating in NGO vehicles crossing the front between PUK and KDP hostilities in 1995. It reminded me of pilots checking with air traffic control and navigating around storms. People did use weather euphemisms to talk about the conflict.

Within Diyarbakir, other Westerners in the city and I were constantly tailed by the secret police, who seemed to believe, even though the United States was clearly on the side of Turkey and no other Western country had openly supported the PKK, that our sympathies lay with the Kurds in the Kurdish-Turkish conflict. Often we would notice a young man wearing a khaki vest loitering nearby. One man in particular was apparently assigned to tail me and another American, a nurse who worked for an NGO in Iraq and with whom I often went to the market and restaurants. Several times other men who were apparently plainclothes police or security forces stopped us and gruffly questioned us. They knew we had spent the initial period of our visit staying in a guest house run by a man who had just been released from prison for allegedly helping the PKK. He had described to us an excruciating experience of being tortured in prison, and now walked with a limp and slightly hunched to one side. I was amazed at how matter-of-factly he told us the story of the horrors he had experienced.

On the street, people used the Kurdish language only in hushed tones and after a surreptitious glance around for anyone who might represent the government. Kurdish music could not be purchased in the open, but was fetched by a shopkeeper from his secret cache only when the coast was clear. One street-cart CD salesman grinned as he pulled back the top layer of Turkish-language CDs to reveal an impressive stash of Kurdish-language CDs for sale. I bought several.

Once while I was riding an inter-city bus with another Westerner, the nurse, and a local guide we had hired to show us around while we waited, the bus was stopped at a military checkpoint. The bus was on its way to Van, but the checkpoint was at a juncture with a road that led to Hakkari, a heavily Kurdish district that was known for PKK activity. These check-points were frequently encountered on any trip between cities; typically one or two members of the gendarmerie (*Jandarma*) would board the bus, look at the occupants' identity cards and passports, and wave us on with-out incident (but often not without a raised eyebrow upon seeing a U.S. passport in the middle of the civil war zone). This time, however, the soldiers summoned two young men outside and talked sternly to them as they stood quietly and submissively just outside the bus. The soldiers then ordered the bus on, without the men. We could hear the men just outside the bus door asking to retrieve their luggage, which remained under their seats on the bus. Some passengers started to pass the bags forward. The driver murmured supportive words on the men's behalf. But the soldiers refused to let them retrieve their bags. One soldier told the men sternly,

"You will not need your things anymore," and repeated the order to the driver to leave. "They will not be coming with you," another soldier said gruffly. After what was probably a few seconds but seemed much longer, we pulled away, with the men's bags placed back under the seats they had vacated. As we did, a chill swept over me, and I sensed a similar reaction in the other passengers. Our guide whispered to us, "They will soon be executed. There is no other possibility for them." He was sweating profusely and had a terrified look on his face. I looked back and saw the soldiers marching the men toward a government building set back from the road. A large Turkish flag flapped above in the breeze.

After my time in Diyarbakir, I took a bus across Turkey in preparation for flying out of Istanbul back to the United States. On previous occasions I had flown across Turkey, but this time I wanted to get a sense of the lay of the land by riding across it. Along the way, I paid a visit to a friend of a friend in the city of Adana, who brought me along to a party that turned out to be attended by political and economic elites, one of whom was a former member of parliament. I had decided not to tell them about my association with Kurds, but they brought up the subject of the Kurdish-Turkish conflict anyway. I listened, continuing to withhold the fact of my close association with Kurdish people, as several of them proceeded to express to me (in English) their opinion that Kurds were, basically, barely human, and that they had a deep desire to see them eliminated.[7] What I heard that evening was nothing short of the sentiments that lead to and sustain a genocide. From then on I understood Turkey's "Kurdish problem" in a new way. Each side had its grievances, to be sure. The state was using terror, and the rebels were using terror (and still are; Turkey regularly bombs PKK camps high in the mountains of Iraqi Kurdistan in response to surprise attacks on Turkish civilians). But only one side saw itself as superior in being to the other. In all of my years among the Kurds, I have never heard the kind of talk from them that I heard from ethnic Turks that night in Adana. I have heard contempt and hatred, but never such pure condescension or desire to annihilate the other. Things appeared to be improving somewhat during the early years of the administration of the current Turkish prime minister, Recep Tayyip Erdoğan, who was elected in 2003. However, the progress was short lived. Government forces and the PKK regularly attack each other, driving the death toll of their decades-old conflict still higher. The government regularly harasses and imprisons Kurdish activists. Among many other indicators that "the Kurdish problem" in Turkey is alive and well, when he made a historic visit to the Kurdistan Region in 2011 to officially open the new Erbil International Airport, which was built by a Turkish firm, Erdoğan did not use the word "Kurdistan" during his entire speech, even though there were many junctures at which it would have been very logical to do so. An analogy would be a head of state visiting California for the purpose of highlighting economic ties with the state and only referring to being in "the United States," never uttering the word "California."[8]

Syria was no better, except that one had the sense that the majority of people, not just the Kurds, were oppressed by the Assad dictatorship. On two occasions, when I was flying into and out of Damascus during the late 1990s and early 2000s, I sat next to a man who told me tales of horrible treatment by the regime. One let out a loud sigh when the wheels went up on takeoff, so loud that I turned to him and asked him if he was okay. We were bound for Europe. "I did not believe I was going to get out of there alive," he said. "I was waiting for the wheels to be up before I would let myself believe it. The government wants to kill me. They will have a harder time now that I have left." Oftentimes, the Kurds were singled out for abuse by the Assad government. Ordinary people made no secret of their disdain for Kurdish people. Once, at a taxi stand, I asked a waiting driver if he spoke Kurdish. He answered me by scowling and spitting on the ground, as though the very idea of speaking Kurdish was vile. On another occasion, in 2003, I spoke to a group of men in the cafeteria of a bus depot in Damascus. I was trying unsuccessfully to place a call from a nearby pay phone, and I hoped they could help me. They did, even rallying others in the cafeteria to give me the additional coins it turned out I needed. I had started speaking to them in my limited Arabic, but then, thinking I had heard one of them speaking in Kurdish to another, I addressed them in Kurdish and asked if they were Kurds. One answered affirmatively with a smile, but another froze and stood there staring at me, as though paralyzed with fear. The man who had already answered said to him in a teasing tone, "She asked if you are Kurdish. Answer her!" That broke the ice and we went on to a warm conversation, but it was clear that even the very question of ethnolinguistic identity, especially coming from a foreign-looking person like me, had initially invoked deep fear in one of the men.

I could also tell many stories of remarks, some subtle and some not, that I heard in Lebanon in reference to Kurds. The Kurds do not comprise a significant proportion of the population, and there is no history of violence against them. On the contrary, Lebanon has long clandestinely hosted the PKK in the Beqa Valley. On a weekend afternoon in late March 2001, I happened across a large crowd of Turkish Kurds picnicking on a football field in the Beirut suburb of Dahiyeh in celebration of Newroz, the Kurdish New Year. Conspicuous PKK flags were flying, and people were dancing and having a good time. Incredulous that there were that many Turkish Kurds in Lebanon, I stopped to talk to them. I was told that normally they stayed out of sight since the vast majority were in Lebanon illegally, but on that occasion, they had received permission to use the field and were thus engaging in a rare celebratory gathering. Most Kurds I knew in Lebanon were not from Turkey or in the PKK, but were Lebanese citizens who had arrived or were descended from a man who had arrived several decades earlier. On more than one occasion, after we had known each other for a while, someone revealed to me that they were of Kurdish descent, letting me know that their Kurdish identity was not something they revealed to everyone. There was a definite stigma associated with Kurdishness. From non-Kurdish Lebanese I got the sense, from all categories of people ranging from cultured, Western-educated colleagues to more "ordinary" people, that they regarded the category "Kurd" as being well beneath their own social status. I found this especially painful coming from other social scientists and scholars in the humanities, who in other settings preached the equality of all human beings. Apparently they believed in equality for people other than Kurdish people.

Modernizing Iraq: Violent and Isolated

Iraq was modernizing rapidly in the 1950s. As interviewees have nostalgically recounted to me, tractors were used to work some fields where draft animals had previously labored, and the use of the radio was becoming widespread and exposing people to ideas from beyond their local area. Women were entering the workplace. Many other changes, both social and technological, changes that people referred to as "modernizing" when they described them to me, were taking place. Then came the revolution of 1958. During the next thirty-three years, Iraq would become increasingly authoritarian and intolerant. With the rise of Saddam Hussein into the vice presidency in 1968 and presidency in 1979, Iraq became a zone of intense totalitarianism. The Kurds were, along with the Shiʻi, one of Hussein's two great internal nemeses. He used all manner of barbaric attacks against them, including mass disappearances and executions, the razing of villages, rape, kidnappings, chemical attacks, and conventional methods of warfare. Most of these attacks took place within the context of the First Kurdish War (1961–1970), the Second Kurdish War (1974–1975), and further hostilities until 1979. Then Iraq went to war against Iran in 1980, and many Kurds died along with the other Iranian and Iraqi casualties in one of the most brutal wars of the twentieth century. It was to get even worse for Kurds, however. In part as an outgrowth of their support for Iran during the war, in 1988 the government launched *Anfal*, a killing spree primarily implemented by dropping chemical weapons and bombs on Kurdish villages, that resulted in around 200,000 dead and hundreds of thousands more wounded and displaced. Anfal was followed three years later by the Iraqi offensive during the Gulf War in which approximately a million Kurds fled to the mountains. Throughout these years, the government detained, tortured, and executed many more people one by one. It destroyed the houses and infrastructure of over 4,000 of Iraq's approximately 7,000 Kurdish villages (Bruinessen 1992a:44), many of them multiple times.

Iraqi Kurdistan as Danger Zone

Even though I first arrived four years after the regime had pulled back from the Kurdish area, the Iraqi Kurdistan I initially encountered in 1995 was a place where people lived with an ever-present fear of violence. The fear emanated from several directions and manifested itself on various scales. My Kurdish associates reminded me constantly that they were survivors of waves of violence stretching back decades. They told horrible stories of repeated aggression by agents of the Iraqi government such as the army and *mukhabarat*. Despite the generality and ubiquity of the possibilities for violence, people spoke of fear not as something in the abstract, but from specific sources, the most frequently mentioned source being at the very top of the regime, Saddam himself. People referred to him by his first name, if they used any name at all, since often they were too afraid to say his name out loud. I still have some Kurdish friends who will lower their voices when speaking of the regime, even though it is long gone. Saddam's brutality is by now well documented (e.g., Adib-Moghaddam 2006).

People I met in Iraqi Kurdistan attributed many types of misfortune, not just the injurious and murderous, to the choices and actions of Saddam. One daily difficulty when the Ba'th regime was in power, and that is to some extent still a problem, was lack of electricity. When I first arrived in 1995, there had been no municipally supplied electricity for four years. Some businesses, organizations, and homes could afford a generator, but Layla and her family could not, so we did without. Over the following few years, many petroleum-fueled generators were installed in neighborhoods, to which households could subscribe. Some municipal electricity became available as well, much of it supplied by the Iraqi government. Most urban households now have two lines, and when one supply goes, you simply flip the switch to the other one (in newer homes, the switch is automatic). When government-supplied electricity first returned in the late 1990s, it came on for only two hours per day. People said they thought the government used the supply to manipulate people in Kurdistan, so when the municipal supply went off, the people around me would often utter colorful curses about Saddam and his family. "Saddam's" impingement on daily life was seemingly thorough and constant.

The people I encountered in Iraqi Kurdistan had thus become accustomed over the course of their lifetimes to the kind of "low intensity panic" described by Linda Green in reference to her experience in Guatemala. This kind of panic "remains in the shadow of waking consciousness. One cannot live in a constant state of alertness, and so the chaos one feels becomes diffused throughout the body" (Green 1999:60). When one is preoccupied in this way, and living in a zone of total media and border control, it is difficult to think or even to know much about the rest of the world. When people in the Kurdish mountains did think about what lay beyond their local area, people had told me, the non-Kurdish majority area of Iraq was often what came to mind. During the years that the Ba'th ruled Iraq, Iraqi Kurds were never entirely cut off from the rest of Iraqi life.

A substantial number of Kurds have always been living in cities such as
Baghdad and Mosul by choice, and pre-2003 Iraqi governments moved
many of them by force or coercion and lured many others away with strong
incentives. The government spent much of its anti-Kurdish efforts trying
to minimize connectedness between Kurds living outside the zones of
Kurdish conflict or autonomy, and those living in the rest of Iraq. It did
this through methods such as prohibiting large amounts of food from
being transported in cars in the direction of where the Kurdish rebels were
fighting.

Not being completely cut off meant continuing to fear the Saddam
Hussein regime even after 1991, after the peshmerga had assumed military
control and (what became) the Kurdistan Regional Government began to
govern. During my research stints in Iraqi Kurdistan while the Ba'th
regime was still in power, which included eleven months in 1997–1998
as well as shorter stints in 1995, 2001, and 2002, I myself lived with a "low
intensity panic," often lying awake at night wondering about and praying
for my safety and the safety of those around me. Although the Kurdish
authorities assured me that they felt it was safe enough for me to be there,
they also warned me to be vigilant because I represented Saddam Hussein's main nemesis, the United States, and his representatives were
known to be working in Kurdistan in a clandestine fashion. The PKK regularly attacked civilians, especially in villages. Other threats waxed and
waned. On a number of occasions I felt heightened fear and experienced
the difficulties of life under threat just as my neighbors did. I have documented my pre-2003 experiences in this regard elsewhere (King 2009).

After the U.S. military unseated the regime and occupied Iraq in 2003,
there was a noticeable shift in the sense of security in Kurdistan. Initially,
it felt like a safer place. On my research trip in late 2003 and early 2004, it
was clear that people in Kurdistan felt liberated. The regime that had
repeatedly attacked them had fallen, and the jubilance was palpable. However, the rest of Iraq was becoming more violent every day. On a visit to
Mosul with some friends from Zakho who had not felt safe enough to travel
there while the regime was in power, there was an altogether different
feel. U.S. snipers were positioned on the tops of buildings with their
guns trained on us as we passed by on the road. Later, we talked to some
U.S. military members guarding their base, a former presidential palace,

and they were noticeably nervous. At one point we saw a plume of flame, large enough to engulf a building, shoot up into the sky followed by billowing black smoke, and smoke was also rising from several other places in the city.

The war brought new threats and fears to Kurdistan, even though the main activity was elsewhere. By my 2005 trip, after some attacks had occurred even in Kurdistan, people had clearly developed a fear of "terrorists," *irhabiyin*. Old friends said they were too afraid to be photographed with me, since they feared that the photographs would fall into the hands of terrorists, who would see that they had associated with an American and later attack them. I, too, felt threatened by former Ba'thists who had opposed the U.S. invasion, as well as the Islamists who had different reasons for enmity against an American. Three years would pass before my next research trip, in 2008, when Iraqi Kurdistan started to feel much more safe and stable than previously. This feeling continued through my last visit, in late 2010. Many geopolitical threats remain, such as a belligerent Iran in one direction and a fracturing Syria in the other, but the effect of these threats on daily life is, for most people, not as intense as the dangers of earlier decades.

3

A Man on the Land

Lineages, Identity, and Place

'Edirê te wekî şerefa te. (Your land is like your honor.)

–A woman's answer when asked why her patrilineage continued to hold in
common, and refrained from selling, its underutilized village land, 2011.
A common saying with several variants in both Arabic and Kurdish.

Kurdistan's valleys and peaks, villages and cities comprise a place imbued
with meaning, meaning that for many people is framed in terms of generations of male ancestors traced backward and forward in time using the
logic of patriliny. In patriliny, biological relationships through males are
regarded as having special significance over other kin relationships. Patriliny
is one of the two forms of unilineal kinship reckoning, among a broader
set of possible ways found around the world of determining who is kin. The
other is matriliny, in which lines of descent are traced through females.
The tracing of male unilineal links, and the relationships that result, make
up the kinship system known as "patriliny" or "patrilineality." One's patriline consists of one's father, father's father, father's father's father, and so
on. Sometimes the line and the men who comprise it are recorded in writing, but in many patrilineal cultures, they are simply remembered and
recited by their members and the surrounding community. In Kurdistan,
both forms of remembering are found, but orally transmitted memory
touches many more people than written lists or charts, which most people
do not keep or see. A man who has had a son has succeeded in extending
his patriline by one generation, and the typical father of a son hopes that
his son, too, will continue to extend the line. Patriliny is traditionally only
understood to consist of biological relationships. Biological fathers are also
expected to be, and are except in the rarest of cases, also social fathers.

In Iraqi Kurdistan, patriliny remains salient, even though some of its features are undergoing new scrutiny in light of new possibilities fostered by globalization. I regard patriliny as one of the most important social and symbolic forces in Kurdish life, the glue that fosters many of the social connections in Kurdistan. Connecting is, perhaps more often than not, made meaningful by patriliny.

In patriliny, a man's generative power is cumulative, and both during his lifetime and in successive generations becomes attached to his reputation. The descendants through males of a particular man constitute a patrilineage. Some patrilineages trace their origins to particularly noteworthy men, and others to ordinary men. Some Kurdish patrilineages recognize several hundred members and trace to a male ancestor several generations earlier, and others comprise just a few individuals tracing only to the youngest living members' father's father. All of the lineage founder's descendants through males (including daughters) receive identities from him of the kind described by Martin Sökefeld (1999:419), "a collection of differences setting them off from varying groups of others." These include association with place (whether urban neighborhood or village), tribal membership (in many cases; some Kurdish lineages, especially urban ones, are not affiliated with tribes), and religion. These identity categories, taken together, constitute a set of features that comprise one's individual identity much like the Moroccan *nisba* concept described by Geertz (1994), which has parallels throughout the Arabic-speaking part of the world, including Iraq. Describing the concept as it is found in Lebanon, Morgan Clarke (2007:382) writes, "It is . . . used to refer to 'genealogy': purely agnatic descent projected backwards in time, seen, in Lebanon at least, as of interest to 'tribesmen' or elites. In much Islamic discourse, *nasab* is viewed as the primordial relationship upon which the wider set of relationships of rights and obligations which form human society is built."

In many patrilineal settings, people may hold to the belief that only men make children. In this understanding, a woman is simply a vessel who "carries" the child, and the father supplies the constitutive element, the essence of the new human. A woman's womb nurtures a new human, until an infant emerges who is the newest member of his or her patrilineage. This idea, called "monogenesis" by some, can be traced at least to Aristotle

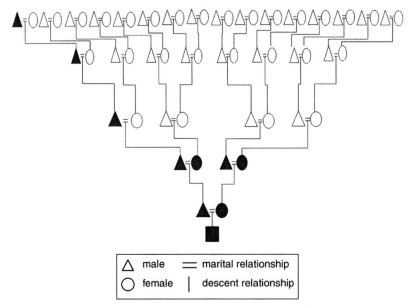

FIGURE 3.1 The hypothetical known forebears of a Kurdish individual. All recent ancestors are known and recognized, but in generations further back, only a line of males, a patriline, is remembered and acknowledged. The unshaded individuals' names are no longer known and collective memory about them is lost, while shaded individuals' memory is kept alive.

(Delaney 1991:47). I prefer, following Joanne Wright (2004), the more specific term "patrogenesis," since it indicates clearly which single parent is seen to be generating life. I argue that patrogenesis may be a powerful contributor to the seclusion of girls and women in Kurdistan and in other societies, most of which are found in the surrounding geographic area. Patriliny and patrogenesis are present and influential in Kurdistan, throughout Iraq, and in a wide area stretching from Morocco to India, the heart of which encompasses Kurdistan.

In this chapter, I explore an interplay between collective memory, patrilineages, and sustained presence on land in the Kurdistan Region. Patrilines are connected to claims of origin in specific places, which, once successive generations of males have called such a place "home," lend identity to the members of the patrilineage. For example, in the village of "Deshta" (a fictional toponym) in the Semel district of the Dohuk Governorate in the Kurdistan Region of Iraq, I began a series of interviews with a couple, Bushra and Loqman, about how they came to be "villagers" in this village. I first visited Deshta in February 1998 and went there most recently in 2010, with many visits in between ranging in length from a few days to a few hours. As I detail in chapter 6, the village had been destroyed, and its members scattered, by the Ba'thist Iraqi government in the 1960s. Those who were expelled were Sunni Muslim Kurds, and the people who replaced them were Sunni Arabs. The Arabs fled during the 1991 Kurdish uprising. Although neither Loqman nor Bushra was able to tell me their age using a number or a birth year, they did tell me that their first child was born in 1966. I think Loqman was born around 1940, and his wife Bushra a bit later, perhaps around 1950.

Loqman gave me the histories of the three members of his patriline whom he could name—his father, Hussein; father's father, Mohammed; and father's father's father, Hassan. He told me that Hassan was born in a village near Ibrahim Khalil, an area now known as the site of the only border crossing shared by Syria and the Kurdistan Region. He left there, Loqman told me, "because the Ottomans took the village." "How long ago was this?" I asked. "This was maybe 200 years ago," he said, but then added, "My father's father had only my father then," which indicated to me a probable date of around the turn of the twentieth century at the very earliest. Loqman went on to recount how Hassan first went to Kani, the next village up the road from Deshta, which is also owned by members of the Haweri lineage. "He was there with Omar Agha Haweri (son of Haji son of Hawer Agha). But when they began to build Deshta, nearly half the village left Kani and moved to Deshta with Omar's brother Idris." "Why did you choose to leave Kani and come to Deshta?" I asked, referring with my use of "you" to an action by a patrilineal forebear as action taken by the whole patrilineage, as I had heard others do. "Because Mohammed's mother and Idris's mother were sisters," he answered, implying that the two sisters were close and wanted to live in the same village. Patrilocal residence patterns, in which a new bride moves to join her husband who continues to live with or near his parents, are a strong feature of patriliny in Kurdistan and throughout the Middle East. Sisters who are both married, then, cannot expect to live close to each other, but in this case, we see an exception made possible by the opening of a new village and perhaps the kindness of one or more husbands. Indeed, I once talked to a husband who was living with his wife's family, and he told me that he felt great shame in doing so. A woman is supposed to follow a man, not the other way around.

Deshta covers a total of 2,200 donums (one donum = 0.618 acre) not counting the adjacent grazing land, which is owned by the government but designated for the occupants of Deshta. Of this, 200 donums are reserved for the "villagers," the people like Loqman who have, or whose lineages have, a history of sharecropping there. The Kurdistan Regional Government has now codified these peasant relationships, and the descendants of the "original" inhabitants now have an official right to live in "their" villages and sharecrop with the owner. In part following Iraqi law, and in part their own innovations on it, the KRG follows modern inheritance practices that grant shares in village land equally to sons and daughters. This change is recent enough, having been codified in villages like Deshta only since the 1990s, that it is still possible to consider the villages as owned by patrilineages. Within a decade or two, however, it will no longer be patrilineages owning villages or having the right to sharecrop there, but groups of people descended through both fathers and mothers from the original patrilineal holders of the land. Deshta's 2,200 donums are held collectively by the twenty-five members of the generation born to three of Idris's sons' sons. (Other patrilineal descendants of Idris inherited shares in Kani. I surmise that this was to even out the ownership proportions in the next generation, since some sons had many more offspring than others.) Both males and females are owners of Deshta. Their children, many of whom are now young adults, number over one hundred, and now that generation is starting to marry and produce offspring. In theory, they are all owners of the village, but until the oldest adult generation passes on, this ownership has little bearing.

In Loqman's account we can see the members of two lineages interacting and shaping each other's histories. The Haweri *agha* lineage, already in place and the owner of a sizable amount of fertile farmland, receives a newcomer, Hassan, to be a sharecropper in one of its villages. "Agha" is Turkish for "lord." In the Iraqi Kurdish context, an agha is typically a Sunni Muslim Kurd, and he is a landowner and tribal chief. The term "agha" is used in both reference and address. In his landlord capacity, an agha typically owns land on which peasants sharecrop. The peasants depend on him for their livelihood. In his tribal chief capacity, he is a

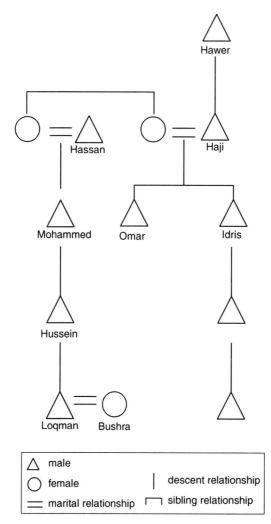

FIGURE 3.2 Individuals mentioned in Bushra and Loqman's narrative about becoming "villagers" in Deshta.

paramilitary leader, and the peasants who sharecrop under him are members of his tribe and are members of patrilineages themselves (all tribes in Kurdistan are comprised of lineages, but not all lineages are in tribes). Male peasants are periodically called upon to fight for him, and female peasants raise the next generation of peasants and tribal members, increasing the tribe's numbers and thus its influence and ability to improve its fortunes. An agha is of high status and a patron, and the peasants under him are of low status and clients, but as I have seen, their relationship may be warm and affectionate. Aghas receive many visitors, mediate disputes, represent the tribe to other tribes and the state, and play other important social roles. Patrilineal descendants of an agha, whether or not they play a similar economic or political role, also carry the title "agha." As Michael Meeker (1976:250) explains it, "As a man recedes in the genealogy away from the present, he at some point acquires the title 'agha,' whether or not he was an agha when alive. All the ascendants of the lineage and the uppermost ascendants of the entire clan therefore are given the title 'agha.'" Women in an agha lineage are not addressed directly as "agha," but may be referred to as "daughter of agha" and addressed by an honorific term such as *khanum*, "lady."

Everyone, peasant and agha alike, carries the identity of the tribe as their own in the broader Kurdistani social context. Kurdish *shaikhs*, Muslim sufi religious leaders, share many of the characteristics of aghas, such as amassing followers, and in the past they would sometimes marshal those followers to act militarily just as aghas did.[1] A shaikh also preaches and is more likely to collect tribute than an agha. An identity as the follower or client of an agha or shaikh is often worn with pride, much as an American might wear the jersey of a favorite sports team. Indeed, many tribes have a uniform of sorts, such as a particular way of wrapping the male head scarf, or a particular waist design in the dresses that women wear for special occasions such as picnics and weddings.

Although Loqman does not mention this, based on the timing, it was probably Haji, Idris's father, who originally received him. Then again, it may have been Idris, since one of Idris's patrilineal descendants, his son's son's son, told me, "Many of our villagers came from Turkey. Many were on the run. Especially in the time of Idris, our family gave them money and assistance, and they became our villagers." Hassan has at least one son, Mohammed, who has at least one son, Hussein, to whom Loqman is born.[2] When Hassan moves to a new village, he does not go far, but only to a new set of village houses built on a portion of bare Haweri land. Omar remains the agha in Kani, and Idris the agha in Deshta. Eventually, I learned from the Haweri family, Omar and Idris's land was put into their names in official state land records, but this probably happened much later. In the early years, the title would still have belonged to their branch of the Haweri lineage, probably the descendants of their father or father's father.

Meanwhile, Hassan and Haji had married sisters. Patriliny should by no means be seen as a system in which women do not have significant influence. Indeed, their decisions and jockeying in certain strategic situations such as the arrangement of a marriage can shape the very constitution of a patrilineage. In this case, although it does not come out this clearly in the interview, we can surmise that Hassan arrived in Kani unmarried, and Haji's father, Hawer Agha, probably suggested he marry the sister of his son's wife. We do not know to which lineage the sisters belonged. Cousin marriage is common in Kurdistan, so they may have been Haweris, too. In any case, because of their apparent desire to live near each other, Hassan's patrilineal descendants have been defined by their membership in the community of Deshta villagers ever since.

Bushra told me a little about her own patrilineal forebears. She was able to name only her father and father's father, who she said were from a nearby village with different aghas. She implied that she had come to live in Deshta at the time of her marriage to Loqman, but did not have much to say about her own history or that of her forebears. We spoke extensively, however, about her ten living children, some of whom were present on that occasion. I have met most of them in my many visits to the village and interactions with villagers in Zakho. An eleventh child, the next to last one, had died in 1991. "He died when we fled to the mountains," she told me, referring to the mass flight by hundreds of thousands of Kurdistanis as the Iraqi military threatened people in Kurdistan. "He became thinner and thinner. He was vomiting and had diarrhea. It was cold, and wet, and snowy, and the air was dirty with soot."[3] Their other children, many of whom I have met, are, overall, thriving.

Bushra and Loqman had lived in Zakho exclusively since shortly after I first interviewed them in Deshta in the late 1990s. I was surprised to learn they had left because they had seemed so much a part of village life, and so happy with it, when I first met them. But they were not alone in leaving, as most of their peers also left for the city around the turn of the century. Bushra and Loqman are still Deshta's villagers, and will be as long as they live. They visit the other villagers, most of whom also live in Zakho now. When I visit Zakho, I, too, visit within Deshta circles. In many ways, Deshta lives on as a social entity in Zakho, even as it has meanwhile absorbed a wave of new inhabitants. In chapter 6, I continue the story of Deshta and the people attached to it, which has recently become interesting again after a lull in the early 2000s, when the village it had dwindled to having very few residents. The village now has completely different tenants, although it still has the same landlord. I am referring more to the story of the village than the story of the people.

Kinship Studies in Kurdistan and Anthropology

In globally connecting Kurdistan, it might seem logical to expect patriliny to wane in importance. Many workers who might have worked in patrilineally organized village agriculture a decade ago are now employed by multinational corporations. Other trends, such as increases in female education rates, might be expected to erode men's claims as the main creators of social categories that are passed on to the next generation. However, that is not what I have observed during my field research. On the contrary, it continues to be the case that each "legitimate" member of society is a member of an identifiable patriline, descended from a particular man, who is associated with a particular location. In Kurdistan, individual identity is strongly shaped by collective identity. In theory, everyone in Kurdistan belongs to a patrilineal descent group. Some patrilineages are "deep," going back many generations, and some are "shallow," going back as few as three generations. Although collectivities can be varied and situational, the identity of the patrilineage in which the individual has membership has an important bearing on a range of individual identity categories. Some of the questions I seek to address in this chapter include: How does patrilineal membership affect people's daily social lives, and what does it mean to people in a symbolic sense? How does patriliny come up in everyday conversation? Most importantly, how does patriliny shape people's social connections?

Patriliny is a very common form of kinship and descent reckoning across Asia and parts of Africa, particularly north Africa. Moreover, Kurdistan lies in the middle of a wide geographical area, stretching around the Mediterranean, across to India, and up through Central Asia, in which all of the otherwise-diverse cultural, religious, and ethnic groups are patrilineal, with only two exceptions in that contiguous area: those sects of Judaism in which Jewishness is passed on by mothers (which includes the majority of Jews worldwide), and the matrilineal Tuareg in north Africa. Closer to home, every ethnic and religious group in Iraq practices patrilineal succession by default. For example, an Iraqi Assyrian Christian is seen by most people as, first and foremost, a person who was born to an Assyrian Christian father, rather than a person who has necessarily chosen Christianity as a belief system.[4] Such a person might well believe the Christian message and practice the faith, but belief and practice are, in a sense, optional. What may be more socially important, what places the individual in the "Assyrian" and "Christian" categories from the point of conception and ensures that he or she will be baptized after birth, married (if he or she marries) and buried in a Christian Assyrian fashion, is that he or she was born to a father who also belonged to those categories. All of Iraq's other faiths, or "sects," Sunni Islam, Shi'i Islam, Yârsânism, Yezidism, and others, also follow patrilineal succession patterns. Iraq's recognized ethnic groups do as well: Kurdish, Turkoman, Arab, and others. Legally, all Iraqis are assigned to one of the recognized sects in Iraq, by default the same sect as their father. Unlike some of its neighboring states, Iraq's Personal Status Law (often referred to by its acronym, PSL) does not treat adherents of different sects differently. It draws partly on interpretations of shari'a but is mainly secular. The state does keep track of its citizens' religion, however, assigning each citizen to officially recognized religious categories. There are, in an official sense, no Iraqi atheists, Buddhists, Hindus, or people belonging to any other faith category unrecognized by the state. Opting out of being assigned a category is not possible. Patriliny helps make sectarianism possible, because it is such a straightforward system, placing every newborn infant for whom male parentage is known into a recognized Iraqi sect. Sects obtain new members much less through attracting new adherents than through male biological reproduction.

Iraqi's PSL contains in Article 71 a section that J.N.D. Anderson (1960:558), an early analyst of the law after it went into effect in 1959, noted is "strange" and "an innovation for which there appears to be no precedent whatever": "*Personal property only* may be bequeathed to one who differs in religion from the testator, while where there is also a difference in nationality reciprocity is a further condition" (italics added). Iraqi law has very specific inheritance requirements and distributes the deceased's possessions among kin. What Article 71 ensures is that no *real property* may pass from a member of one religion to another. Suppose the son of Muslim parents, who would have been classified as a Muslim under Iraqi law, converts to Christianity. He can only inherit "personal property" from his parents, not land. I interpret this law to mean that land in Iraq and the Kurdistan Region (neither of which have amended this portion of the PSL as of this writing in 2012) not only lends identity to patrilines, but that land is considered by the law to be religious territory as well. A "man on the land," or even a woman on land that she owns, stands before the state as a religious adherent, and passes that land on only to his or her fellow religious adherents.

Since men beget members of their ethnic and religious group and women do not, ethnic and religious identity remains, in theory, singular from generation to generation. People understand the daughter or son of an "Arab" man to be unquestionably an "Arab," no matter the ethnic identity of that daughter or son's mother. In the patrilineal Middle East, there are no "half" ethnic categories. The child of a Kurdish man and an Arab woman (and there are many such children) is "Kurdish." He or she might often say, "My mother is Arab," but would be unlikely to say, "I am half Kurdish and half Arab." In actual practice, interviewees have reported to me a variety of cases in which a patrilineal ancestor's ethnicity changed. One man told of a patrilineal forebear several generations back who was "a Turk," but he migrated to a Kurdish area and his patrilineal descendants "became" Kurdish through learning the Kurdish language and acquiring land in a Kurdish-majority town. Today their legal ethnicity is Kurdish, and they are recognized as Kurds in the community. Other interviewees reported similar transformations in the past. Saddam Hussein's Ba'thist government tried to force ethnic change on thousands of Iraqis. In most of those cases, it changed the documentation of people who had previously been "Kurds" and made them into "Arabs" so that it could boost the "Arab" population of Iraq as a part of its ethnic cleansing efforts. For example, in the censuses of 1977 and 1987, Yezidis in Sinjar were forced to register as Arabs and prohibited from speaking Kurdish (Savelsberg, Hajo, and Dulz 2010:104). (In post-Ba'thist Iraq, many of these forced ethnic changes have been rectified, and others are in the process.) Martin van Bruinessen (1992b) cites many examples of ethnic change and flexibility, even in individuals during their lifetime, in late twentieth-century Turkey,

Iran, and Iraq. These examples are important to note. It is also important to note that ethnic change may not be fully accepted and recognized by the community in one lifetime. I have never met an Iraqi who claimed to have *voluntarily* changed his or her personal ethnic identity, nor have I heard of such a change in individual identity taking place.

Kinship studies, which included the study of patriliny, as well as matriliny and more complex forms of descent reckoning (such as "dual descent"), were once a major focus in anthropology, especially during the mid-twentieth century. Within the kinship literature, "segmentary lineages" were very well represented in the 1950s, 1960s, and 1970s, with E. E. Evans-Pritchard (1940) and Meyer Fortes (1953) leading the way. Anthropologists observed in diverse settings that lines of males traced back in time were finite. They led to an apical ancestor, who often served as the lineage's namesake. Additionally, many lineages were subsets of larger lineal categories, such as clans, that claimed lineal descent through either males or females, from a common ancestor even though people could no longer recall the precise links to that ancestor. What caused a lineage to break off from another lineage into its own segment to become, over time, distinct? Did marriages in the context of lineages mainly serve the purpose of alliance, or descent, or both? Debates addressing these questions were carried out mainly by anthropologists working in the patrilineal cultures surrounding the Mediterranean as well as other locations in Asia and Africa. A materialist vein of this literature linked patriliny to scarce resources in arid landscapes and competition between groups (e.g., Schneider 1971; Sahlins 1961).

By the 1980s, however, the conversation on lineages had largely disappeared from the anthropological literature. In part, it had seemingly run its course. Its demise was greatly hastened, however, by strong critiques. I went to work in Kurdistan having been trained after David Schneider (1984) and Adam Kuper (1982) had attacked "kinship" and "descent" as anthropologists had understood them to that point. Schneider argued that kin relations are constituted symbolically to a much greater degree than biologically (1984). Kuper wrote, "My view is that the lineage model, its predecessors and its analogs, have no value for anthropological analysis. Two reasons above all support this conclusion. First, the model does not represent folk models which actors anywhere have of their own societies.

Secondly, there do not appear to be any societies in which vital political or economic activities are organized by a repetitive series of descent groups" (1982:92). Even Edmund Leach, who had started his anthropological career in Kurdistan with fieldwork in 1938, wrote in 1961 after fieldwork in Ceylon that "it might even be the case that 'the structure of unilineal descent groups' is a *total* fiction" (1961:302) (italics in original). Another line of criticism simply claimed that anthropologists had overstepped their bounds when looking for lineages: "Extreme concern with kinship has given rise to an overapplication of descent theory and the 'discovery' of lineages where they did not exist," based on surname and inheritance patterns but in the absence of other evidence of the tracing of lineages (Loizos and Papataxiarchēs 1991:3).

By the turn of the millennium, while kinship was no longer a major area of interest within cultural anthropology, a new vein of kinship literature had nevertheless begun to emerge, led by Janet Carsten (2000, 2004), Sarah Franklin and Susan McKinnon (2001), and others. Linda Stone (2010) continued Jane Collier and Sylvia Yanagisako's (1987) project of merging kinship and gender studies. Marilyn Strathern (2000) and Marcia Inhorn (1994) pioneered the study of new reproductive technologies, which has now developed into a rich literature in its own right (e.g., Clarke 2011; Inhorn 2003). Lineages, however, for the most part remained in the background of kinship studies, perhaps failing to draw a great deal of attention because of their association with "structure," which had gone out of fashion with the poststructuralist turn in anthropology and related disciplines.

It is my contention in this book that anthropology, especially Middle East anthropology, turned away from an emphasis on kinship and descent too soon. In so doing, I follow a few others who have continued to point out its importance. The ethnographic record makes clear that people throughout the Middle East continue to trace patrilines and to value lineage membership, even as talk of them is couched in conversations about the modern, oral histories are written down and thus lose their fluidity, and the modern state shapes them and is shaped by them, as Andrew Shryock (1997) shows for Jordan. Lila Abu-Lughod notes in her ethnography of Egyptian Bedouin life that despite the many changes taking place in the Bedouin world during her fieldwork in 1978–1980, "Agnation has an indisputable ideological priority in kin reckoning. Descent, inheritance, and tribal sociopolitical organization are conceptualized as patrilineal, extending the strong relationship between father and son (and father and daughter) back in time and outside the immediate family. The significance of agnation is reflected in how rights are distributed among members of a family . . . paternal kin have jural rights to all children born of agnates" (1999:51–52). She further notes that "kinship is still the dominant ideological principle of social organization" (1999:70). Marcia Inhorn (e.g., 2011, 2012) and Morgan Clarke (e.g., 2008, 2011) have drawn attention to patriliny in their work on new reproductive technologies.

In Kurdistan, Martin van Bruinessen apparently brought some doubts about the importance of kinship and descent to the field, but came away from his fieldwork in a variety of locations across Kurdistan to write, "I am aware of the many cases where other factors outweigh kinship or lineage segmentation . . . but time and again I was surprised to see not only how pervasive the kinship ideology is, but also to what extent it actually shapes behaviour" (Bruinessen 1992a:317). David Shankland, whose fieldwork in Turkey was mainly with Alevis in the Kurdish-majority area, writes (1999:143) citing Ernest Gellner (1989), "Gellner asserts . . . that societies opposing the state characteristically possess a lineage organization and mediators who can reconcile disputes, yet who may also lead a rebellion. This model is not in favour in anthropology today." (Shankland mentions Kuper [1996] as an example in a footnote here.) "Nevertheless," Shankland continues, "the Kurdish material in Turkey appears to offer an abundance of material to support Gellner's position."

I have found in my fieldwork in Kurdistani homes and other settings that the degree to which an individual may value and be affected by lineage membership can be highly variable. Ideas and practices associated with patriliny may be very important to one person, and much less so to another. However, after many interviews like the one with Loqman and Bushra as well as countless references that I have heard in everyday conversation, I can assert that cognizance of one's patriline, the names and associated information about the men stretching back to one's apical ancestor, and patrilineage, the people descended through males from that ancestor, are widespread in Kurdistan. In some families, parents make a point of teaching their children to be able to recite the names in their patriline at a very young age. If you ask a child in such a family, he or she will proudly recite the names, starting with the previous generation, his or her father, and proceeding backward in time to the earliest ancestor who can be recalled. In other families, such knowledge is not held by everyone, but is kept by certain "experts" who are usually elderly. Derek P. Brereton argues that in general, societies that recognize lineages linked to places generally trace no farther back than five to seven generations (2005:136). I have found this to be the case with all but a few lineages in which people are able to name a few more than that. Some lineages, especially those with *sayyid* status, which indicates a claim of patrilineal descent from the Prophet Mohammed, claim a much deeper line of descent stretching to the sixth century. Kurdistan, like many other places with a Muslim population, is home to a number of sayyid lineages. However, I am not aware of any Kurdish sayyid lineages in which members claim to know *all* of the links of ascent between themselves and the Prophet.[5]

Some members of prestigious lineages keep a chart or a "family tree." The lineage members' names are written at the base of the chart or onto a drawing of a tree, with the apical ancestor (lineage founder) at the base or trunk, and his descendants farther up and out, culminating with the most recent generation on the outer and upper edges, or on the leaves. The analogy is of a seed that long ago germinated to start the lineage, which each successive male has kept growing until it has become a tree. I have seen a number of these charts and trees in Kurdistan, although they do not seem to be very common. None of those that I have seen contain women's names. As I argue in the next chapter, patriliny is a system that in a number of critical ways affirms maleness and denigrates or at least downplays femaleness. To see a genealogical rendering of ancestry that completely omits the female is to see the power of patriliny to make history into "his story."

Land, Lineages, and Individual Identity

Patrilineages are not "free floating" but are, or were in each lineage's recent past, emplaced on land. Members of each patrilineage have a narrative about the place or places to which the lineage belongs and that have lent it identity. People belonging to a lineage whose members have lived for sufficient duration in a village located within certain tribal lands, for example, are highly likely to be considered members of that tribe. Lineage identity implies tribal identity. Just as expressions of identity, including Kurdish identity, are bound up with the spatial in an urban setting to which people have recently migrated (Secor 2004, 2007), so too are they inseparable from the spatial in the heart of the Kurdish homeland. Kinship theorists have long emphasized relationships between lineages and place (e.g., Bohannan 1954:3).

Women do not impart identity categories to their children. Therefore, a woman changing locations for a purpose that is sanctioned by her lineage and later her husband, as a bride and later as a wife, has no implications for the identity of future generations. A man moving, however, does. A man's sustained presence in a particular location, whether that location is rural or urban, and whether he owns a house or rents it, becomes consequential if he has male offspring. Those male offspring, and their male offspring, go on to constitute, with time, a patrilineal group with a new identity, an identity derived in part from its location. It is also derived from the relationships that allow for sustained presence in that location. In the past, presence in a rural location, which would describe most locations in Kurdistan where residences are found, meant that an invitation to remain in that location was granted by a powerful patron. "Places are not inert containers," writes Margaret Rodman. "They are politicized, culturally relative, historically specific, local and multiple constructions" (1992:641). It is patrons in the form of aghas, shaikhs, and other wealthy landowners including the state (presently, in the form of the Kurdistan Regional Government) who grant the land and its attached people a political and cultural identity. Clients receive the right to dwell on the land, and in the process receive its attendant identifying categories.

Hierarchical Identities

When two strangers meet in Iraqi Kurdistan, they are likely to begin the conversation with a few identifying questions about place, lineage, and other social categories such as tribal membership and position within the tribe. Such categories range from low status to high, and include peasant (*fellah*) or agha, sayyid status, or membership in a shaikhly lineage.

At the bottom of the Kurdistani status hierarchy are the *qereçi*, or *hosta*, people with low social status who often occupy a particular economic niche. The former term is sometimes translated "Gypsy" and is considered pejorative, and the latter means "craftsman" and is the more frequent autonym. I visited some hosta whose main occupation had been the making of sieves for use with local grain. While they showed me some of their past work, beautiful sieves made with local leather, they complained that demand had slowed to a trickle because of cheap imported substitutes. Other occupations may include playing music at weddings or beating a drum on the streets of Muslim neighborhoods to wake people for the presunrise meal during Ramadan. Hosta were once nomadic, and many lived in tents as squatters near towns and cities, but in recent years the Kurdistan Regional Government has provided them with land and housing. Next in ascending order are the *fellahin*, peasants (sing. *fellah*). Fellahin work the land but do not own it, and are usually compensated through a sharecropping arrangement. The Iraqi government has long involved itself in the allocation of land, and the two Kurdish administrations spent much of the 1990s developing new land policies, modifying some of the Iraqi land reform law promulgated in the 1970s and keeping the rest. A Dohuk Governorate official told me in the late 1990s that his administration had begun a long and involved process of redistributing some land that was seized from owners whose plots were bigger than the law allowed and given to "original inhabitants of the land," fellahin, who had previously not held title. Since then, in both the KDP and PUK administrated areas, the KRG has redistributed vast amounts of agricultural land. The recipients are former sharecroppers, IDPs (internally displaced persons), or others who had previously been landless. It has also, like its predecessor, the Government of Iraq, organized many types of collective agricultural enterprises and has many assistance programs for individual farmers that facilitate the sharing of equipment, acquisition of seed and fertilizer, and the like. As a result, the idea of the "peasant" is in flux. Many people whose income comes from the land are no longer in an exploitive relationship with a landlord. However, they may be heavily dependent on the Kurdistan Regional Government, having a small plot but a large number of mouths to feed. Many have rented out their land, and their rental income is very small. They remain poor and/or unable to live off agriculture alone. Despite all of the changes of recent decades, then, one still meets many people in Kurdistan for whom the label "fellah" still seems apt in the present, and whose patriline is comprised of men who previously comprised the class of sharecroppers dependent on, and often exploited by, large landowners. They now comprise a large proportion, probably the largest proportion, of the urban poor.

At the other end of the economic spectrum, Iraqi Kurdistan now has many urban social climbers and nouveaux riches. Each time I go there to carry out fieldwork, I see new evidence that the prosperity level of some families has surged dramatically upward. The most ready evidence is the new luxury neighborhoods under construction in every city, evident since approximately the middle of the 2000s. In many cases, a newly prosperous family occupies an economic niche that it acquired initially through political connections. The granting of business licenses and concessions is tightly controlled by the Kurdistan Regional Government. Many people have told me that prosperity in business is very difficult without membership in the KDP (in Dohuk and Erbil Governorates) or PUK (in Silemani Governorate), and without favorable relationships within the party in question. Following the 1991 uprising, both parties rewarded men who had displayed fighting prowess in the Kurdish resistance movement of the preceding years with opportunities for employment, for business ventures, or both. Many of the nouveaux riches are former peshmergas and their descendants.

As old landowners and their patrilineal descendants, aghas are the antithesis of the new rich. Many individual members of agha lineages also belong to the new economically prosperous class. Members of the two groups, the newly prosperous who lack prestigious patrilines, and the prosperous whose patrilineal forebears also occupied an honored social place, often scrutinize and rank-order each other. I have heard many remarks from members of agha lineages in which the speakers put down the new rich. "Who are they?" they ask. "They have no 'esil [pedigree, attested patrilineal origin]!" Agha lineage members who have not managed to parlay their past high status into economic prosperity in the present may feel intense jealousy toward the newcomers. I have also heard the newly successful distance themselves from the aghas. Pointing out past abuses by the aghas, emphasizing the present over the past, or recounting peshmerga heroics and sacrifice are frequent strategies. Many aghas were chete, mercenaries of the Baghdad government, and peshmerga and their descendants often disparagingly point this out. In the chete system, aghas were paid by the government to arm, and sometimes mobilize, the members of their tribes against the KDP and PUK peshmerga. (Chete are often called *jash* by their detractors. This term means "donkey foal," which insinuates that by siding with the government, they are traitors to the Kurdish cause.)

Religion and religiosity are additional measures by which people categorize one another. Is the speaker Muslim, Christian, or Yezidi? If Muslim, does she or he appear to have Islamist leanings, primarily indicated by more restrictive clothing for women and beards for men? These categories can also produce sharp divides in certain social settings. In other settings they may not matter. Many Christian men fought as peshmerga. They are not ethnic Kurds, but they were part of the Kurdish body politic, on behalf of which they fought. Yezidis are ethnic Kurds, and many also fought as peshmerga, but they are not part of the Muslim *umma* (community) like the majority of their fellow Kurds. Religious categories in Kurdistan cut across, and adhere to, other categories in specific ways rooted in particular local histories. In all cases, place matters. A Christian is highly likely to be from a village or neighborhood comprised mainly or entirely of Christians. An Islamist belongs to a patriline just like anyone else, which is likely to be mentioned even though the person may prefer to emphasize religious identity over other identity categories.

Two people who meet for the first time in Kurdistan draw on the above categories and more as they reveal their own place and learn about the other's place in the local set of social hierarchies. In the dialect spoken in Dohuk and the surrounding area, the initial question in such a conversation is often worded, "Where are your people from?" "*Tu xelk e li kîve ye?*" This is a way to ask about place, but it is also an entrée into questions of more specific social positioning. The answerer's accent may reveal immediately that they are from a part of Kurdistan that is distant, and with which the questioner may not be familiar, and in that case the categories that one initially offers would be broader. If the speaker's Kurdish is very familiar, then one might mention a more locally known category such as the former fellahin of a notable agha. Many encounters between strangers take place in Hewler, since it is a meeting point for people from all areas of Iraqi Kurdistan and Kurdistan at large. In any case, each will likely come to identify the other in terms of space and status. "*Ez xelkê Zebariyê me,*" the person might reply, giving the name of his or her *aşiret* (tribe) if the speaker seems to be from far away, whereas to someone from close by, a village would find mention instead. Further clarification would be needed to determine the person's place in the hierarchy of the category given. For example, if the speaker reveals that he or she is from Bamarne, a town famous for its powerful and influential Naqshbandi shaikhs, then the questioner knows he or she is either talking to a member of a lineage of villagers who were clients of the Bamarne shaikhs, or a member of the shaikhly lineage. The questioner might ask a further question to place the person in either the relatively low-status former category, or the high-status latter category, asking, "*Binemala kiye?*" "Which patriline?" The answer at that point for a person belonging to a high-status or well-known lineage would be the name of the lineage. "*Mala Babile,*" "the Babil lineage." A person belonging to a lower-status patrilineage might say, "*Cema·atêt Beşar Agha,*" "Beshar Agha's group." The individual agha named Beshar could have lived several generations ago, but his name is still offered both by his direct lineal descendants and the lineal descendants of his client peasants in an explanation for their individual identity in the present. The second speaker to answer will do the same, positioning himself or herself in Kurdistani place and social status, based on his or her patrilineal membership.

Introductory conversations almost always include information about the individual in addition to lineage information. A woman with adult children might mention her children, especially her sons. A teacher might mention his or her occupation and school. A young man might mention the occupation of his father. Lineage membership is given alongside such information, and in certain settings, the information pertaining to the present might be offered before the lineage information or instead of it. In urban settings this is increasingly the case. However, in my observation, the majority of introductory conversations still turn very quickly to place and, indirectly, or at least with deft use of language designed to smooth any obvious differences, social status. Patrilineal identity categories can carry great meaning in the everyday social relations of children, women, and men and affect people's understanding of appropriate roles and even individual potential.

Place, implicitly traced to an arrival of a man on a particular spot of land and fused with lineage membership passed on over time, is intimately bound up with social role, and the two come to influence heavily the relations of the two meeting strangers. The short introductory conversation may reveal the speakers to be members of lineages with a long history of cooperation and friendship, enemy lineages, lineages with vastly different social status, or lineages with similar status. The revelation of major differences in status would immediately influence the interactions of the two. The lower-status person would likely show deference and express respect for the other person's high-status lineage, and the higher-status person would, in most instances, graciously receive the respect but utter some expressions of kindness designed to put the lower-status person at ease.

Lineage and Spatial Histories Intertwined

In the nineteenth century, some important power shifts took place vis-à-vis the Ottomans and the local Kurdish polities, the principalities that dotted the Kurdish areas of the Taurus and Zagros mountains. For a period of several hundred years, the Ottoman and Persian empires had been in conflict, and the consequences for Kurdistan, positioned between the two, had been bloody. As Amir Hassanpour writes, "Pursuing a policy of expansion and centralization, these two states engaged in a destructive war in Kurdistan, Armenia, and Azerbaijan that lasted until the 19th century. . . . The populations of entire principalities were massacred and many conquered tribes were forced into migration to the eastern borders of Iran" (1992:53). During those tortured centuries, average people in Kurdistan were likely to have experienced the rule of Kurdish princes and tribal chiefs to a much greater degree than they experienced imperial governance. But during the 1830s, political changes occurred that would eliminate one of the tiers of power operating in the region. Mohammed Pasha, leader of the Soran Principality headquartered in Rowanduz, waged a campaign to dominate the neighboring principalities that was, for a time, successful. By the middle of the century, however, the Kurdish principalities had fallen and the Ottomans had introduced direct rule, leaving the heart of Kurdistan under unmediated control by non-Kurds for the first time in hundreds of years.[6] The Tanzimat legal reforms were under way, and removing the princes took place in the context of overall modernization efforts taking part across the beleaguered Ottoman Empire.

My research interviews, and references I have heard in everyday conversation in Kurdistan, suggest that many of the tribal chief (*agha*) lineages currently living in the area came to power during the period in the mid-nineteenth century directly following the demise of the principalities. One member of a lineage founded by a man who came to the area near Zakho, with which the lineage is now associated, told me that the land was "empty" when the lineage founder came. At first, hearing this sounded to me like the idea of *terra nullius*, long used to justify colonization in areas that actually were already populated. However, an account of observations made by a Western traveler in 1844 makes clear the devastation he found in the area as a result of recent conflicts between Ottoman and local powers: "The town has shrunk far within the ruined rampart of former days. Even the island is but half covered with houses; so it was ruin, ruin everywhere" (Laurie 1853:342). Into this ruin came settlers who may well have found a void that was not of their own making, and who successfully established themselves, had sons who had sons, and were later recognized as lineage founders.

Most of the oral accounts I have heard in my research of lineage forebears of people of diverse levels of social status, from peasant to town dweller, tend to go back to a period around the turn of the twentieth century. This period is a few decades later, on average, than the typical chiefly lineage. It is possible to infer from these accounts that chiefs filled local power vacuums resulting from the fall of the principalities and the unprecedented exertion of Ottoman control at the local level. Several interviewees who were members of high-status lineages mentioned that the Ottomans had allowed the placement of or installed an ancestor in a chiefly position, and the role of agha was passed down the patrilineage to successive generations. Early generations of lineage members would have lived through the fall of the Ottoman Empire in World War I and the emergence of a modern Middle East presided over by the European Mandate powers, represented by the British in Iraq. Most of Kurdistan's lineages, in other words, are thoroughly modern, created by modern events during the past two centuries, even though the basic elements of the patrilineal motif are not new at all.

The intertwining of lineage structures and spatial histories has an ongoing and powerful bearing on group and individual identities and experiences in Iraq and Iraqi Kurdistan. Perhaps no greater symbol of the Kurdish nation exists than the Kurdish village. During the 1970s and 80s, millions of people throughout the Middle East left their villages and migrated to urban centers (Shami and Center for Migration Studies 1994). But during this same period, Kurds fought vigorously for the right to remain in, and to be sovereign over, their own villages. That thousands were deported involuntarily by the Iraqi government to "collective towns" only served to whet many people's appetite for return, and produced a longing for the lost traditional lifestyle perhaps unmatched anywhere else in the Middle East. I heard many expressions of this type in the 1990s. People in a town would tell me how they were anticipating the completion of their village house by a European or American NGO, and that they were excited at the prospect of returning to village life and reviving their orchards and planting new crops. Many kept a few head of sheep or goats in the city. In my first neighborhood, Barushki, I witnessed a delightful ritual each dusk. Hired herders would escort hundreds of animals down the mountainside on the back side of the neighborhood. The sheep and goats would loudly baa as they made their way home. Once on the edge of the neighborhood, the individual animals would then fan out, making their way home on their own, where someone in the household was waiting to open the gate and let them into their pen for the evening. Those neighborhood houses that had such animals only had room for a few. Some families had only one. In the morning, the animals' owner would let them out to be herded en masse up the mountain again. Many people such as the owners of these animals seemed to feel out of place in the city, and excitedly resumed village life once their village houses were reconstructed.

From statements I have heard from Iraqi Kurdistan's political leaders in both casual conversation and in political speeches and other means of communication, village resettlement was in the years after 1991, and to some extent still is, integral to their vision of the Kurdish nation's identity. Villages, especially mountain villages, have long served as havens where

PHOTO 3.1 Boys herd sheep and goats, bringing them down from the slopes above the city of Dohuk, summer 1995. (Photo by the author.)

Kurds could live in relative safety and with a great deal of autonomy. However, a new vision, of an urban, petrodollar-funded life of luxury is taking its place alongside the ideals of safety and autonomy. Many of the people who returned excitedly to their villages in the years following the 1991 uprising were in for a rude awakening. Despite a major campaign of school construction and reconstruction in the 1990s and 2000s, many villages still lack access to adequate schools. In many places a primary education is available, but nothing beyond that. Other challenges awaited the returnees, who had become used to modern conveniences in the city. I have observed that village return has been coolly received where villages are not outfitted with modern infrastructure, schools, and other amenities. The result has been that many people, after reoccupying their villages in the late 1990s or early 2000s, have again abandoned them. Others, probably the majority, use their village house like a weekend retreat. A large family may be able to leave a few of its members in the village all week during the warm season, especially if crop yields make it worthwhile. Many members of the Barwari tribe, for example, live in Dohuk and Zakho. They still maintain homes in their villages up the road in the mountainous Barwari territory an hour or two's drive away. A few members of their lineage are likely to reside there full time, except in the

PHOTO 3.2 Maqula Mirza works on her knitting in the courtyard of her village house in June 2008. The boy is her neighbor. (Copyright 2009 American Anthropological Association. Reprinted from *Anthropology News* 50, no. 3, with the permission of the American Anthropological Association. Photo by the author.)

dead of winter. Others make the trip occasionally to tend their crops. Apples are one of the main agricultural products of the Barwari area, and it is possible to tend an apple orchard on weekend trips from the city, or to hire out the work to others present in the village. Wintering in remote mountain villages, away from roads and snowplows, is now virtually a thing of the past for everyone but the PKK rebels who continue to occupy some high-elevation Iraqi Kurdish villages. Iraqi Kurdistanis are choosing modernity, living in cities on or near the plains, over their mountains and their villages, some of the potent symbols for which they spent decades fighting.

Claims of patrilineal origin are built up over several generations, and once solidified through emplacement, can be portable for at least one generation. Members of a patrilineage who now live in the city will probably continue to claim patrilineal origin ('esil) in their specific village, even if none or few of them actually continue to reside there. On a visit to a secondary school in Zakho in 2010, I asked the students in two classrooms of approximately forty students each to raise their hands if they had been raised in a village before coming to Zakho. None raised their hands. Then I asked how many had one or two parents who grew up in a village. In each

PHOTO 3.3   A man poses with an old plow, which he made many years before, in his ancestral village in October 2008. He noted that he wants the viewer of this photograph to know that he has long used a more "modern" plow, and that he divides his time between the village and a house in town. (Photo by the author.)

classroom, two students raised their hands. Finally, I asked how many had grandparents who were raised in a village. Only a few hands went up in both classrooms. When I expressed to the students my surprise at the low numbers, one female student summed up Kurdistan's recent strong trend toward urbanization by saying, "In Kurdistan you don't *live* in a village, you *have* a

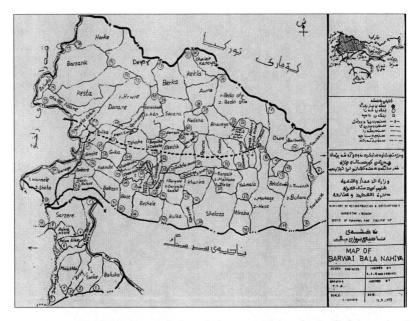

FIGURE 3.3 Barwari Bala, a tribal area, has several hundred villages, each of which is home to the members of between one and several lineages as well as women who have married lineage members. This map was produced by a government office. The modern Iraqi state has recognized tribes and tribal territories throughout its history, although to what degree, and for what purpose, has varied. (Courtesy of Kurdistan Regional Government Ministry of Reconstruction and Development.)

village." The village still lends your lineage identity. You go there occasionally and still own land, or have sharecropping rights in it. Just as Loqman and Bushra still have Deshta, you have the village and the village has you.

Tribal and Urban Leaders, Place, and Collective Identity

It appears from interviews I have conducted that a majority of the twentieth century's major landholding patrilineages, whose members by definition hold the title *agha* or *beg* (a title very similar to agha that in Iraqi Kurdistan connotes a slightly higher level of status) acquired the original title to their land during the late nineteenth century or during the first half of the twentieth century. This demonstrates a remarkable resiliency when one considers the many regime changes that have taken place since 1858, and it suggests that while aghas' roles may be changing, it is presumptuous to assume that they will fade away quickly. During the British period, from the fall of the Ottoman Empire during World War I to 1932 (and to a more limited degree until 1958), most landholding families were not challenged for their land; in fact, the tendency of British colonial administrators to prop up local chieftains resulted in their safeguarding the aghas' land ownership (McDowall 2004:297). Toby Dodge (2003) describes a two-stage process in which the colonial administration first discerned who the locally recognized owner was of a given plot of land, and formalized his ownership rights (105).

The 1958 revolution deposed the British-installed monarchy and brought the nationalist Abd al-Karim Qasim to power. The new regime ushered in land reform, which especially affected the Kurdish areas after the 11 March 1970 agreement between rebellious Kurdish leaders and Baghdad (Bruinessen 1992a:29). Peace between the government and the Kurdish rebels was short lived. Within a few years many of the plains villages had been emptied of Kurds by the government, which placed Arabs on formerly Kurdish lands as a part of its ethnic cleansing efforts. Some Haweri men I know served as chete during the period from the 1960s to 1991. As aghas, some were leaders in the chete brigades. During this same time period, Deshta was annexed and given to Arabs as a part of the Iraqi government's "Arabization" program of ethnic cleansing. The high salaries that the government paid out under the chete program only partly placated them. Their reoccupation of the village with the support of the KDP after the 1991 uprising is recent evidence of the enduring power of the agha role and its ability to weather regime changes.

Although not everyone in Kurdistan belongs to a tribe, the tribe is an extremely important and salient feature of Kurdish life. Ernest Gellner's description of Middle Eastern tribes is a good fit with what I have observed in Iraqi Kurdistan: "The commonest pattern is the existence of a chiefly segment or lineage, which is traditionally empowered to provide the leader for a wider group also comprising other lineages and segments. It is characteristic of this system that there is no clear and unambiguous rule of succession" (1990:110–111). All of the Kurdish tribes of which I am aware do fit Gellner's description, but there are many variations on the ideal-type Kurdish agha and tribe. A tribe may be split into two or more divisions and thus have more than one leading agha. The leading lineage may be concentrated in one or a few villages, or it may have members living in a large

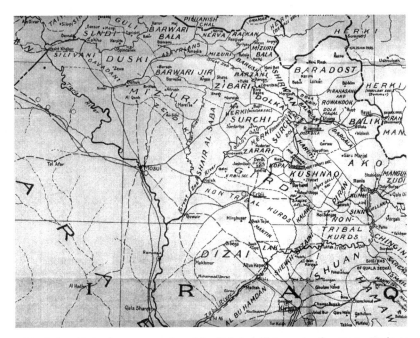

FIGURE 3.4 Part of a map produced by U.S. intelligence in the 1940s. Today's tribal territories are very similar. (United States Military Attaché Office 1944.)

number of villages due to earlier patterns of colonization. Other variations are found as well.

Agha influence waxes and wanes depending on the political situation. In addition to being a group defined by its territory and leadership, a tribe is a military entity. As Edmund Leach states in reference to Iraqi Kurds, "The members of the clan or tribe are aware of their unity largely in terms of their common enmity to some other group" (1940:55). Martin van Bruinessen (1992a) has further argued that modern aghas owe much of their power, and in some cases even their existence, to the state. This was manifested most clearly in Iraqi Kurdistan in the decades before 1991 in the form of the chete system.

Kurdish tribal membership entails making a claim to particular territory and specifically to a village in that territory. Traditionally, aghas have made such claims themselves and also validated claims of tenancy for the peasants they chose to absorb as their own. The legacy of these claims is still in play all over the Kurdistan Region. On the plains, aghas have presided as landlords over the other members of the tribe. In the mountains, where land is scarce, they have had other sources of income, which included thieving and brigandage in the early twentieth century and earlier.

The persistence of the saliency of the agha social category challenges old social science paradigms, from Weberian ideas on political legitimacy to the primitive-modern dichotomy such as that articulated in the article "The Grocer and the Chief" (Lerner 1958), in which the charismatic leader was predicted to be on the way out, and the modern capitalist on the way in. The Kurdistan Region has become an example of what Rogers Brubaker (1996) has called "nationalizing states" in which claims are "made in the name of a 'core nation' or nationality, defined in ethnocultural terms, and sharply distinguished from the citizenry as a whole. The core nation is understood as the legitimate 'owner' of the state, which is conceived as the state of and for the core nation" (5). In such states, members of the core nation engage in a legitimization process, shoring up their claims through such ethnic markers as language and dress. As Andrew Shryock (1996) has demonstrated through his work in Jordan, the recognition of tribal pedigrees is an especially potent form of identity building. Kurdish aghas have been, and remain, indispensably and essentially a symbol of Kurdishness, despite—and perhaps dialectically because of—their sometimes fraught relationship with other Kurdistanis. They are men who attached themselves to the land before a Kurdish nation coalesced and founded a statelet in a fractured modern Iraq, and no one can take this away from them.

At the same time, aghas have been losing ground as arbiters of elite sensibility. Since 1991 they have been losing it to a variety of people: former peshmerga, newly successful urbanites, returnees from abroad, and people with strong connections to the KDP or PUK (and to some extent the smaller political parties such as the Kurdistan Islamic Union). Since it takes several generations for a patrilineage to form, and for the descendants of one man in the past to claim descent through his patriline, it is too soon to tell which men alive now may be claimed by future Kurdistanis as apical ancestors.

Patrilineal memory, like other forms of collective memory that are passed orally from one generation to another, may be subject to what Jan Vansina calls a "floating gap": "For earlier periods one finds either a hiatus or just one or a few names, given with some hesitation. There is a gap in the accounts, which I will call the floating gap. For still earlier periods one finds again a wealth of information. . . . Because the limit one reaches in time reckoning moves with the passage of generations, I have called the gap a floating gap. For the Tio (Congo), c. 1880, the limit lay c. 1800, while in 1960 it had moved to c. 1880" (Vansina 1985:23–24). I argue that a patri-lineage is started, is "segmented" off from another patrilineage, when a man who did something memorable is recognized by his patrilineal descendants as their founder. These descendants keep his own memory alive, but in many cases they do not trump his accomplishments. His story may be told for several generations until his descendants are numerous enough to claim and be recognized by others as constituting a patrilineal descent group with him as their apical ancestor. As Vansina goes on to argue, "There are many accounts for very recent times, tapering off as one goes farther back until one reaches times of origin for which, once again, there are many accounts" (Vansina 1985:168).

In urban settings there are also some lineages that have risen in social status and wealth to produce men who function in many ways like aghas. Town dwellers may make a claim to an urban, nontribal identity based on a claim to several generations of fathers' and sons' residence in the town, which might be coupled with a deliberate erasure of a patrilineal forebear's identity as a "villager." One such lineage whose members I know had several men who became relatively wealthy in the construction busi-ness. They employed large numbers of young men and became patrons to their employees in a way similar to the relationship between a landowning agha and the peasants under him. Just as a peasant/client of a landlord/ agha pays regular visits to his *diwan* (council chambers) to drink tea and eat fruit in the evening, the employees would visit their employer.

Some townspeople I know who do not claim tribal affiliation seem to go out of their way to emphasize the urbanness of themselves and their lin-eage, an identity they see as superior to being a "villager." In interviews, some members of urban lineages told me that they were able to trace their patriline to a tribe and thus to a village, but that this was not something they regularly talked about in the community. In each town, specific events in the twentieth century led to the galvanizing of the identity of the urban lineages.

Many of today's leaders in the Kurdistan Region are the sons and sons' sons of men who were politically involved in the beginnings of the Iraqi state. They in turn are now involved in state building at the regional or national level. The Iraq Directory (Iraq Ministry of the Interior 1936), which was published by the colonial government as a general guide to the country, contained a "who's who" section. By looking in the directory at Iraq's leading men (and they are all men), and identifying their patrilineal descendants in Iraqi politics today, one can see the power of patrilines in the modern(izing) Iraqi state.[7] While there are many such examples throughout Iraq, here are two Kurdish ones: Hazim Shamdin [sic] Agha is listed as deputy to the Iraqi Parliament (581). His son Nijyar represented the KDP portion of the KRG in the United States, serving as a de facto ambassador, from 1997 to 2006. Like many Iraqi elites in the early twentieth century, his lineage was a large landholder. In a table of holders of agricultural land in Iraq, Batatu (2004:58–60) lists the forty-seven families owning more than 30,000 donums (one donum = 0.618 acre) in 1958. One, the family of Shamdin [sic] Agha, is from the area that today comprises the Dohuk Governorate. It is listed as holding 53,040 donums.[8] Another lineage, that of the Barwari begs, owned much less land due to the mountainous topography of its territory but was nevertheless very influential because it led a populous, influential tribe. Haj Rashid Al-Barwari (Rashid Beg) is mentioned in the Iraq Directory as being a member of the Constituent Assembly (605), which was charged with making legal the relationship between the new state of Iraq and mandatory Britain in the early 1920s and presiding over the transition to a parliamentary system.[9] His son's son 'Adil, whom I came to know while living in his neighborhood in Dohuk, is the current paramount chief of the Barwari Bala and has had a long career as a paramilitary leader, first with the Iraqi government and later with the KDP.

In another account, from anthropologist Henry Field (1952), the connections between a prominent man and a swathe of land in Kurdistan are clearly illustrated. Field lists the tribes of Kurdistan, their territories, and their leaders, including, in the case of some of the leaders he lists, the names of the men in their lines of patrilineal descent. Virtually all of the land mass of Iraqi Kurdistan is covered, except for the highest and least habitable mountain areas. In the personal introduction conversations I described earlier, many of the men on Field's list are still mentioned, or if they are not, their son or another successor is mentioned. (Sometimes a chief's successor is not his son but another member of the same patrilineage.

The Middle East has a long history of this type of succession, as opposed to the pattern of primogeniture more common in Europe [Goody 1983]). To look at Field's list is to see the names of fathers and fathers' fathers of men who are in power now. The names on Field's list are some of the names that people in Kurdistan mention when someone asks them who they are—either because the men are their patrilineal forebears, or because their patrilineal forebears were fellahin or otherwise in a client relationship to them.

Population, Aghas, and Connecting

When a society is organized into lineages, more people become "knowable" than they might be otherwise. My sense is that the degrees of separation between any two people in Kurdistan are far fewer than the stereotypical six. I argue this despite the fact that the population of Kurdistan has risen very significantly in the past century. Because lineages take as their reference point a man who lived at an earlier time, they can allow a large group to continue to feel small. In addition, when most people identify with a local leader such as an agha, shaikh, or urban leader, or they belong to such a lineage themselves, the degrees of separation are reduced still further. Land remains an important part of the equation because, even though it is a finite resource, increasing numbers of people can claim the same piece of land as their own, as the point on the earth from which their identity springs. As income rates from rural land decrease, people may move to the city, but they still meet there as people belonging to lineages that belong to certain places. In short, lineages and land-connected leaders such as aghas represent tremendous forces as connecters of people. They knit people together within the given space of Kurdistan in a way that is, in my view, every bit as powerful as the forces of economics, nationalism, language, and shared experience.

During the twentieth century, land reform took place concurrently with rising birth rates in Iraq. This put the aghas in a quandary: it allowed agha lineages to retain land they would otherwise have lost, because every adult individual was entitled to the maximum-allowed share. However, the ratio of yield to individuals became increasingly unfavorable as each new birth meant the land and its yield had to serve yet another individual. Deshta, with its 2,200 donums, is considered a rather small village, which has allowed the Haweris to withstand the various implementations of land reform since 1958. An individual may own no more than 3,000 donums, of which 1,000 may be irrigated and 2,000 dry. In contrast, a paramount agha from the mountains told me that his personal spread totals 700 or 800 donums of dry land and 200 donums of irrigated land. This agha presides as a symbol and to some extent a political leader over half of a mountain tribe and its many villages, as opposed to the aghas of Deshta who have only a single village and whose lineage no longer has a paramount leader. Even though his land is smaller and sloping, the mountain agha stands a better chance of receiving a decent income from the apple orchards on his land because there are fewer people splitting the proceeds. Geography has allowed the mountain aghas other advantages. The mountain landscape is a natural fortress against intruders, the terrain makes it more difficult for authorities to track down smugglers, and, before brigandage tapered off in the mid-twentieth century, its canyons allowed for easy ambushes.

During the past several decades, the aghas' ability to extract a generous income from their land has declined precipitously. In addition to land reform, high fertility and polygyny was a large contributor. Many paramount aghas married multiple wives in the mid-twentieth century. It appears that the practice may be tapering off, although it is still a prerogative frequently exercised by a successful man who occupies a prestigious position. Land was passed on patrilineally until the Personal Status Law of 1959, and, since then, many daughters who have inherited have allowed their brothers to retain control and in some cases to enjoy all of the benefits of their share. The law still allows for some male advantage in certain situations. For example, Article 91 states, "The husband is entitled to a quarter of the legacy when there is an inheriting descendent to his wife; and to half when the latter does not exist. As for the wife, she is entitled to one-eighth of the legacy when there is an inheriting descendent; and to a quarter when the latter does not exist" (Government of Iraq n.d.:22). The phenomenon of many landowners having multiple wives led to their having more children. More children in a patrilineage led to increasing numbers of people sharing a limited amount of land, to the point where in some cases the harvest yielded to each individual only a token sum.

During the same period, the population of Iraq as a whole increased significantly. More people existed, but not necessarily more lineages. In many cases lineages simply became larger, rather than segmenting off into new lineages.

Let us imagine a person alive in the present who is a part of a lineage that traces its identity to a man who was born in the second half of the nineteenth century and whose children were young adults by the 1920 census. Let us assume that four of them were sons (for the sake of this argument we will exclude his daughters because they do not pass on patrilineal membership). By the 1947 census, the population had more than doubled. Not all men have children, and not all men have sons. Some lineages die out. (I once interviewed an elderly woman who was a member of a lineage that had been strong several decades earlier, but due to very high male mortality in the previous generation and out-migration to the West by the few remaining members, it had become nearly extinct.) Successful lineages grow faster than the rate of population growth. So, let us assume that by the 1947 census, our hypothetical lineage has been successful, both economically and reproductively, and the next generation has sixteen men. They marry and have children. Since the lineage is successful, some of them may have polygynous marriages. Interviews I have carried out with some members of large lineages have revealed a high fertility rate in the mid to late twentieth century.[10] If the sixteen men have twenty wives collectively, who each bear them an average of six children, then the next generation could have 120 individuals (approximately 60 of whom are males who will pass on lineage membership) by the mid-1960s. The generation of 60 men born by the mid-1960s could have produced another 360 offspring, and their children would be in the process of reproducing. By now, the lineage would have hundreds of members, both male and female. Throughout the decades, the lineage members would have kept their lineage founder's name and reputation alive through oral tradition. In addition, the Iraqi state, as it registered people in the process of making them citizens, would have begun to document the lineage's growth in its own records. Each state identity card carried by Iraqi citizens, including those in the Kurdistan Region, includes the name of the individual's father and his father, and mother and her father. By now, state records contain patrilineal membership stretching back in time to the first Iraqi Nationality Law, promulgated in 1924.

A British survey of the Mosul *vilayet* (Ottoman administrative unit) in 1920 yielded a population figure of 703,378 (Keltie and Epstein 1920:1330). The vilayet was one of three whose approximate territory came to comprise the new state of Iraq. It was divided into five governorates (*liwas*). According to the General Census of 1947, by midcentury the five governorates' total population was 1,351,100, of whom 804,240 were Kurds (Edmonds 1957:438). The same land area today is approximately equivalent to the Iraqi governorates of Ninewa, Dohuk (split off from Ninewa in 1969), Erbil, Sulaymaniyah (Silemani), and Tameem (Kirkuk), which were reported to have a population of 7,934,400 in 2007 (United Nations Office for the Coordination of Humanitarian Affairs 2007, [OCHA]).[11] During the past century, the population of the area that encompasses the Kurdistan Region has approximately doubled every twenty-five years.

And yet, how many new lineages have formed during the same period? Many, to be sure, but the number of lineages has not increased nearly as quickly as the population itself has. Rather, those lineages that have been successful in reproducing now have more members who carry their reputation as lineage members into more corners of the society. Their members' individual identity is in large part connected to their collective identity.

Lineages make vast numbers of people "knowable." Even I, an outsider, have worked hard to learn the names, associated places, and reputations of many lineages in Kurdistan, because I found that knowledge of other people's lineages was an important social skill. I once met an elderly Kurdish woman just after we had crossed the Tigris River and entered Syria. We were sitting in the van belonging to the KDP, which was about to leave for the Syrian town of Qamishli, and from there each of us would travel by road to Damascus and by air to the United States. I asked which lineage she came from, and it was one I had heard of. I told her a little of what I had heard about her lineage forebears, and that people had said they were respectable men. She brightened, and within a few moments, I had a warm invitation to visit her and her family in San Diego. She had started out a stranger but very quickly left that category and became for me a representative of a group about which I already had some information. We connected, and a man, who arrived on a given piece of land a long time ago and had sons, helped us to do that.

4

Gendered Challenges

Women Navigating Patriliny

[W]e can say that a woman has the right to be proud of her social status and prestige in Kurdish society. She is equal with men in most rights, and in fact, there are certain rights granted exclusively to women. These rights are entitled to the woman as long as she maintains her virginity and chastity.

—Government of Iraq (1973) publication,
Dohuk after March 11, 15

Historic shifts have taken place in the gender system of Iraqi Kurdistan. While the Iraqi government during much of the twentieth century promoted girls' education and encouraged women to come into the public sphere (Al-Ali 2007), those efforts had little impact on Iraqi Kurdistan. Since 1991, however, education rates for both males and females in Kurdistan have increased significantly. In the past, a son was much more likely to attend school long enough to achieve literacy than a daughter. By the turn of the twenty-first century, in most families both sons and daughters were attending school long enough to become literate, and longer. Illiteracy rates were estimated at 18.4 percent in 2011 (Kurdistan Regional Government Ministry of Planning 2011:132). Female education rates (along with education rates overall) have steadily increased in Kurdistan (Kurdistan Regional Government Ministry of Planning 2011). This has created stark intergenerational contrasts. I have observed that both nonliterate older women and highly educated younger women are now found within many families. Many women are called upon to maintain a difficult balance in a Kurdistan that is connecting to the world. I argue that the logic of patriliny impels women to cloister themselves and their male kin to enforce their

PHOTO 4.1 Girls studying to become teachers of English, Zakho, 1998. (Photo by the author.)

cloistering. At the same time, women's observations and experiences as a part of the new and globalized world invites them to exercise their "freedom" as "modern" women.[1]

In recent years, significant numbers of women in the Kurdistan Region have begun to drive. Before the turn of the millennium, the only female drivers in the small cities, towns, and villages of Kurdistan were employees of NGOs and UN agencies, and most of them were not from the local area. Women drivers were very rare in Kurdistan's two major cities, Hewler and Silemani; in fact, I do not recall seeing any local female drivers in either of those cities before 2000, although people have told me that there were a few. Now, in the second decade of the century, the streets are still overwhelmingly male-dominated, but a few women drivers can be seen here and there, and this is new.

When a woman drives, especially when she drives by herself, she has much more personal freedom than when she is reliant on others to drive her. The standard mobility options for Kurdistani women include walking, being driven by a male relative or household employee, or taking a taxi or bus. (They do not include the bicycle, about which I will have more to say later.) Especially for girls and women of child-bearing age, the various transportation options usually involve a tight schedule or supervision, so that her family knows where she was (in the taxi or bus, which took her to an agreed-upon destination) and what she was doing (riding) during a given block of time.

A woman who drives a car can drive somewhere to have an illicit sexual relationship. This was a point made to me several times in the 1990s when I probed people as to why women should be prevented from driving, as they apparently were then. People would not say so openly, but they hinted at it, until, in several cases, I asked: "Do you mean that if a woman were able to drive a car, then people would wonder if she was driving it somewhere to have sex with someone who was not her husband?" I said this only to a few people I was close to, who I thought would be tolerant of the directness of my question. "Yes, that's it!" was always the answer of my embarrassed interlocutor.

Many added that a girl or woman who drove would surely feel şerim, an emotion prompted by the scornful gaze of others in the community, or at least the perception that a gaze was scornful. Others associated with her, especially the lineage into which she had married (if she had) and members of her own lineage, would feel it too. Şerim's most common and logical translation in English is "shame," but that term seems inadequate. Şerim, and its Arabic equivalent eyb, are talked about constantly by many people in Kurdistan, especially parents talking to their children. Şerim is something to fret over, and to try one's best to avoid. It can be brought on by any number of things, although, for adolescents and adults, the accusation that a female has had sex outside of marriage, or has even been open to having sex outside of marriage, is probably the most powerful inciter of feelings of şerim, for the person herself, and for anyone associated with her, especially her husband (if she is married) and members of her lineage.

Today, the vast majority of women still do not drive, and the usually-left-unstated reason of sexual suspicion may be the main explanation, in addition to the fact that many girls and women have simply never learned to drive in the first place or do not have access to a vehicle.

From the start, it was clear from my conversations with girls and women in Kurdistan that many dreamed of driving. Driving seemed to be forbidden, but then again it seemed possible, too. Iraq was not Saudi Arabia; it was not against the law or any policy to drive. The situation was simply that individuals and their kin, both women and men and people in lineages both urban and rural, all conspired through omission (the women) and commission (the men, by driving the women around) to keep women from behind the wheel.

Myths helped enforce this. One myth I heard from several men was that women simply were not skilled enough to drive. It was not part of their nature. If they joined men on the roads, they would frequently crash and create chaos. Once in 1998, I was riding in the back of a shared taxi. I was the only female passenger in the full vehicle. We were in a rural area between cities when the driver trained his rear view mirror on me and asked, "Do you know how to drive?" I was an American in my thirties who was from car-saturated Southern California and I had driven hundreds of thousands of miles in my lifetime. "Yes, of course!" I said to him, trying not to sound offended. "No!" he said, sounding genuinely incredulous. He kept pressing me. "I really know how. I have a lot of driving experience!" I told him repeatedly. "What kind of car can you drive?" he asked. "Any kind!" I asserted. At that, he slammed on the brakes, pulled over to the side of the road, got out, opened the rear door, and ordered me with a good-natured smile to take his place in the driver's seat. I did as he requested, and he in turn settled into my former seat in the back. The other passengers were grinning ear to ear as I settled in at the controls. The car had a manual transmission. I will admit that I deliberately pulled away abruptly, just so there would be no doubt about my abilities. The clutch engaged perfectly smoothly and soon we were zooming down the road just as we had been a few minutes previously. The driver and the other men howled with delight. "This is amazing!" the taxi driver said from the back seat. "I have never seen a woman drive before! And you even know how to drive a man's car!" "What do you mean by a 'man's car'?" I asked as I drove, unaware that there was such a thing. "A stick shift is a man's car. I know that women drive in other parts of the world, but I understand that they drive cars with automatic transmissions only, because shifting is too difficult for them. Until now I thought that only men could work the stick shift!" We talked for a bit longer as I drove. I was not comfortable driving us for more than a few minutes, however, because I had seen and heard horror stories about accidents. Not only were they frequent, but auto insurance was unknown, and tribal justice was sometimes applied after an accident. I had heard a number of stories of a driver accidentally hitting and killing someone, and the relatives or tribe of the deceased might then try to negotiate for blood in return, leading to the death penalty for the survivor. Whether anyone had received such a sentence, I did not know; but I found these stories daunting. In light of them, it made sense to me why so many high-status people did not drive themselves, or at least did so rarely, but were driven around by professional drivers from a lower economic echelon. In a situation that led to tribal justice proceedings, someone of lower status would be the loser, not they themselves. With these thoughts in mind, I pulled to the side of the road after a few kilometers and the taxi driver drove us the rest of the way.

The glass ceiling that had previously prevented women in Iraqi Kurdistan from driving started to crack in the late 1990s. In the Dohuk household of Layla and her daughter Zahera, driving was a frequent topic of conversation. Zahera yearned to drive, and her mother told me in 1998, when Zahera was only seventeen, that she was not opposed to the idea. One day in January 1998, driving suddenly started to seem like a possibility. Layla's son called from Denmark and said that he was about to send them $10,000 to buy a house or a car. Zahera was giddy and lobbied hard for a car. She and her mother hatched a plan: they would buy the car, and at first, only I would drive it. I would teach Zahera, and by the time I left at the end of my fieldwork, she would be skilled enough to drive it on her own. I found the idea intriguing, but I worried about their reputation. Wouldn't Zahera's driving cause them to feel şerim, shame, in the face of the watching community? Layla, who was more open-minded than virtually any other woman in her age group whom I knew in Kurdistan, insisted that it would not. She added that this would especially be the case in the neighborhood to which we were about to move, Girebasi, since it was considered the most "modern" area of Dohuk. Layla was ready for her daughter to be the first female driver in Bahdinan, an area with a population of around 800,000.

Layla could not know then that her and Zahera's time in Kurdistan was limited, and within a year, they would be accepted as refugees in neighboring Syria, and off to the United States not long after that. In the meantime, they decided to use the money for a house instead of a car.

Zahera got her wish, but not in Kurdistan. She has now been an American driver for over a decade.

Other cracks in the ceiling appeared. A friend in Dohuk who worked as an obstetrician told me in March 1998 that she and her husband had just bought a new car, an Oldsmobile. "Neither of us really knows how to drive it yet," she said with a laugh. "But we are learning, outside of town where we can't hit anything."

By June of that year, I had seen Nesreen Barwari, who eventually became a cabinet member in the regional government and later minister of public works for Iraq, driving around Dohuk in her capacity as director of the local United Nations Habitat office. I later asked Nesreen if she knew of any local woman who drove before she did, and she said that she did not. I, too, did not see any in the Bahdinan area before I saw her. Sightings of female drivers were still rare for the next several years. Here is a field note I wrote in Zakho:

Field Note, Wednesday 27 February 2002:

[W]e saw a woman driving. She had her head covered and was driving a late-model Mercedes. This is the first woman driver I have ever seen in Zakho! When I first arrived this time I asked "Nahela" and "Sabeha" what is new. They said, "Women are driving here now." Since this is the first one I have seen in the twenty-five days since I began this research stint, I imagine you can count the number of women drivers here on two hands.

One woman told me in 2002 when I asked her why she thought women were starting to drive: "They are driving because they want to be a part of the modern world. They see on television that women in most other places are driving. They have heard about it from people who went out to the West. Maybe these women themselves have been out, and that is where they learned." Lara Deeb notes in her ethnography of women in Hezbollah who deftly combine a pious life with a modern life: "A person, community, place, or thing is always modern as compared to some other thing, another that is defined in the comparison as not modern or less modern" (2006:17). It seems that the Kurdish women who are driving are engaging in a comparison of their own.

Sabeha still does not drive, but shortly after I wrote that field note in 2002, Nahela was inspired to try driving herself, and it is now an important part of her life. Her adventures as she starts to exercise some new free-doms, which includes learning to drive, illustrate some of the changes now taking place in the Kurdistani gender system. Nahela is a teacher in Zakho. Born in the mid-1960s, she is a member of the Haweri lineage. She is unmarried and has always lived with other members of her family, which at the moment includes one of her brothers and his wife and their young adult children. She and her household have been hosting me during my research trips for years now. She has long provided friendship, humor, and a constant running commentary on Kurdistani life. Nahela is politically skeptical and cynical. She has an uncanny ability to reflect on her own society and its place in the world, which belies the fact that she is not well traveled despite a deep desire to be. Here is a conversation we had in 2005, about a hypothetical trip to America that she hoped to make (but as of this writing still has not):

NAHELA: I think I will be able to travel to America without one of my brothers traveling with me. My family is becoming more open minded. They let me wear pants in school, they let me take driving lessons, although I haven't driven anywhere yet.

DIANE: Who is letting you do these things?

NAHELA: By God, I didn't ask anyone. I just started doing them and smiled and no one stopped me.

DIANE: But who *would* have stopped you?

NAHELA: Everyone! But no one stopped me. Anyway, I am almost forty. How can they stop me from doing everything when I am almost forty? I am not going to cause a problem [a euphemism for becoming preg-nant] now. They think I am too old!

DIANE: [Jokingly] Let's not tell them about my friend who is also forty and pregnant.

NAHELA: No! We must never tell them! [Laughter] I am changing little by little. Slowly, slowly [she said wryly]. By the time I am sixty, they will let me go to Baghdad!

In 2008 Nahela and I traveled to Hewler, several hours to the south-east. Each of us had business in the passport office there. I needed to update my own immigration status, and Nahela was applying for a "G" passport, the only type of Iraqi passport that would allow the holder to apply for a U.S. visa. She had long wanted to visit the United States, where she has a brother and many other relatives. While in Hewler, which is several hours from Nahela's home in Zakho, we stayed with her cousin, her father's sister's son and his wife and child. Over a two-day period, Nahela managed to pass successfully through several of the required bureaucratic steps. She had filled out many forms, and had her picture taken, when she hit a road-block: the person behind the counter informed her that Iraqi law requires a close male relative to authorize the issuance of a passport for any female under the age of forty-five. Since she was not married and her father was dead, one of her brothers would be required to sign. Her nearest brother was far up the road in Zakho. "I had no idea about this law!" she told me, with clear frustration in her voice. "I mean, I thought there was something like this, but that the age was forty, not forty-five!" I urged her to ask if there was some way around this. Her three brothers who were in Kurdistan knew she was trying to get the passport. We had come to Hewler two days earlier in a taxi that one brother had arranged for us; it was driven by his friend and he had entrusted us to him. Her fourth brother was in the United States, but she could not visit him without the passport. What if she were to reach one of the three on the phone, right there? Although the people behind the counter were sympathetic, they ultimately told her that there was nothing they could do without bringing her brother in person. And with that, Nahela's plan was postponed until she and a brother could make another time-consuming, costly trip to Hewler.

On the third day of our trip, I had a research interview scheduled in one part of town, and Nahela needed to return to the passport office one last time to pick up some of the paperwork that had been in process. Our appointments were overlapping and neither was flexible. Nahela had told me the previous day that it would not be appropriate for her to take a taxi alone in Hewler. We had a logistical problem on our hands. I could escort her to the passport office in a taxi and then proceed to my research inter-view. Her family had regularly entrusted her to me in this manner, and I was grateful, since many families would only allow a related male to play such a role. But what would happen when she was finished there? The office closed in the early afternoon. I would be busy virtually all day, with-out a defined ending time. Finally, that morning Nahela announced that she had changed her mind: she would take a taxi in a big city by herself for the first time. I went with her in the morning and gave her instructions as to how to find me later. I was in the middle of a research interview with several highly educated and influential policy professionals, talking about issues of civil society and governance in the new Iraq, when Nahela slipped quietly into the back of the room. Everyone had consented earlier for her to sit in on the research interview should she arrive in time, so they paid little attention to her. As I glanced over at her, however, I thought about the momentousness of the occasion. Not the occasion of talking about Big Subjects with Big People, but an occasion that remained a secret in that room: my forty-three-year-old friend had just taken a taxi, a taxi driven by a stranger in a big city, by herself for the first time.

Perhaps paradoxically, by that field visit that began in May 2008, Nahela had been the owner of her first car for about six months, having purchased it around the beginning of 2008. She drove it only in Zakho, and almost always with passengers along, unless she was going a very short distance known to her family, such as to her sister's house a few blocks away. She had almost finished paying off the car's $6,000 price tag out of her $400 per month teacher's salary and some savings, and was in the process of trading it in for a second car. She was driving the new one, a 2004 Mitsubishi, "with '*ful otomatik*,'" as she told people proudly during a two-week trial period on agreement with the owner. She kept the Mitsubishi in a pristine state, one that seemed in complete contrast to Zakho's rough, dusty streets. At one point she reprimanded me for slamming my passenger-side door in what I thought was a relatively gentle fashion. "Don't do that!" she snapped! "What?" I said defensively. "You must close the door very, very carefully, like this," she said, closing her driver's-side door delicately, as though a sleeping baby were lying between us. "I will tell you why," she continued, seeing the look of confusion on my face. "People here care very much about those parts of the car that you can see. They will notice the tiniest scratch. This is not my car yet, so I have to be concerned about what the owner will think, but even if I buy this car I will still keep it perfect, absolutely perfect!" She did buy it, and she did keep it perfect. Vehicular aesthetics had not struck me as a big concern for Kurdistanis in the past. It seemed that Nahela's car was not only a sign of new liberties being taken by some women, but also a sign of a marked increase in consumption that was readily visible. People had placed great emphasis on some forms of aesthetics all along. Many women were fastidious house-keepers, and when they got dressed up for a special occasion, they went all out. Many men went to great lengths to stay neatly groomed and to keep their cars clean. For a woman to care about the cleanliness of a car as well as its overall aesthetic and functional condition was a reminder of the embededness of gender conventions in broader patterns of consumer values, some of which were brand new.

One morning in June 2008, Nahela and I went shopping in Zakho's old bazaar (sîk, souq). After two months of fieldwork in various locations in the Kurdistan Region, I was preparing to leave in two days, and there were things I needed to buy first. Afterward I wrote this field note:

Field Note, 18 June 2008:

She drove, and we did not have anyone with us. We bought batter-ies and other little things. What a luxury it is to be able to just take off in the car! . . . Before, we had to beg and cajole (even if I paid them as research assistants) her brothers to take us somewhere, and/or we had to take taxis, which was limited to daytime and had to be approved by the family. As we drove, Nahela offered a running commentary on the other drivers. "Shameless dog!" "Dog, son of a dog! . . ." she would say to reckless male drivers, such as the driver of a truck heading our way, in our lane, which would swerve into its own lane at the very last millisecond with seemingly a hair to spare. It seems she is in more culture shock over the driv-ing here than I am. She drives carefully, slowly. "All of the women in our family like to ride with me," she said, straightening with pride. "They trust me. I swear if I am ever in an accident, I will scream at everyone watching, 'How many people die every year because of men's dangerous driving?[2] How many? And how many die because of women's driving? Tell me!' I will scream this in the street, I swear!"

The car had an MP3 jack, and there was a small hard drive attached to it that belonged to one of Nahela's nephews. Most of the music on it was American hip-hop music. As we drove, the sounds of rapper 50 Cent's song "Candy Shop" boomed in the background. I protested that the song was vulgar. "Do you know what he is actually saying?" "I have no idea," said Nahela, who had majored in English at university.

"Yeah . . . uh huh. So seductive," thumped the song. "I'll take you to the candy shop, I'll let you lick the lollypop, Go 'head girl, don't you stop, Keep going 'til you hit the spot. . . . You can have it your way, how do you want it. . . . I'll break it down for you now, baby it's simple, If you be a nympho, I'll be a nympho, In the hotel or in the back of the rental . . ."

I "translated" some of the lyrics for her by offering my own interpretations of some of the song's milder metaphors, skipping over the more explicit ones. Even a few of those were enough to make my point. "Wow!" she said. "I am glad no one else here knows what he is saying, either. 50 Cent is very popular now. Everyone loves his music! But if they knew what he was saying, they might feel differently."

The American military was just outside Zakho on a base at the Ibrahim Khalil border complex. Most of the personnel working there came and went from the war zone in Mosul, bypassing Zakho and having little influence on everyday life in Kurdistan. So while it might have been logical to assume a connection between the sudden popularity of American rap music and the presence of the U.S. military, I knew from many other observations and encounters that an important source for Western imports such as the MP3 player and music was people from Kurdistan, now living in the West (cf. King 2008). Coveted cultural goods would arrive in their own luggage when they came to visit, or it was couriered by family members and friends. I thought back to the late 1990s, when the movie *Titanic* was popular and Celine Dion's theme song, "My Heart Will Go On," could be heard wafting from what seemed like the most unlikely places in Kurdistan.

Gender Roles in Iraqi Kurdistan

This is a paradoxical time in the gendered history of Iraqi Kurdistan—the proverbial best of times and worst of times. Kurdish society has long fit the classic sex/gender archetype of the Mediterranean and Middle East. Kurdish men appear to experience and exhibit the dominance typical across the Middle East, where "there is a strong linkage between the patriarchal construction of gender roles and authoritarianism" (Ghanim 2009:6). As David Gilmore has written of men in the Mediterranean region,

"[A] man is expected to spend his free time outdoors, backslapping and glad-handing. This world is the street, the bar, the fields—public places where a man is seen. He must not give the impression of being under the spell of the home, a clinger to wife or mother" (1990:52). Gilmore might also have added military or para-military service to his list, from which few men in Iraq, including in Kurdistan, have been exempt. The converse of this is that a man is not a man without being socially legitimized outside the home. A man is not a full man without the public sphere, but a man does not make the public sphere so much as the public sphere makes a man.

Idealized Kurdish women's roles, in contrast, are relatively straightforward: a woman is charged with maintaining a home and with upholding the honor and purity of her and her husband's patrilineages through her proper behavior. My sense from conversations with women about the past is that the expectations placed on a woman went relatively unchanged even during the years of upheaval prior to 1991. Even when they were displaced by conflict, as thousands were, wives continued to be homemakers wherever they were, even when their husbands were away fighting or working. Suad Joseph (2000:6, citing Layoun 1992 and Peteet 1991) writes, based on her fieldwork in Lebanon, that a woman is that person who authenticates "a community of kin, a safe haven for family, a 'home.'" A home is not a home without a woman in it. A home is legitimized by a woman, and from my observation this assertion applies as strongly to Kurdistan as to Lebanon. Polish anthropologist Leszek Dziegiel wrote the following about the Kurdish homes he observed, which, despite his use of male terminology, were surely maintained by women: "One had the impression that both the rural and the urban Kurd treated his home or property as a closed, miniature world of his own, an oasis surrounded by an indifferent, if not entirely hostile external universe" (1982:48).[3] The vast majority of the Kurdish women I know spend most of their waking hours preparing food and cleaning their homes. Most girls do as well, when they are not in school. In villages, homes are smaller and therefore need less attention, but there is agricultural labor to do on most days. I have noticed that city women are confined to their homes, and complain of boredom, much more than village women. Al-Khayyat (1990:112) also found this to be true for women in Baghdad.

Patrogenetic Logic and Its Influence on Gender Relations

In patrogenesis, the father is regarded as the main or only contributor of biological substance to the child, so only fathers, not mothers, are regarded as having generative power. The ideas of semen and fetus are conflated into one. Conception occurs when the man inserts the makings of a new human being into a woman's womb, where the new human is nurtured and grows. Patrogenesis is a common idea in the Middle East and circum-Mediterranean, and evidence from ancient writers such as the authors of the Jewish scriptures to the Greeks (Wright 2004) suggests that it has been around for a long time. Fertility is both emphasized and interpreted in ways that privilege the male. Like the Turkish villagers described by Carol Delaney (1991), I have heard Kurdish people speak of sexual intercourse as a process in which the man inserts "seed" into the "soil" of the woman. I learned that to comment an infant resembles its mother was to imply a lack of virility on the part of the infant's father, the implication being that his sperm was not robust enough to fend off influence by the enveloping womb. Many other hints in everyday conversation suggested that, as valued and idealized as mothers were, people regarded fathers, not mothers, as imparting essence and being to their offspring. Andrea Fischer-Tahir also notes parallels between Kurdish terms and concepts having to do with conception, pregnancy, and birth and those that Delaney describes, and argues that "in Kurdish beliefs, the body of a woman is considered the fertile possession of 'man' and 'society,' similar to the soil wanting to be cultivated, covered and defended as a forbidden domain against attacks from the 'outside'" (2009:74–75). On the same pages, Fischer-Taher offers a wonderful inventory of relevant Kurdish words and phrases that clearly demonstrate the logic at work.

Unilineal kinship systems tend to emphasize a person's role as a son or daughter because each individual is a member of his or her lineage by virtue of the person's role as a daughter or son. (In all kinship systems, other roles, such as sibling or parent, do not apply to everyone, but everyone was born to someone so the roles of daughter and son are more universal to begin with.) As daughters, women are full citizens in a patriline and fully responsible for the maintenance of its reputation. A patriline, however, can be thought of as a male body writ large, coursing through time. The bodies of men are the source of seed which, when it is planted and grows into another human, produces an extension of the patrilineal body. In other words, only men are fertile. Women's contribution to life-generation is severely deemphasized. Women are, like mules, by definition infertile. They are not generative persons like men (Delaney 1995:183–184); but mere "carriers," through pregnancy, of the next generation.

While women *receive* just as much patrilineal membership as men, femaleness may be denigrated because women are not able to produce new members for *their own* line of descendants. They can only produce new members for *their child's father's* line. (Sometimes members of the same lineage marry. The most common of these types of marriage is between the children of brothers. When a union of a woman and man who belong to the same lineage yields children, the woman is raising children with whom she shares a lineage. However, each infant produced by such a union is still a member of the patriline by being born to his or her father, not mother.) In patrilineal systems in which patrogenesis is emphasized, females may simply be regarded as less valuable to their families and communities than males, because while they are full persons with regard to their full receipt of patrilineal membership from their fathers, they cannot pass that membership on.

Not only do men have the advantage of the ability to pass on patrilineal membership to their offspring, but each man is also a potential lineage founder. It is the rare man who is so privileged as to start a lineage or part of a lineage whose members later come to claim him as their founder, but, in theory, every man is the potential founder of a lineage. Linda Stone and I have argued that a patrilineage is, most basically, a group of people who claim descent through males from a man who did something memorable (King and Stone 2010). We argue that men can build up and pass on "lineal masculinity" to and through their agnatic ascendants. Placing the emphasis on the lineage founder having done something memorable simplifies what we feel was an overly complex debate about segmentary lineages in anthropology in the mid-twentieth century, which sought to answer the question of why a lineage segment formed out of a previously recognized lineage. Echoing that vein of literature's main assertion, that segmentation happened for reasons that were mainly structural, Hildred Geertz wrote that patrilineality is "a cultural model for group formation that is based on a systematic elaboration of the chain of father-son links into a branching tree form, with group segmentation programmed to occur at each forking point" (Geertz 1979:348). Stone and I disagree with Geertz that segmentation is "programmed to occur." Rather, it occurs when there is either an incident such as migration or conflict that causes a rupture in the line, or a tremendous achievement that elevates one individual, who through sons creates a branch that may come, in time, to be recognized as a separate lineage. Interviews with Kurdish people who recounted to me the histories of their lineages have produced many examples to support this. Not every man who does something memorable is later remembered as the founder of a new lineage. However, he may, if the remembered action or occurrence is heroic or at least viewed in a positive light, bring renown to his whole lineage.

In the lineal masculinity model, masculinity in patrilineal cultures takes on a quality that is extracontemporaneous. It is received by a male infant from his father, and passed on by a man to his son. It is *not* individualized or automatic in the sense that it depends for its maintenance on the proper behavior of the lineage members, most notably the sexual restraint of the lineage's female members. It *is* individual, however, in the sense that each individual man builds on, maintains, or diminishes whatever lineal masculinity he has received from his lineage at birth (or, more accurately, conception). Because a man's accomplishments and reputation can have such long-standing effects, gender roles take on an importance they might not otherwise. My sense is that both men and women in Kurdistan face pressure to be certain kinds of men and certain kinds of women who can be located in their membership in lineages. All gender systems, everywhere in the world, place demands on people to conform, but in this system, people yet unborn, the people who may comprise a lineage in the future, are seen as participating in the application of gendered social pressure on both women and men.

Collective Identity, Class, State, and Nation

Numerous writers, including Sherry Ortner in her classic article, "The Virgin and the State" (1978), and others such as Anh Nga Longva (1993) and Leslie Peirce (2000) have pointed out that the seclusion of women as a method of sexual control has long been linked to the maintenance of collective identity—whether of the Kuwaiti women in the presence of lower-status migrant workers that Longva describes, or the social elites under the Ottomans analyzed by Peirce. By controlling sex, the community controls reproduction and thus the introduction of new members into groups. Rarely, however, have analysts of female seclusion analyzed the specific theory of reproduction at work in the particular cultural setting that produces seclusion. Peirce, for example, simply notes that a married childbearing woman's seclusion was stringently enforced because she was "considered to have an awakened sexual appetite" and "reproductive capacity was a potential threat to the integrity of her husband's blood line" (2000:62). A patrogenetic theory of procreation, especially when bound up with other features of patriliny, is an assertion that carries with it a host of ramifications for individual, household, and group life.

As Marcia Inhorn's extensive body of work has clearly shown (e.g., 1994, 1996, 2003, 2012), Middle Eastern men seeking treatment for infertility in the Middle East are extremely uncomfortable with the idea of using a sperm donor. Most will not even consider the idea, and explain that in such a case the child would not be "theirs." Instead, they will pursue other options aimed at increasing their chances of siring a child. They may choose to take an additional wife, a relatively common practice in response to a current wife's presumed infertility in Iraqi Kurdistan. Many wives who have been unable to become pregnant fear that their husbands will announce a decision to marry polygynously. Some first wives appear to be happy to have a co-wife join the family, or they at least come to accept her and the arrangement over time. However, I have heard many married women express anxiety at the thought that their husband may decide at any time that he wants to marry again. Fertility treatments and marital patterns aimed at fostering male procreation are but two of the many aspects of kinship and social relations engendered by patriliny and patrogenesis.

The valuing of female virginity before marriage and chastity afterward are widespread values that have proven sustainable through myriad changes in the Kurdistani socioeconomic milieu. In an article in which he asserts that the structure of the Kurdish language reproduces female subjugation, Amir Hassanpour notes that "a semantic field has developed around 'virginity,' which lies at the center of the definition, social construction, and disciplining of females" (Hassanpour 2001:238). Patriliny and patrogenesis can shed further light on this field. When group membership is reckoned patrilineally, you know who is in your group (tribe, class, lineage) and who is not in your group by knowing to which father each person was born. Therefore male parenthood must be known. One way to be confident of male parenthood is to control the autonomy, and thereby the virginity and chastity, of women in their childbearing years.

When the constitution of a "nation" is in question, or when patrilineally defined groups are in conflict or are rivals who can slip into conflict when an incident triggers it, people may sense an even greater need to make sure that everyone knows which individuals were born to which fathers. Because patrilineages are themselves potential fighting units, and groups of patrilineages comprise larger fighting units, when conflict is increased the policing of reproduction increases. The Kurdistan Region of Iraq is experiencing a period of relative stability, but, as I detail in chapter 2, its past is very bloody. Some kinds of group conflict remain, however, in the form of blood feuds between patrilineally defined groups. A lineage or tribe that is mobilizing for a blood feud against another lineage or tribe wants to be sure of who its members are, and it wants to keep its child-bearing women, both those still living among the lineage or tribe's population and those who are elsewhere because of, for example, marriage or attending the university, from producing offspring for possible rivals. Rather, they must be pressed into service for the group through endogamy (or strategic exchanges, such as the giving and taking of brides to and from other lineages). At the lineage level, endogamy is accomplished through agnatic cousin marriage, and at the level of the tribe or nation, through marriage to another member of the tribe or nation. The nationalism literature makes a clear link between pronatalism and nationalism, especially in times of conflict (e.g., Kaufman and Williams 2008). As Jan Pettman writes, citing her own work and that of Wendy Brown, "The nation is feminized, and the male/state must fight for her honor. In an identity shift, women are also constructed as mothers of the nation, especially in times of conflict or mobilization. Women's bodies become the territory on which national work is done. This is seen most graphically in systematic war rape, designed to demonstrate to enemy men that they are unable to defend 'their' women, and to disorganize the nation by introducing 'enemy seed'

through forced pregnancies (Pettman 1996c; see also Brown 1992)"
(Pettman 2000:260). In the mid-2000s, systematic war rape took place in
Iraq, although not in Kurdistan, as Sunni and Shi'i militias attacked each
other's populations during the U.S. occupation. For Mary Layoun (2001:18),
the social construction of nations and states can be a process in which
"purity is sovereignty, rape is the violation of sovereignty, and consumma-
tion is possession of pure and sovereign land." Patrilineages sometimes
constitute or contribute to fighting groups. Their women members can
bring renown to their own lineage if they maintain virginity before marriage and chastity afterward. That way everyone knows which infants
belong to which lineages. How can a lineage stand tall, and act as a fighting force if necessary, if there is doubt as to who constitutes its membership? "Nationalist rhetorics often portray a core of males who embody
the nation," write Georges Fouron and Nina Glick Schiller, "while female
bodies are possessed by the nation" (2001:541).

Islam and the Supernatural in Women's Lives

For most of the women among whom I have worked, the religious and
supernatural realms are of great importance and are a part of their lives on
an everyday basis.[4] For many women, judging by the frequency with which
I have heard them acknowledge God and other spiritual forces in everyday
speech, unseen spiritual forces may come to mind throughout the day
every day. Indeed, it would be difficult to speak the Kurdish language as it
is spoken colloquially without making frequent reference to the role of
God in events. Like other people in the Middle East, most people use the
phrase "If it is God's will" when speaking about the future. Both the Arabic
("*Enshallah*") and Kurdish ("*Heke Xwedê ḥez ket*") are frequently used.
People seem to have a strong belief in fate as well.

Kurdistan has often been characterized as one of the Muslim-majority
places in the world in which Islam is not taken very seriously. I have heard
such characterizations mainly from foreign men who are employees of
international organizations and businesses working in the Kurdistan
Region. Islam and Kurdish nationalism, the promotion primarily by men of
Kurdish political power in public spheres, have had an uneasy coexistence.
I have heard many people, most of them men, deride the famous military

leader Ṣalāḥ ad-Dīn Yūsuf ibn Ayyūb (Saladin), adversary of Richard the Lionheart in the Third Crusade and founder of the Ayubid dynasty in the twelfth century, for doing more to advance the cause of Islam than the cause of the Kurds. Other observations I have made suggest that for many men in Iraqi Kurdistan, there is social pressure to refrain from being too religious. I once overheard a conversation between two middle-aged men in Zakho that went like this: "So, do you pray?" said one man. "No," said the other. "I don't believe in it because so much of it is just for show. I believe God cares more about how I am on the inside, not whether people see me at the mosque or not." "I agree completely!" came the reply. "Once during Ramadan a couple of years ago, I decided to go to the mosque to pray. I never go, but this time I decided to. So I went. I noticed that everyone was staring at me. I felt uncomfortable. Then after that, for days people were congratulating me, mocking me—everyone had to make something of it. One of my friends said to me, 'So . . . I heard you were at the mosque. . . .' You would have thought that a Christian went to the mosque that day! So that was the end. I will never go back. There is no need. You are right. Prayer is for God, not for people."

My sense as a woman researcher, and from having spent significant time with both women and men in Kurdistan, is that, while highly variable from individual to individual and household to household, Muslim women have an overall higher degree of religiosity than men. Most of the women I know well will do the Muslim prayers at least once a day, if not all five required times. Many of the men I know will go to Friday prayers, although perhaps not every Friday, and they may or may not do the prayers during the week. During Ramadan, women seem to be much more diligent about keeping the fast than men. In Deshta, I once watched as a group of men ate meat declared to be *haram* (forbidden) because it was not butchered properly, while their female relatives looked on, refusing to partake even though they were hungry.

Islamic parties are very active in seeking new members in Kurdistan, and Islamist influence is having some success. The Islamic Union of Kurdistan is the party that has attracted the most attention among the people I know. Although it and other parties are quite visible, they do not have large numbers of members. Their main accomplishment has been to build thousands of mosques since 1991, reportedly with funding from

Saudi Arabia.[5] Iran has sponsored some mosques as well, especially in the Hewler and Silemani areas. In 2011, Islamists clashed publicly with the KDP-dominated KRG and some violence was perpetrated and both sides were blamed. For the most part, the KDP and PUK have promoted their own brand of "moderate" Islam, involving themselves, just like other governments in Muslim-majority areas, with *waqf* (charitable endowments) and other public aspects of the faith. Nowadays, this mainly takes place through the KRG Ministry of Endowment and Religious Affairs.

When I taught at Dohuk University in the 1990s, some of my students were involved in Islamic parties, and a woman in my neighborhood was very vociferous about her beliefs and support for Islamist causes. For the most part, however, the Muslims I know in Kurdistan who are more religious than their peers are not members of Islamist political parties. They simply cover their heads, read the Quran (those who are able to), and pray regularly. They may attend neighborhood study groups. Some of these groups are sponsored by the parties, but many people who attend them are not members of the parties, but are rather seeking to increase their own personal piety. While I was living in Layla's household, Layla went to a neighborhood study group and would sometimes bring along one or more of her daughters. One of her teenaged daughters went through a period of trying to be more observant. She listened to Islamic teaching on the radio, and made an effort to do all five daily prayers right after the call to prayer was emitted from the local mosque. One day during Ramadan, she announced that she was beginning a campaign to stop swallowing her own saliva during the daylight fasting period, since doing so could be considered eating or drinking. For a few days, she carried around a cup into which she would periodically spit. I remember her sisters and mother loudly mocking her for this behavior, and telling her that they thought this was taking the idea of fasting much too far. After a few days, she quit.

Many Muslim Kurdish women, like many other Muslims, believe in spirits, *djinn*. A djinn is "an invisible spirit with a will of its own that may lurk at the bottom of your teacup or seep through your pores to possess you" (Drieskens 2008). Like other peoples from the circum Mediterranean to South Asia, many people also believe in the evil eye, a force possessed by some people and transmitted through a gaze. The evil eye can be invoked if a person who has it feels jealousy. Amulets can ward off the evil eye. Blue amulets with an eye in the center can be seen all over Kurdistan, from one made of cloth pinned to an infant's clothing, to a large one made of steel welded onto a truck. If I ask a woman how many children she has had, she may report that one or more had died at a young age (the rates are higher in the case of older women). In such conversations I typically ask if she knows the cause of the death of her infant or child. Quite a few women have answered that the cause had to do with intervention by the djinn, or the evil eye. Many women told me that the djinn were seen as particularly active in the bathroom, and in a woman's life around the time she gives birth.

The question of whether Islam contributes to women's subjugation, and if so, how it does and how much it does, is the subject of an extensive debate that I will not rehash here. However, I would like to make the following point about Kurdistani women's practices relating to and beliefs about Islam and the supernatural: a woman who exhibits piety in her behavior, speech, and dress elicits more sexual trust from the community. Based on both direct comments as well as insinuations in conversations with a variety of interlocutors, it seems to me that most people in Kurdistan believe that a woman who is more religious will be less likely to engage in sex outside of marriage. Some women who wear the head scarf have told me that they feel it gives them an extra measure of freedom to come and go, because their families trust that the piety they display in their dress will be matched by sexual restraint. A woman who works in an office—and there are growing numbers of such women—can easily cut down on the chances that she will be sexually harassed by covering her head. Based on comments I have heard from a variety of people, covering one's head may to some women seem to be in conflict with the modernist impulses that also influence the few women who work outside the home. Probably the majority of such female laborers do not cover their heads, but those who do may reap an advantage in that their virginity or chastity will less likely be questioned.

Sex and Marriage

Patrilineal kinship systems require the control of activities that can lead to reproduction. Of course, the most obvious of these activities is sexual intercourse, but my sense is that people in Kurdistan see a wide array of other activities as leading to, or at least inviting, intercourse. Driving and other forms of mobility are chief among these. A woman who is seen going to the bazaar two days in a row may be gossiped about as possibly having an ulterior motive for going there. Might there be a man working there with whom she will rendezvous? The typical historic bazaar found in each city and town is a male space full of dark warrens and a few back rooms, which makes it very sexually dangerous for a woman. The women I know go quickly, with another person if at all possible. Young women virtually never go alone. Women of all ages typically buy what they need, do not linger, and leave as soon as they have acquired their purchases.

Human sexual activity can be limited by social and religious conventions in many ways and for many reasons, as the global ethnographic record bears out. The limiting of sex to marriage is not a novel idea in the world, but a common one. A familiar justification for this limitation as practiced and adhered to by many Christians, for example, is based on the biblical idea that "the two will become one," among other ideas. Sex is understood to produce a oneness that is only appropriate within marriage.

PHOTO 4.2 Shopkeepers and shoppers in the fabric section of the main bazaar of Dohuk, June 2008. (Copyright 2009 American Anthropological Association. Photo by the author.)

In contrast, an argument that sex should be limited to marriage that is based on patriliny follows a logic based on reproduction to a greater degree than based on the two people engaging in sexual activity per se. It is based more on a third party, the couple's potential offspring.

In theory, Kurdistan is a conservative Muslim society in which sexual activity is only supposed to occur within marriage. I find that standards for talking about sexual matters vary widely. In one interview I conducted with a middle-aged couple from Deshta, they spent much of the interview teasing each other sexually under their breaths. Their ribald comments had seemingly little to do with the interview content. Neither held back as they referred to real or imaginary events from the previous night, as I and several others within earshot listened and I struggled to keep the interview on track. They seemed thoroughly amused with themselves. I also heard joking of this nature by other "villagers," people in villages or who had lived in a village recently and still used the title "villager" to refer to themselves. All of it seemed good-natured and relatively harmless—not the kind of talk that could be categorized as gossip and therefore damaging, since the people were talking mainly about themselves. Later, I was talking with a Kurdish friend who had grown up in Baghdad and Dohuk, and she mentioned in passing that people in the area were reluctant to talk about sex. I told her some of what I had heard from some villagers. She expressed what seemed to be thoroughly genuine shock, and stated repeatedly that she had never heard such a thing. She is representative of many people I have met in more urban settings, who seem to avoid such talk completely and may exhibit great shyness if the subject comes up in conversation. Some men will not even refer to their wives directly in public, avoiding mentioning their wife's name, and speaking instead about their "family" (mal).

Despite the restraint shown by many people in sexual matters, patriliny can lead to a double standard, in which many men are not really limited, but most women are. Men can go to prostitutes, they can have foreign girlfriends, or they can have clandestine relationships whether they are married or unmarried, because the onus of avoiding conception is not on them. Şerim regulates sexual behavior for both women and men, but much more so for women. Of course, other kinship systems are associated with double sexual standards, but I see patriliny as fostering it perhaps to a greater degree than others.

In an interview I conducted with a middle-aged man in Zakho in 1998, he argued that recent changes had led to many men having more sexual partners than just their wives:[6]

MAN: Maybe more than 95 percent of the females here are virgins when they marry. But for males, now 50 percent of males are virgins. From 1961 to 1990, 80 percent were virgins. Before that, 99 percent were virgins, because all of the families knew each other. From 1950 to 1961, if I was engaged to a girl, I would not even go to that area of the city. To be seen anywhere near her house would be very shameful. Nowadays, no. They are coming and going together, sleeping together, dancing. . . . Before, the sexes were totally separate. Dancing was only with the same sex. At weddings the men would dance together in one area and the women together in another area.

DIANE: The math doesn't add up—95 percent versus 50 percent. How do you account for that?

MAN: The men are sleeping with *married* women, not with girls! Ninety-five percent of them are paying money to married women for sex.

I have heard many other references to prostitution since that interview. In 2010, I was speaking with an Arab woman who had lived in Mosul in the late 1990s. She told me that the house across the street from her was a brothel run by a Kurdish woman. The women who worked for her as prostitutes were Arab. The clients were men who made the trip from Kurdistan. I wondered if this was the same brothel I had heard some Kurdish men talk about in earlier years.

One way in which members of patrilineal cultures control reproduction is to place great emphasis on the hymen. A girl or woman's hymen may be the most important part of her body. "Whereas boys learn to acquire space with their bodies," writes Andrea Fischer-Tahir based on her research in Silemani, "girls are permanently reminded of the value of the hymen and hence the threat to their bodies and social status" (2009:81). On her wedding night, a bride's hymen is supposed to bleed, which "proves" that she was a virgin. Many Kurdish families still practice the ancient custom that was, or still is, practiced in Europe, Asia, and Africa, in which a cloth is placed under the couple on the night of first intercourse. The girl is coached and comforted ahead of time by an older woman, called a *serspî* (white head), and the soiled cloth is shown to her and to other relatives who are waiting, often right outside the door.

One woman gave the following account of her sister's experience: "My sister had a good situation. They didn't make her show them the cloth. She only had to show it to her mother-in-law, not to the whole group that wanted to see it. She refused and got away with it." Later I asked her what she thought is at the root of this practice. "That's easy," she said. "Females have a way to prove that they have not had sex, and males do not." The same person noted in another conversation, "The hymen is important simply because it carries the proof that a girl has not had sex. I cannot lie about it, it is there to speak for itself."

I have argued (King 2010) that a hymen serves as a border to membership in a patrilineage. Beyond that border is the zone in which a new human, a new member of someone's patrilineage, can begin life. Whose patrilineage? The patrilineage of a man who had sexual relations with the woman. Of course, the state of a woman's hymen does not "prove" anything. Some hymens do not bleed on first intercourse, and some do. Injuries can occur that alter the state of the hymen. Several women have mentioned the bicycle as a danger in this regard; while some very young girls are allowed to ride, most parents stop allowing their daughters to ride a bicycle well before their teen years. Hymenoplasty operations, long practiced in a clandestine fashion across the Middle East and elsewhere, are becoming increasingly common, even in the West. "The reified hymen becomes a sign . . ." writes Wendy Weiss (1990:416), "concealing [a] complex set of relations between men, and between men and women. Its penetration and defense become a struggle waged with romantic poetry and songs, on one side, and a bulwark of restrictions on a daughter's behavior, on the other."

One Kurdistani woman told me this about a friend of hers: "She is to be pitied greatly. She is unmarried, and she had a hysterectomy, so she cannot have children. So that means that there is absolutely no man here who would even think of marrying her. Not one! If she could keep it a secret maybe she could marry, but everyone here knows about it. Besides, she would have many problems later after her husband found out that she could not have children. If that isn't enough, to make matters worse, she lost her virginity in the course of the operation, because they had to cut up through the vagina." This short narrative reveals several aspects of the gender system in Kurdistan: It is pro-marital. It is pro-natalist. Men are said to want "virgin" brides, that is, a bride whose hymen has not previously been ruptured, and which will bleed on her wedding night. Having such a hymen seems to be even more essential to the definition of "virgin" than the definition that would likely come to mind for most English speakers, "a person who has not had sexual intercourse." A potential husband has the right to full knowledge about the state of his potential bride's hymen before marriage, and to full control over her movements and activity after marriage. A wife does not have the same right to knowledge about, and restriction of, her husband's sexual activities. This system seems set to change, or to cause widespread victimization of unsuspecting wives, when HIV-AIDS arrives in force. A few cases have already been reported. As of 2010, the KRG Ministry of Health was aware of seventy-six cases of HIV-AIDS in Kurdistan, and STDs were sharply on the rise (Baban 2010).

As the above narrative also affirms, marriage is popular in Iraqi Kurdistan. Most of the unmarried women I know have told me that they would like to be married. Weddings tend to be joyous occasions, mainly for the groom's family. A generation ago, the bride's family did not attend the wedding itself, but hosted a large engagement party beforehand. Now brides' families are starting to attend weddings, and many grooms' families attend engagement parties.

Virtually all unmarried adults live with their parents or siblings (or both). The residence patterns in Kurdistan are like those elsewhere in the region, the chief rule being that no one lives alone, and children only move out of their parents' house when they are married. There are now some exceptions to this, such as when an adolescent or young adult goes off to college, but most families still follow the traditional residence pattern. A daughter moves at marriage, and a son may move several years after marriage, or never. The pattern is patrilocal, and sons are expected to stay near their parents even if they set up a separate household, and take care of their parents as they age. Patrilocal residence goes hand-in-hand with patriliny in most parts of the world where patriliny is found. Like other features of patriliny, it is more about the next generation than the couple. Patrilocality ensures that the next generation will be raised among their father's people, not their mother's. If their mother is from another group, whether tribal, linguistic, or even religious, the children are highly likely to feel close to that group, but they will be surrounded by people belonging to their father's category, in their father's place. As I argue in chapter 3, much of Kurdish collective identity assertion is about land. Patrilocal residence patterns ask a wife to move to her husband's land, which is the most logical place to perpetuate his patriline.

Plenty of marriages in Kurdistan are happy, and I would not be surprised if a poll would show that more married couples in Kurdistan are happy with their marriages than American couples. However, when things do go wrong, patrilocal residence can put a wife at a great disadvantage. As Jane Fishburne Collier puts it, "Marriage in a society with patrilocal extended households is a traumatic affair for everyone, but particularly for a bride. She must leave her natal home to take up residence among strangers who rightfully regard her coming as a threat to their solidarity and who expect her to . . . produce children to strengthen the group. A bride . . . is at the bottom of the domestic status hierarchy and knows it. But as a woman bears children, her interests change. She now has something to work for, because her future power will depend on the status of her sons. The ambitious woman will use all her political knowledge to increase her sons' inheritance and all her feminine wiles to persuade her husband to set up a separate household where she may have more control over family resources . . . she seeks to bind her sons securely to her" (1974:93). In Kurdistan's cities, increasing numbers of young couples, and even larger numbers of couples who have been married a decade or more, now live neolocally, in their own apartment or house. They may have stayed in the husband's parents' house for up to a few years, but after that they set up an independent household. Collier's description echoes many complaints I have heard and problems I have witnessed. People who choose neolocality are opting for a different way of life that benefits a young wife, among other benefits—as well as challenges.

Collier uses the term "political" and, indeed, matters of residence in Kurdistan can be highly so. Nahela and I were once having a conversation about the rivalry between the two main political parties, the KDP and PUK, when she mixed macro- and micropolitics to make a point. Although they are working together quite admirably these days, everyone remembers that the parties went to war against each other in the 1990s, and that to this day they are competitors of a sort. Jalal Talabani, head of the PUK, became Iraqi president in 2005, thereafter spending most of his time in Baghdad. Mes'ud Barzani, head of the KDP, became president of the Kurdistan Region that same year, continuing to spend most of his time in the region. Nahela said she thought that their separation, and that they nevertheless both had important roles, was a smart arrangement and used some of the problems she had seen in patrilocal households to make her point: "Listen, Diane, in Kurdistan two women can't share a kitchen. Do you think two presidents can share a country?"

Preferential father's brother's daughter (FBS/D) marriage is another feature of some patrilineal societies that is practiced in Kurdistan and the surrounding area.[7] A young man is generally assumed to have the right to marry one of his father's brother's/brothers' daughters if he wants to and his father wants him to (and in most families his mother also has a strong say in the matter). Put differently, in many families, a man who has a brother with a son, and who also has a daughter, must check first with his brother before agreeing to give his daughter in marriage to non-kin or kin of a different kind. As Scott Atran points out, citing Murdock's famous study (1949), FBS/D marriage is found in only a small minority of societies worldwide, just 3 percent, is "restricted to the Arab world and immediately outlying areas," and yet the practice is "historically robust" and "a powerful factor in the area's politics and economics (Atran 1985:661). Anthropologists engaged in a vigorous conversation and debate over FBS/D marriage in the mid-twentieth century, with some of the ethnographic examples coming from Kurdistan (e.g., Barth 1954).

In a review of theories pertaining to parallel cousin marriage, Pierre Bourdieu (1990:32) cites Fredrik Barth's work among the Kurds (1979 [1953]). Barth saw the Kurds' FBS/D marriage patterns in terms of "alliance," as a way for a lineage to promote cohesion and thereby strengthen itself in preparation for conflict. Murphy and Kasdan (1959) criticize Barth, placing their emphasis on fissioning patrilineal segments. Bourdieu notes that Lévi-Strauss (1969) saw these theories as essentially the same, and concludes that "both admit that parallel cousin marriage cannot be explained within the pure logic of the matrimonial exchange system and that any explanation must necessarily refer to external economic or political functions" (32). This represents just a small fraction of the debate touched off by Murphy and Kasdan, whose article was highly cited within anthropology. More recently, Morgan Clarke has seen FBD marriage as promoting "closeness." He cites a Lebanese informant who told him that cousin marriage is about "morals" and "know[ing] everything" about the potential spouse's family (Clarke 2011:39).

As with segmentary lineage theory, I think something much simpler is afoot than complex matters of lineage "alliance" or "descent" or even an overarching notion of the moral. For one thing, cousin marriage seems as popular as ever in Kurdistan, but the types of cousins that people are marrying seem to me to be becoming more diverse. I know of many examples of consanguineous marriages in which the couple are related through a woman and are thus not (necessarily) in the same lineage. I think confidence in the bride's virginity is a major part of the reason that consanguineous marriages remain popular. In other words, I think that *all* types of cousin marriage, or marriage between close consanguineals, can be argued to shore up patriliny if confidence in the virginity of the bride, and her future chastity as a married woman, is an influence in the decision of one or more of the parties to marry.

Neither Barth nor Leach make any mention of virginity as a factor in marriage patterns. For many people I have known in Kurdistan, however, the virginity or possible lack thereof of the unmarried women they knew has appeared to be a near obsession. Quite a few people have made assertions to me that sound like the one made to Clarke, but in those cases when I pressed the speaker as to what he or she meant by "moral" and related terms, I was told that this kind of talk encompassed a way of alluding to female virginity. While in some families marriage is forced on young people, usually girls, I found that it is more often entered into willingly by the bride and groom, but that does not mean that many people in the bride's and groom's family are not involved in discussing and consenting to the marriage. In a culture that still has very little "dating," in which young people spend time with prospective marriage partners, a marriage is often preceded by highly complex negotiations, and "detective work," discreet information gathering about the prospective spouse, often precedes it. How better for both sides to ensure that the marriage will weather the crucial moment of revelation on the wedding night than to encourage marriage to a trusted relative? And besides, even if the groom had concerns, if the bride did not bleed very much, for example, wouldn't he do his best to cover for her, knowing that they share the same grandparents? What young man has the nerve to drive a wedge into his family like that? And what bride would not want the security of knowing that her husband, whom she may have known all her life and for whom she may well feel great affection, would also be kind to her for the purposes of family cohesion? I think the often-pointed-out advantage of FBS/D marriage, that it allows resources to stay in the same patrilineage, also applies. Perhaps the new diversity in types of consanguineous marriage in Kurdistan also has something to do with the fact that in the mid-twentieth century Iraq made it much more possible for women to inherit land than in the past.

Honor Killings and Modernity

An "honor killing," a killing for *namûs*, is a form of domestic violence. In the classic pattern of an honor killing, first, a girl or woman is suspected by her family and community of being open to having sex outside of marriage, or, more rarely, she actually has sex outside of marriage.[8] People start to gossip about her. As a result, her lineage's reputation suffers. In such a situation, pressure mounts for her lineage mates, especially the male lineage mates closest to her, to kill her. The most directly responsible person in this instance is her father, but he (and his wife in many cases) may incite one of his sons, the girl or woman's brother, to do the deed. The girl or woman is killed. Afterward, her lineage's honorable reputation, its namûs, is restored.

A new bride can be killed for namûs if her hymen does not bleed on her wedding night. This is why showing the bloody cloth the morning after the marriage is consummated is an important part of the wedding event in its classical form. The display of that blood may well save a new bride's life. Such killings are very rare, but they loom as a possibility nonetheless. Most grooms and families will find a quiet, nonviolent way to defuse a situation in which they have asked a bride to display the cloth and no blood appears, but a few will reject the bride, setting up a situation in which her father, brother, or someone standing in for one of them is called upon to kill her. More rarely, the groom may kill her himself. Young Kurdish men may be socialized to understand that they must be ready to kill their sister should the need arise. Mustafa Mirzeler (2000), drawing on his own childhood growing up in a Kurdish village in Turkey, describes a system in which violence against women is justified through stories and songs sung in the village. Among other lessons, a male child learns the logic of namûs, and that he might be called upon to kill his sister should she besmirch the family's reputation through perceived or actual sexual misconduct.

The aforementioned chain of events leading to and culminating in an honor killing is now quite well known, even in the West, where honor killings occasionally take place among immigrant populations from the Middle East and South Asia. Honor killings persist in Iraqi Kurdistan, and some people say that they are on the rise there. In any case, they are now a hot topic. In some Western and Middle Eastern nationalist and modernist narratives, they symbolize backwardness. In the new globalizing Kurdistan, many people now know that honor killings are not practiced by many societies in the world, which has brought the practice into sharper relief than in the past. But why do honor killings occur? The main explanation given in the press and other sources is that people who commit them have a cultural attachment to honor defined as sexual control. I have argued in earlier work (King 2010) for a much more specific explanation linking honor killing logic to patrilineal logic. Specifically, I locate the impetus that causes a father or brother, who may well have been a loving father or brother to his daughter or sister, to transform into a killer in maintenance of the sovereignty of the lineage. As I noted above, a girl or woman is just as much a member of her lineage as her brother. However, when it comes to producing the next generation, she can only produce children for the lineage of her children's *father*, not hers. Lineage sovereignty is exercised when the members of her own patrilineage decide whom they will allow to use their female member to produce more members of another lineage. Once that decision is reached, a wedding follows. A wedding is a sovereignty-affirming event in which the bride's lineage displays their consent to the watching community that her husband's patrilineage may use her reproductive capacity increase its numbers.

Egyptian feminist Nawal el Saadawi simply conflates the ideas of namûs and an intact hymen in a chapter of her classic book, *The Hidden Face of Eve: Women in the Arab World* entitled "The Very Fine Membrane

Called 'Honour'" (2007:38–49). In it, she describes a virginity and chastity complex in the Arab world that is nearly identical to the one in the Kurdish world. In Iraqi Kurdistan I observe that namûs, lineage sovereignty, defined in this way is upheld by what seems to be an overwhelming majority of people. From villagers to urbanites, on countless occasions I have heard people affirm their support for virginity and chastity linked to lineages, and I have heard numerous people, many of them female, affirm support for honor killings and indicate their disrespect for a lineage that would allow one of its female members to have sex outside of marriage and not kill her. One unmarried friend told me, "My family is good, therefore they would kill me if I made a mistake." "Making a mistake" is a common euphemism for having sex outside of marriage. "Trust" is often invoked as well, as in, "My family trusts me not to make a mistake," which I have often heard from young women who now have a measure of freedom, for example, to come and go from school or the university on their own.

"I will tear you!" (*Ez dê te dirînim*) is a phrase that some people say when they are very angry, much in the same way that an American might say, "I will kill you," but not mean it literally. "I will tear you" is a death threat as well. It literally means, "I will tear your hymen." Said to an unmarried female, it means, "I will set you up to be the victim of an honor killing," or at minimum, "I will sharply reduce your chances of marrying and having children." This saying is so common that I have heard both sexes say it to both sexes, and to married and unmarried people, even though its literal meaning only applies to unmarried females (who have never had intercourse, but this is assumed of an unmarried female).

In a conversation I had with a woman in her thirties about another young woman who had left Dohuk to travel to the West for graduate school, the woman said that she had heard gossip accusing the student of leaving for reasons other than education. It seemed that she, too, believed this. "I think the main thing people are saying is that she ran away because she is not a virgin," the woman told me. "Believe me; if she comes back here she will never, ever marry." "And maybe someone will kill her?" I asked. "No, no one will kill her. That is the job of her family, and since they have not objected to anything she has done, she will not be harmed. It's just that people will gossip about her and no one will marry her." In this example we can see the power of gossip, which can transform a woman's mobility, which in this case was both socioeconomic and physical mobility, into an imagined sexual transgression. Most girls and women in Kurdistan never get so far as to invite this type of gossip. Weathering it can be very difficult. My sense is that thousands of girls and women who would like to travel away from home to further their education or pursue a career never do so out of fear of inciting this type of gossip. Without the support of her family, it could lead to her death at the hands of her brother or father. Many of Kurdistan's women are on lockdown, setting aside their dreams in order to be able to live without fear for their lives.

As I further argued in my 2010 piece, as Afsaneh Najmabadi (1998) has argued for Iran, Esra Özyürek for Turkey (2006:145–146), and others have argued for other settings, the logic of namûs can be extended to the level of the nation. A middle-aged woman from Silemani told me about a classmate of hers who had gone off to the University of Baghdad after they both graduated from high school in the late 1980s. "During the girl's first year away, her parents divorced, and neither one of them cared about her," the woman told me. "So, she began to sleep around, and people suspected prostitution. Expensive cars with important men would come and go from her house. One day even Uday, the son of Saddam Hussein, came to her house. Eventually the peshmerga in Silemani announced on the radio that she was on their wanted list and that they would kill her if she returned. They said that they even wanted to kill her in Baghdad, but that that would be too difficult given her connections there. So, she stayed in Baghdad and is probably still there." This young woman's reputed behavior was perceived as a threat to the Kurdish nation, and if this threat was actually issued, she needed to remain at a distance to stay out of danger.

As honor violence has increasingly entered public debate, the question has repeatedly been raised as to the relationship between it and Islam. Does Islam promote honor violence? The question presents itself because the countries that have the highest rates of such killings are mainly populated by Muslims. However, the ethnographic record demonstrates that non-Muslims honor kill as well. For example, if a woman in Hindu Gopalapalli, India, "has extramarital relations, she might be deserted if not killed by relatives," consequences a man would not face (Säävälä 2001:134). The same question is raised about FGC. FGC, specifically the clitoridectomy procedure, occurs in Kurdistan, mainly in the Sorani-speaking areas.[9] I interviewed an older woman who had performed the FGC operation on her three daughters in the 1970s and 1980s, two of them at age seven, and one at age four. She spoke approvingly of the practice. "If you don't cut off the clitoris when a girl is young, it will grow very long when she is older," the woman told me. "A girl who has this done becomes *miskîn* (well behaved; gentle)."

When it comes to the question of Islam and the practices of honor killing and FGC, I think that scholars and publics alike would do well to ask a better question, a question rooted in kinship and gender conventions rather than religion. Both of these practices fit neatly within the logic of patriliny. The global ethnographic record is clear: they are practiced by members of groups that reckon descent patrilineally. Many members of such groups are Muslims. Islam was born into a thoroughly patrilineal culture, that of Arabia in the seventh century, so many Muslim values and practices overlap with patrilineal values and practices. However, to implicate Islam for honor killings and FGC is wrong and overly simplistic. Patriliny certainly existed before Islam, and it certainly exists in places with no or few Muslims. A better question asks how kinship is implicated, and what other sociopolitical and economic forces may be at work in the modern states where people who engage in these practices live. To argue that honor killings are an outgrowth of patriliny raises other questions as to how the setting of the modern state may be changing, or upholding, patrilineal meaning systems and practices. Activists in diverse settings would do well to consider how the practices they are opposing are part of a much larger and comprehensive set of ideas that shape people's lives in profound and impactful ways. This is especially urgent in settings where Muslims may face discrimination (e.g., Ewing 2008).

In June 2008 I was staying with Nahela's family during my last few days in Kurdistan after several weeks of traveling around the region. One research objective had eluded me to that point: I wanted a better glimpse into the Region's burgeoning oil industry than I had managed to get so far. I suggested to Nahela that we drive out to Tawke, the oil extraction and exploration site near Zakho run by DNO, a Norwegian oil company. Nahela was hesitant because this meant driving about twenty minutes out of town, on dirt roads in an area that was remote until one arrived at the bustling oil facility. But I had an international flight to catch the next day. I thought there would be no time to arrange an alternative if we did not seize the moment right then.

Field Note, 19 June 2008:

> After expressing some reluctance, Nahela agreed that we could drive out to the Tawke oil field. Her cousin (father's sister's son) worked there. She called him up. It just happened that he was about to get off work, and was happy to show us around if we would drive out. "Bring some boys with you," he said as he signed off. So, Nahela asked her brother's son, fifteen-year-old Nizar, to come with us. But he didn't want to come. Nahela offered to let him bring a friend along, and he agreed. We were off. We picked up the friend a few doors down. "I wonder if his mother even knows where he is going," I said rhetorically to Nahela in the front seat as the boy got in the back of the car. "Imagine, these boys are somehow our guardians. We are grown women! What can they do for us?" Nahela added with exasperation in her voice.

We got to Tawke and found that it was not possible to go inside without a lengthy security process. The day was waning, everyone was antsy to get home, including me, since I needed to pack and say my good-byes. Visiting the Tawke facility would have to wait. On our way back to Zakho, the 50 Cent song came on. ". . . Soon as I come through the door she get to pullin on my zipper, It's like it's a race who can get undressed quicker . . ." went the song. "I love this song!" gushed Nizar. Nahela mumbled that the lyrics were dirty. There was no reply from our two chaperones in the back seat. Did they fully understand their responsibility to Nahela? Did they understand their duty to make sure that she did not do anything on that trip to show that she might be open to threatening the reproductive sovereignty of her and Nizar's lineage? That ultimately, they were responsible for making sure that her brothers, one of whom is Nizar's father, did not face any social pressure to kill her? Or were they too lost in a sexy American rap song to care about that? For me to ask them directly about their responsibility would have been embarrassing to everyone. So I simply pondered the rich irony of the situation as we rode, the way in which Nahela's comments betrayed a clearly critical stance toward her own gender system despite her deep embededness in it, and the challenges faced by everyone in the Kurdistani gender system at a rich yet confusing moment in history.

5

Politicking

> But Mosul [the Ottoman *vilayet* encompassing today's Iraqi Kurdistan] has always been against the government, whatever form it should happen to assume; the begs have always played with the authorities as you play with a fish on the hook, and the fact that they were now constitutional authorities gave an even better zest to the sport and barbed the hook yet more sharply.
>
> –Gertrude Bell, *Amurath to Amurath* (1911:284)

The Kurdistan Region is abuzz with politicking, a form of, and impetus for, much of the social connecting that takes place there. By "politicking," I mean political activity in the form of conversations and actions. Politicking is by definition active and always in process. Politicking comprises the political stuff of state, local, tribal, and lineage governance, aspirations to such governance, as well as economic jockeying both licit and illicit. In one sense, politicking is patriliny's counterweight, because it is highly agenic and in motion, whereas patriliny makes claims to fixedness and immutability. But politicking also makes, shores up, and to an extent depends on patriliny. The two work in concert in Kurdistan, and as Kurdistan connects to the wider world.

A bureaucrat or politician's office is usually rectangular, with the entryway at one end, and a desk at the other. Along the sides are comfortable chairs and small coffee tables. Such an office can usually seat at least eight guests, and many can handle a much larger crowd. If you are welcomed into such an office, you will be invited to sit and make yourself comfortable. Within a few minutes, an attendant will appear and ask whether you prefer tea or coffee, and sometimes a soft drink or water is offered, too. A few minutes after that, he (the person in this role is usually male) will bring your preferred beverage and possibly some candy or cookies. If it is winter, he is also likely to slide an oil-fueled space heater (*sope*), near you. In summer, an evaporative cooler is likely to be on. The politician or bureaucrat may be finishing up talking with whoever preceded you, and once that is finished, will warmly welcome you and ask you to state your petition. A short conversation ensues in which you explain what you hope the politician can do for you, and the politician offers some kind of solution, one that may or may not be satisfactory. Sometimes matters are left open ended. You are unlikely to be openly rushed, especially if you have not yet finished your beverage, although the social atmosphere may indicate to you that it is time to leave. Many other people are likely waiting, some possibly sitting there in the same room. If all is relatively quiet, some small talk, or even a lot of small talk, might precede or be mixed in with the "business" conversation.

A modern political office in the Kurdistan Region is reminiscent of a shaikh or agha's busy, guest-filled diwan, except that a traditional diwan in the village has floor cushions rather than chairs, which allows a large number of people to squeeze into the room. A popular agha's diwan may be bursting with people on any given evening. They will eat, laugh, tell stories, gossip, and drink nonalcoholic beverages late into the night. The main diwan area is for the men, but the women may be socializing in another room.

The modern state representative's office, and the shaikh or agha's diwan (or the diwan of an influential man in the city) are the traditional spaces for politicking in Kurdistan. As a longtime "politically unstable" place, Kurdistan has long had much to contest. Since 2003, Iraq itself has again been "unstable," and a great deal of life and the political order is again contested there, after the more stable and predictable Saddam Hussein years. Kurdistan now interacts with Baghdad as part of the same country and has many representatives serving in the Iraqi government. To be sure, Kurdistan and Iraq's relationship is not unproblematic. It is beyond the ambit of this book to do justice to the number of issues between Iraq and the Kurdistan Region that remain unsettled, but most of them have to do with territory and oil revenues under overarching issues of sovereignty. However, as of this writing the Iraqi state and the KRG are grudgingly working together, which is a great improvement over the past.

Early Kurdish Nationalism: Erratic and Bloody

Iraqi Kurdistan's current political leaders are heirs to a rebel movement that began in the mid-twentieth century. It, in turn, arose out of previous nationalist efforts, none of which succeeded in founding an enduring Kurdish state. The business of defining early "Kurdish nationalism" has long occupied historians. One difficulty lies in the impossibility of distinguishing whether the leader of a conquest saw himself as mainly operating on behalf of a Kurdish nation, or acted for some other purpose. For example, Shaikh Ubaydallah is today regarded as an early Kurdish nationalist. His conquests began with a failed attempt to retake the city of Amadiya, former seat of the Kurdish Bahdinan Principality, from direct Ottoman control in 1879. After this initial failure, he became "the acknowledged leader of a vast Kurdish nationalist movement" (Jwaideh 1960:253) as he went on to success in battle against the Persians. In 1880 he attacked the city of Urmiah with 12,000 men (Nikitine 1929, cited in Jwaideh 1960:258), including Nestorian Christians from the Tiyari valley (McDowall 2004:54). Robert Olson (1989:1) agrees with Jwaideh and sees Ubaydallah's ascent as "the first stage of a greater consciousness of Kurdish nationalism," arguing that his nationalism was more clear-cut than that of Bedir Khan Beg, who preceded him and is often regarded as the greatest nineteenth-century Kurdish nationalist. David McDowall (2004) and Wadie Jwaideh (1960) are more skeptical, attributing his actions at least as much to personal ambition as to nationalism. Whatever his motives, the conquests of Shaikh Ubaydallah are described by McDowall (2004:54) as a "carnage" in which more than 2,000 villages were destroyed and 10,000 people were made homeless before his power diminished when he was exiled. Although historical accounts give little indication of the toll of suffering on the general population, it must have been tremendous. In a world more connected by globalization, it might well have led to large-scale flight out of the region.

Other efforts followed in all four of the quadrants of Kurdistan that by the 1920s constituted parts of the new states of Iran, Iraq, Syria, and Turkey.[1] Kurds in Iraq rebelled against hegemony by the Baghdad government off and on starting with the formation of the Iraqi state following World War I. In 1946 the ascendant Kurdish leader Mulla Mustafa Barzani founded the Kurdistan Democratic Party (KDP), which proceeded to carry out an insurgency against Baghdad. In the 1960s, Barzani and his peshmerga also fought rivals from nonloyal tribes and fended off challenges from within the party, most significantly from rival Jalal Talabani. The 1970s were marked by a catastrophic setback for the KDP in the form of the collapse of a covert, U.S.-supported campaign against Baghdad, and by the formation by Jalal Talabani of a new party, the Patriotic Union of Kurdistan (PUK). The PUK soon established itself as a rival to the KDP, asserting military control in and from the southeastern portion of Iraqi Kurdistan, while the KDP did so in the northwestern portion. In the early years their areas of dominance were roughly correspondent with the territories where the two major Kurdish dialects are spoken, with Behdini Kurmanji in the northwest, and Sorani in the southeast.

The ensuing years were marked by conflict on a variety of fronts. Mulla Mustafa Barzani died in 1979 (of cancer in a hospital in Washington, D.C.) and was succeeded by his son, Mes'ud. In the 1980s the Iran-Iraq War raged, becoming the longest interstate war of the twentieth century. The Baghdad government led by Saddam Hussein turned against the disloyal Iraqi Kurds with systematic brutality, behavior Eric Davis calls "savagery" (2005:11). It destroyed thousands of villages, using all military means at its disposal, including chemical weapons. Thousands of Kurds died, and several thousand villages were leveled. While continuing to control separate territories, during the late 1980s the KDP and PUK set aside their rivalry, which was not to flare again until the 1990s.

Politicking in the Ba'thist state was straightforward: join the party, talk the talk, never question the regime no matter what it did or asked you to do. In other ways, however, sociopolitical stability was as elusive as ever for Kurds in Iraq. Military service in the Iraqi army was required of all Iraqi men. Some Kurdish men had another government-endorsed option, service as fighters in the chete brigades comprised of tribes contracted by Baghdad to fight its war against the peshmerga. Kurdish men who resisted these two choices usually joined the peshmerga of either the KDP or PUK. In numerous households and patrilineages, male members served in opposing forces; in many cases brothers who met as kin in their natal households met as enemies on the battlefield. Kurdish people, especially men, thus faced continual dilemmas of loyalty. Principles were a luxury. Mistrust and violence were a way of life.

In conversations and life history interviews covering the decades prior to 1991, some of my interlocutors reported fleeing their homes and losing all of their possessions multiple times over a lifetime; for the elderly, this may have happened as many as seven or eight times. At the same time, there is hardly a "typical" story. Some people, particularly town dwellers, remained largely unscathed physically, but no one escaped experiencing an overlay of constant political intrigue and the *threat* of violence—a violence that stemmed ultimately from a claim to territory emanating from Baghdad. Life for most Kurdish people in Iraq was characterized by constant uncertainty.

A few people in Kurdistan, especially those living in mountain villages, were able to avoid direct interaction with the Ba'th, but many more lived under direct Ba'thist rule. This meant living in a political milieu in which little was open to negotiation, under a regime that valued "adherence to party discipline, and submission to the will of a strong leader who acts as the embodiment of the nation" (Rohde 2010:130). A "citizen" was actually a subject who received fiats handed down through intermediaries from the top. Here is an example of some of the regime's propaganda, taken from one of the books in the regime's official English course, as taught to millions of schoolchildren:

"Why do you want to join the Air Force?"

"To serve my country and to protect the Arab Homeland. We all follow the words of our beloved leader, President Saddam Hussein who says, 'All Iraqis are loyal to great Iraq and to the glorious Arab Nation and they are also ready to take the path of sacrifice.'"

"That's great. I'm sure you'll be a good pilot." (Al-Hamash et al. 1993:5–6)

There is little room for negotiation here. The leader's words are followed, and the political tone is set. There is little jockeying, little compromise, little room for questioning. The regime was brutal, to be sure, killing thousands. But it was also obsessively controlling, and this control touched everyone, even those not obviously victimized by it.

All along, Kurdish politicking was taking place in the mountains, clandestinely in the cities, and abroad. Kurds plotted and strategized and rebelled and rose up all the way through the twentieth century. There are

too many rebellions to inventory here, too many adversaries, too many
well-laid plans, too many strategies. "There is some cause for apprehen-
sion as there have been no less than six armed Kurdish rebellions, some
common to several of the four governments involved and quelled with difficulty, in the past twenty-five years," wrote anthropologist William Murray
Masters in the 1950s (1953:172). Masters wrote these words before the
Kurdish movement's campaign under Mulla Mustafa Barzani began its
three-decade-long effort encompassing many more rebellions, their
number depending on how they are counted.

The neighboring state governments that have vied for control of
Kurdistan during the past century have provided an opportunity for
Kurdistan's leaders to play one power off another, resulting in loyalties that
rapidly shift to the highest bidder. The following is a condensed version of
the events leading to today's two main political parties in Kurdistan, the
KDP and PUK (these events are covered in greater detail in van Bruinessen
1992:26–31.): Mulla Mustafa Barzani rose to prominence as a nationalist
leader in Iraq in the early 1940s. In 1946, Qazi Muhammed's Kurdish
nationalist movement in Iran, supported by Barzani, resulted briefly in the
Mahabad Republic. The movement was encouraged by the Soviets, who
were occupying neighboring Azerbaijan, but it fell after only a few months
and the Soviets withdrew their support. Barzani retreated to Iraq, but then
marched with 500 men to the Soviet Union, where they were harbored as
refugees for the following eleven years. In 1958, Iraq's pro-Western government was overthrown in a coup led by Abd al-Karim Qasim. Barzani was
invited back to Iraq and gained popularity with urban, educated Kurds,
becoming president of the KDP. During the following years, a pattern
developed that was to repeat itself several times: the Iraqi government
attempted to appease the Kurds, who were then drawn into a war that
resulted in a coup d'état. In the 1960s, Jalal Talabani emerged as Barzani's
rival within the KDP, eventually splitting off to form a new group, which
became the PUK. The two sides clashed repeatedly until 1968, when
Talabani negotiated the support of the Iraqi government in pursuing
Barzani. The government recognized Barzani's influence, however, and
negotiated an agreement that granted the Kurds a fleeting peace and semi-
autonomy. In 1971, tensions between Iran and Iraq increased, and Iraq nation-
alized its oil operations that were previously controlled by the British,

Dutch, French, and Americans. These countries then responded with a boycott. Barzani secretly contracted with the shah of Iran, who wanted to revive the war between the Kurds and the Iraqi government. Through the shah, Barzani won the support of the CIA and met with U.S. Secretary of State Henry Kissinger in Tehran. In 1974 a war erupted between the Barzani-led Kurds and the Iraqi government, this time with sophisticated training and weapons on both sides. Barzani suffered many casualties and eventually surrendered, and thousands of Kurdish refugees poured into Iran. Although they would continue to rebel for the next decade and a half, the Iraqi Kurdish movement would not see definitive success until 1991.

In these events, loyalty functioned as a commodity. This is easily observable in the sequence of events I just recounted. Barzani appears on the stage as the ultimate bargainer, asking the polarized nations around him to name their price. He swings back and forth on at least two axes: between the United States to the Soviet Union, and between Iran and Iraq. (This process has continued well beyond where the above scenario leaves off, and there are many more examples even from the period covered here.) They, in turn, are bargaining with him: when his allegiance is no longer useful, he is quickly jettisoned and must seek another bidder. The population that the Iraqi government attacked was an active one. It fought, and fought back. It drew on a memory stretching back to Ottoman times, during which Kurds were known not for their victimization, but as bandits, smugglers, and fighters. Even Kurdish religious leaders, or perhaps one could even say *especially* Kurdish religious leaders, were wily characters then. Shaikh Said, the famous Kurdish rebel leader executed by the Turks in 1925, once said that the Naqshbandi sufi order in Kurdistan, which produced revered holy men, some of whom became rebel leaders, "resembled more a 'gangster ring' than a religious order" (Olson 1989:101). The Barzanis and Talabanis, today's leading shaikhly lineages, have produced the main leaders of today's Kurdistan. They no longer hide in the mountains but live and work on ornate compounds in cities, Mes'ud Barzani as president of Kurdistan and Jalal Talabani as president of Iraq. Mes'ud's son is head of security for the Kurdistan Region, and his brother's son is prime minister. Jalal's son represents the region in Washington in an ambassador-like role.

Politicking in Kurdistan was largely violent for more than a century but is largely nonviolent now, despite its political system having "developed

under conditions which may be considered difficult and anomalous"
(Stansfield 2003:3). In 1992, the first modern elections were held in Iraqi
Kurdistan (cf. Hoff et al. 1992, for a comprehensive report on the elections).
The KDP and PUK emerged as power sharers, with several smaller parties
also having representation. The KDP and PUK's peaceful cooperation was
short lived, and for the next several years they were at war in a conflict that
cost more than 3,000 lives (Agence France-Presse 2000). They signed a
peace agreement in Washington in September 1998. Politicking in Kurdistan
has been, with very few exceptions, peaceful since then. It now takes place
in offices, diwans, coffeehouses, guest rooms of homes, streets, and the
media. It takes place in a social milieu deeply connected by a sense of
shared history and yet in some ways also deeply divided. The old PUK-KDP
conflict simmers beneath the surface. A new party, Gorran (Change) was
founded by disaffected PUK figure Nawshirwan Mustafa in 2009. It offered
the first significantly powerful option to the two main parties (as opposed
to the many small political parties in Kurdistan, whose power is quite
limited). Many young adults are dissatisfied with their government in
comparison with other governments in the world, while many older adults
focus on how good things are now in comparison with the past. Urban
people and rural people's lives are increasingly disparate. The rich and the
poor live very, very differently. Politicking takes place among, between,
and across differences and similarities. The Kurdistani achievement of
nearly a decade and a half of peaceful state building is more remarkable
considering that it follows over a century of nearly constant conflict.

Politicking in the Everyday

One of my first impressions of interpersonal interaction in Kurdistan still
holds: I sensed that when I was meeting someone new, or interacting with
someone I had met but did not yet know well, they would invariably be
gathering information from me in a strategic fashion that would not be
fully revealed at the time. I came to see my own mainstream American
culture's way of interacting as unsophisticated and based comparatively
on face value. I was used to just blurting out an unreflected-on answer if
someone asked me a question. In contrast, my Kurdish friends seemed to
make decisions in the blink of an eye about how to answer a question in

the most strategic way possible. Sometimes the person would tell a white lie that I would later come to understand had concealed higher-stakes drama behind something seemingly trivial. As an example, I could recount any number of real situations, but here is a hypothetical one. Suppose I ran into my friend Fatima on the street and asked her where she was going. Her real destination was the butcher, which meant she was going to purchase a relatively expensive food, which meant she had important guests coming over, which meant those guests might be coming to propose that their son marry her daughter. But she would not reveal to me that she was going to buy meat, because that might cause me to start theorizing, and I might theorize correctly, and then her family would be embarrassed if the marriage proposal came to nothing. So, she might tell me that she was going to the store to buy potatoes instead—an everyday foodstuff that would not arouse much theorizing.

It also seemed that when people took in information, the process worked in reverse. They would assume that the full story was not being told, and that it was up to them to imagine what the other person might be withholding. Again, a marriage proposal can serve as an example. A family who are acquaintances but not very close friends with my host household might knock on the gate (or, today, call ahead) and pay a visit as evening guests. They might say at the outset that they just wanted to come over to catch up, since it has been a long time since they have seen my host family. But then, in the third hour of their visit, if the visit was going well, one of them would broach the question of a possible marriage.

All the world's a stage, but in Kurdistan the play is often shot through with intrigue. At every political level of scale, much is in process and much is contested. Political alliances and enmities in the public sphere also form in a social context of tremendous scrutiny and theorizing. Little is certain and little is settled. Negotiations are necessary in order to proceed. Intense politicking may occur in everyday relations between individuals and families, and it may bear similarities to the kinds of politicking that take place in semipublic and public spheres. These spheres range from tribal chief roles such as feud mediation and other types of decision making, to activities ranging from rebel movements to state building.

Martin van Bruinessen has described the political jockeying that took place (and still takes place) at the level of the Kurdish tribe: "[T]here were perpetual struggles for leadership of the tribe. Each of the rivals tried to manipulate the socio-political environment in order to get the better of the others. For such ambitious chieftains the important dichotomy was not between 'the rival tribe' and 'my own tribe' but 'the power sources my rivals are tapping' vs. 'the power sources I might tap.' . . . The manipulation of the central state in order to get the upper hand in a local, tribal conflict is a recurrent theme in Kurdish history" (Bruinessen 1992a:75).

High-Stakes Politicking

Much of the politicking in Kurdistan before the Ba'th dictatorship was deposed was high stakes. The loser in a given political game might die, or cause others to die. Diplomacy meant trusting the other side enough to put one's safety and life on the line. Sami Abdul Rahman was an important Kurdish nationalist leader. I interviewed him in February 2002 when he was KDP deputy prime minister, and two years before he was killed by a suicide bomber. Our conversation was wide ranging. At one point we started to speak about the Saddam Hussein regime, which, unbeknownst to us at the time, was entering its last year of power. Sami had been a high-level negotiator for the KDP, and at one point, he and several others went to Baghdad for a scheduled meeting with the president. This is what he told me:

> We were ushered into a waiting room. There was almost nothing in the room except for a TV and a cassette recorder. The TV was turned off. We waited and waited. One of my colleagues was becoming very nervous, and started pacing the floor. Then he touched the recorder. We heard a "click." We all looked at it and looked at him. He pressed some more buttons and discovered that it had been on the whole time, and recording our conversation as we sat there! All of us were extremely unsettled by this. We sat there in silence trying to remember what we had said since we entered the room. Thankfully, we had not said anything incriminating. In fact, I had always thought about how the regime could be spying on me. I would look up to see if maybe there was a "bug" anywhere on the wall. I would look for a recording device in a potted plant. So this discovery of ours was not surprising at all, but it was chilling.

After that, the party did meet Saddam Hussein, but Sami said little to me about that. It was clear that, even though he was an eminent figure in Kurdistan and Iraq, the chilling discovery in the waiting room before the diplomatic visit had thoroughly unnerved him. Politicking can be risky for anyone. Sami's political identity did eventually lead to his demise, since the suicide bomber who killed him specifically targeted a high-level political gathering, and he may well have been the main target.

A place with many alliances, such as Kurdistan, is a place with more possibilities for betrayal than one with fewer alliances. The largest betrayal in recent decades may be what the KDP did to the PUK in 1996, when it made an alliance with the Saddam Hussein government to take the city of Hewler that I described in chapter 2. Had Sami been in Baghdad to orchestrate it, or was he there for some other purpose at a different time? He did not tell me. In high-level politicking, ordinary people (and anthropologists) may not be privy to what happens backstage between parties that, to the casual observer, are enemies.

The KDP and PKK were enemies for decades, and their relationship is still somewhat strained. During my field stints in the 1990s, the PKK would actively seek out and kill KDP peshmerga and attack villagers in the mountains who would not acquiesce to their various demands. The two parties' enmity and the PKK's fierceness seemed total. Not only did the PKK leader Abdullah Öcalan kill his enemies with abandon, including with many suicide attacks on Turkish civilians, he was known to execute those within his ranks who did not display complete loyalty. I was affected by PKK attacks on Iraqi Kurds myself, since the original village in which I planned to do fieldwork was evacuated under threat from the PKK, and I knew many people who were affected by their violence. Once, the PKK announced it would begin to blow up fuel tankers on a particular road. I was traveling on that particular road not long afterward, when, sure enough, we came upon the fresh ruin of an exploded fuel tanker. The KDP fought back in a variety of ways. In 1998 it even helped Turkey, the PKK's main enemy, capture a major PKK figure, Şemdin Sakık.

In 2008 I was invited to lunch with the prime minister of the Kurdistan Region, Nechirvan Barzani. The two other American academics with whom I was traveling at the time and I were ushered onto his compound in Hewler. The state of education in the region was one of our main topics over lunch. Then, the topic turned to the PKK, and this is how our conversation went:

> "In the mid-1990s," the prime minister said, "the PKK was doing very awful things. They were attacking us again and again. We did not even know why! Why were they attacking us? We did not know. So I went to Damascus." "Wait, you went to try to talk to him?" I interjected. "But you were serious enemies at that time! How is that possible?" The prime minister just grinned, and continued. "I asked the Syrians to see Öcalan. They said, 'We do not know where he is. *Wallahi* [by God] we do not know where he is.' But I saw him in a mansion in Damascus." "You mean the *asayish* [KDP intelligence forces] saw him there," I said. The prime minister grinned again. "Yes, that's right. So I went there to meet with him. When I opened my mouth to speak to him, I said, 'Öcalan.' He looked at me with a look on his face indicating he did not like that. Then I said 'Apo' ('Uncle,' Öcalan's nickname). He seemed to like that better. Then I said, 'Serok' ('Leader,' a title often used by his followers) Öcalan, and he sat up like this." As he spoke, the prime minister straightened in his seat to show us how. "It was clear he liked that very much. I saw there in his mansion that he had a big TV, the biggest TV—I could not *believe* how big this TV was—and he had a telephone next to his chair. With this phone he could make one call and Kurds all over Europe would come out into the street and demonstrate. Then he would watch them on TV. So he had the phone, and he had the TV. After I saw this I thought, 'This is the problem. The TV is the problem. Because he makes that call and then he sees the results and he is so proud. The TV is the problem!'"

This story brims with political intrigue on several levels. First, Öcalan's location was hidden at that time. He was wanted by numerous countries, including the United States. There was widespread speculation that he was in Syria, but Syria would not admit he was there. He was the hidden leader of a very active political, paramilitary, terrorist group active on multiple continents, and the state of Turkey's enemy #1. The following year, 1999, he was captured in Kenya, where he had fled, and since then he has been in solitary confinement in a prison on the Turkish island of İmralı. To me the most interesting angle to this story is that Nechirvan

Barzani, who was a major figure in the KDP even in the late 1990s, would go
to see Öcalan. Presumably he risked his life to do so, especially since he
went without an invitation. Nechirvan is the son of Idris, son of the great
nationalist leader Mulla Mustafa Barzani, who founded the KDP and led its
fight against the Iraqi government for decades. Nechirvan was clearly leading a more peaceful life than his forebear. But perhaps this clandestine
visit is not so surprising after all. During the 1990s, while they were still
"enemies," the KDP gradually increased its trade with Baghdad until the
goods crossing its territory amounted to billions of dollars' worth each
year. Thousands of commercial vehicles came and went each week, shut-
tling goods from Turkey, into Kurdistan, and on to the Iraqi government-
controlled area. Most were large trucks that returned with petroleum in
special tanks that fit underneath their beds. Most of this trade was against
international law, specifically the economic sanctions levied against Iraq
by the United Nations. Someone high in the KDP had to deal with the GOI
in order to make this trade work. This meant interacting with the regime
even though it was a sworn enemy.

Others had, and have, similar designs on passageways through the
area. The prime minister continued:

> Do you know what Öcalan said when I asked him why they were
> fighting us? He said that people had told him that people in the
> villages were not loyal to us. He thought that if he attacked them,
> they would come over and support the PKK's cause. He wanted Iraqi
> Kurds to join his cause, but he was attacking us. This did not make
> any sense. I told him, "Believe me, if you continue to attack us, we
> will sign an agreement with Turkey and start attacking you. Believe
> me, we will do it!" Unfortunately, he did not stop the attacks. So,
> later that year, as you know, we signed the agreement and started
> fighting them. . . . You know, they have support from Syria and Iran
> because Iran wants a land route to Syria. Iran knows that if they
> could really take some territory there, then they could have access
> to Syria and their people in Lebanon. So they want this very much.
> Of course, this will not happen!

Deals with neighbors who double as enemies are in abundance in
Kurdistan and the surrounding area. There are only frenemies in the area,

not enemies or friends. In 1996, the KDP even struck a secret alliance with the GOI. The alliance became very public once the plan that resulted from it was executed. The PUK controlled the city of Hewler, which the KDP wanted. The deal went like this: Iraqi troops would temporarily enter Hewler. Their numbers and equipment would be relatively modest, so that the American planes overhead would not bomb them for violating the no-fly zone. They would stay only briefly, taking care of their own business while they were there, which mainly involved assassinating local people who had been associating with the CIA. The KDP, in on the secret that the GOI was only coming in temporarily, would rush in as the PUK fled, taking the city. The plan worked flawlessly. The cost, however, was a general sense that one no longer knew whom to trust. Many people, especially those allied with the PUK, were outraged at the KDP's "deal with the devil." Many PUK-allied people in Hewler fled to Silemani, where some remained for years as Internally Displaced Persons, too afraid to return home.

Somehow, the KDP was able to do this and remain an unofficial American ally. It went back to being the "enemy" of the Iraqi government within a few days, although travel restrictions between the government and KDP-controlled areas were significantly loosened. The KDP dominates Hewler and the KRG to this day. Many PUK-aligned people have not forgotten, but the fact that the post-1996 order of things has held for over a decade and a half suggests it is here to stay. In all likelihood much of the back-channel reason for the KDP-Baghdad deal centered on trade and smuggling. Iraq was heavily restricted in international markets due to the sanctions placed on it by the UN Security Council. The PUK's outlet to the world was Iran, another pariah state that was also under trade sanctions. But Turkey, which bordered the KDP area, was open for business and open to the world. The KDP was and is positioned in one of the most strategic land passages in the world. Turkey has a broad-based economy that is one of the world's fastest-growing. Iraq has some of the world's largest oil reserves, and its problematic relationship with Iran means that shipping through the Gulf could be cut off at any moment. Notwithstanding that the KDP and PUK territories are now producing oil themselves, is it possible to imagine a more lucrative place for middlemen, traders, smugglers, traffickers, and brokers? The skills that allowed people to survive and thrive in the Kurdistani mountains during centuries of imperial contests now come in handy on a whole different scale.

Descent and State

In chapter 3 I referred to anthropology's turn away from a widespread interest in the study of kinship in the late twentieth century, and to some of the critiques that were leveled against the study of lineages. Another aspect of that turn is relevant here: links between descent reckoning, the way in which descent is given meaning within a kinship system, and the state. In his book *Primitive Social Organization* (1971), cultural materialist Elman R. Service outlined four types of political organization: band, tribe, chiefdom, and state. This typology became very well known and was soon a basic element in most introductory anthropology textbooks. Service saw lineages as belonging to the "tribe" category. The "state" was portrayed as a more complex structure that came after the tribe. The state was more evolved than the tribe, encompassed the tribe, and was eventually supposed to replace it. But a central argument of this book is that lineages, specifically patrilineages, have and have had tremendous importance in Kurdistan and the Middle East, even though the state is not only present, but present in full force and as the main overarching political form. Lineages seem well adapted to the Middle Eastern modern state and vice versa. As I have noted, many of the key political figures in the Kurdistan Region belong to patrilineages that have a long history of producing political figures. Nechirvan Barzani is just one of many cases in point.

The Ba'thist Iraqi state oppressed people on the basis of their membership in certain patrilineal categories. Political leaders in the Kurdistan Region have said that they seek to chart a different course from the Ba'thists, and in many ways they have. The Kurdistan Region is, in comparison to the rest of Iraq, a place where a person is vastly less likely to be targeted for violence or oppression on the basis of a patrilineally conferred ethnicity or religion. As I elaborate in chapter 6, the region is a refuge for people fleeing such discrimination in the rest of Iraq. It also harbors people who have fled Iran, Syria, and Turkey. The direction of their flight speaks for itself.

Patriliny is still integral to the political system in the Kurdistan Region. The Kurdistan Parliament has seats reserved for people belonging to certain ethnic and religious categories, which the Ba'thist state never did. These are the Member of Parliament (MP) seats currently reserved

for ethnic minorities, as represented by the following parties, in the
Parliament:

Turkoman Democratic Movement: 3 MPs 4

Turkoman Reform List: 1 MP

Turkoman Erbil List: 1 MP

Chaldean Assyrian Syriac Council: 3 MPs

Al-Rafidain List: (Assyrian Democratic Movement) 2 MPs

1 Armenian independent MP: Mr. Aram Shahin Dawood Bakoyian
    (Kurdistan Regional Government 2012)

Kurdish officials have asserted in conversations during my ethnographic
work in the region that they believe that having quotas in the Parliament
is a step toward a more just society. In these conversations they have often
made direct references to the extreme violence perpetrated by the Ba'thist
Iraqi state. But could quotas also be considered a form of sectarianism,
which has caused entrenched conflict in Lebanon and elsewhere? The
question of sectarianism, or a related concept, consociationalism, is the
subject of a rich debate in political science that began with an article by
Lijphart (1969) and has also had more recent proponents (e.g., McGarry
and O'Leary 2004). This debate is too extensive to cover in depth here, but
we can raise one related question regarding Kurdistan and Iraq. Which is
more just: a strongly Arab Sunni-dominated Iraqi government with a
Chaldean Christian deputy prime minister (Tariq Aziz, 1979–2003) whose
patrilineally conferred identity was seen as an "exception," or a system in
which a seat in the Kurdistan Parliament is specifically and explicitly
reserved for an ethnic Turkoman? I think that each system has its draw-
backs, and that justice may ultimately lie in a more flexible system than
either of these. While questions such as this are ultimately for Kurdistanis
and Iraqis to ponder, the latter system has been instituted during a period
of undeniable rectification for Kurdistan, in which very few people have
been killed based on their ethnic identity category, compared to hundreds
of thousands in the period before. Many young Kurdistanis have recently
protested, especially during vigorous street protests in Silemani in 2011,
that their government does not perform to their expectations. In contrast,
many people in the older generation remember a voraciously violent state

and see the present as an improvement. Can the people of Kurdistan find a way forward that builds on recent gains, and institute a systemic rather than a merely palliative remedy for the horrors of the past? Can sectarianism be a remedy for genocide?

"Rarely do analysts using supposed ethnic names probe their actual usage," writes Richard Tapper. "[I]t is too easily assumed, for example, that Baluch, Kurd and Pathan are comparable identities, that each one keeps the same meaning wherever it is used, and that each represents a 'real' unity of origins and culture. An examination of the immensely varied and complex popular discourses shows that cultural identities, whether 'ethnic,' 'tribal' or otherwise, make sense only in social contexts. They are essentially negotiable subjects of strategic manipulations; individuals claim status and present themselves, in different ways in different contexts, and how they do so depends particularly on power relations and on local hierarchies—but also on policies and categorisations by the state" (Tapper 1988:1030). Tapper is right to point out the flexibility and constructedness of ethnic categories in modern states, which I have emphasized in this book as well. But there is a flip side to state-recognized ethnic categorizations. The state may reserve the right to manipulate ethnic categories, and when it does, it may do it in bad faith or coercively or suddenly, as the Saddam Hussein regime did. But during times of stability and stasis, the state's use of categories for its citizens that are conferred by one (and only one) parent constitutes a claim to immutability of those categories. When the state assumes, as most Middle Eastern states have, that men make their own categories, it does not pose any questions to those father-made individuals. It does not ask them, "With which ethnic community or communities do you most closely identify?" "With which religious confession, if any, have you freely chosen to affiliate?" On the contrary, the state sees categories, and it sees offspring of fathers as constituting those categories, no questions asked. No mothers confer identity categories that might differ, and thus no hybrid categories exist. The state makes for its citizens a claim to autochthony in the Lévi-Straussian sense, a claim of being born to only one parent (Lévi-Strauss 1955).

In a system that assumes that individuals receive identity categories from one parent or both parents, I can think of only two ways to ensure that offspring belong to predictable, whole categories: allowing only one parent to confer the relevant category is the simplest and most straight-forward way. If that parent is the father, then ensuring paternity is para-mount. A more complex method is two-pronged: preventing infants from being born to unmarried parents and simultaneously disallowing inter-marriage/exogamy (which can be accomplished by requiring one member of the couple to convert to the other's category; generally this only applies to religion, not categories seen to be more "fixed" such as ethnicity). In the former case, one parent does the conferring, and in the latter, both par-ents could. The two-parent model is found in Kurdistan within Yezidism, which does not allow conversion in or out and which requires endogamy by everyone who marries. A Yezidi person who lets it be known that he or she wants to marry (not to mention create a child with) a non-Yezidi may be heavily pressured, shunned, and is sometimes even killed by members of the Yezidi community. Yezidism is deeply patrilineal, but the Yezidi descent system does not leave the door open even a crack for any other identity category to be passed on to the next generation. It is a perfectly closed descent system. Many Muslim Kurds look to Yezidis as "true Kurds" who represent a purer, pre-Islamic Kurdishness. (Many Muslim Kurds also look down on Yezidis; the relationship between the two groups is multifaceted and can be contradictory.) Since a Muslim man can marry a Christian or a Jewish woman without asking her to convert, Islam can be considered patrilineal in this regard and not overly concerned about the influence of mothers. It has full confidence in the male Muslim parent to confer religious identity on his children.

Borders and Descent

The issue of how categories are passed on and represented in the state is related to issues of the geographic borders of the state. A state border encir-cles a populace that must be defined. Patriliny has provided the framework for that definition in the state of Iraq since the state was founded. At pres-ent, the status of the "disputed territories," areas that both Kurdistan Regional Government and Iraqi government authorities claim should be governed by them, is a key political issue in Iraq and Kurdistan.

During the first half of the twentieth century, Iraq's internal borders, in the form of governorates and smaller municipal areas, became fixed and defined by maps. The country was divided into fourteen *liwas* (provinces or governorates), each of which was administered by a governor. Each liwa was divided into several *qadhas* (districts) administered by a deputy, and each qadha contained *nahiyas* (boroughs), each of which was administered by a *mudir*. There were 45 qadhas and 125 nahiyas in Iraq (Government of Iraq 1953). The Ottoman administration had had similar divisions at the local level. The line established by the advance of the peshmerga and the retreat of Iraqi forces in 1991 approximated, but only loosely, the line separating the governorates of Dohuk, Erbil, and Sulaymaniyah from the rest of Iraq. These three governorates became known as the Kurdistan Region. The majority of Iraq's Kurdish population lived there, but many, perhaps 40 percent of the ethnic Kurdish population of Iraq, continued to live in the government-controlled area, some in places to which they had recently moved, and others in their ancestral homes.

When the permanent Iraqi constitution became law in 2005, it contained a provision in Article 140 that allowed the question of disputed territories to be postponed for later. It stipulated that in 2007, Iraq would hold a referendum in which people living in the territories would decide whether their areas will become part of the Kurdistan Region or be rendered as officially outside it. Kurdish leaders made it clear that they would not support the 2005 Iraqi constitution without such a provision. As of this writing in 2012, the plebiscite has been postponed multiple times and it is not currently scheduled. Thousands of people live in limbo, under undefined local jurisdiction.

Iraq is legally a federation, and official regions are allowed by the Iraqi constitution to exercise a great deal of autonomy. To date, the Kurdistan Region is the only recognized region, although there has been talk in other parts of Iraq of forming additional autonomous regions. The disputes over internal borders center around those that the Kurdistan Region shares with the rest of Iraq. The city of Kirkuk is the most prominent of the disputed areas in Iraq. Kirkuk was "Arabized" by the Ba'thist government over the course of three decades. One of the world's largest oilfields lies beneath Kirkuk, and if Iraq were an "Arab" state, then in the state's view the resources that it held most dear had to be under "Arab" land. How was "Arab" land made? By putting Arab men on it. When the Iraqi government began to play up ethnicity in the expression of its identity, Iraq was an unstable state attempting to find its feet following the 1958 revolution. Successive governments seized power in a series of coups—most notably in 1963 and 1968. But republican Iraq, while on the one hand officially recognizing the rights of Kurds, on the other hand declared itself to be an "Arab" state. War began between the Kurdish rebel movement and Baghdad in 1961, and Saddam Hussein became president in 1979, ruling in a totalitarian fashion and espousing pan-Arabism and socialism. The Ba'th government forced or induced Arab men and their households to move to Kirkuk from other parts of Iraq, and it forced Kurdish men and their households to leave the area for Kurdistan. Following the 1991 Kurdish uprising, an estimated 120,000 people, most of them Kurds, were forced out of Kirkuk (Mufti, Bouckaert, and Human Rights Watch 2003), moving north and east across the newly erected internal border to Kurdish-controlled Kurdistan. Since the deposing of the Ba'th regime in 2003, this process has reversed itself, and thousands of people have returned. Kirkuk remains unstable as it awaits the referendum. The issue of who is eligible to vote is one factor in the delay. In October 2008, I spent time in the office of Merdan, a regional government official whose staff members were computerizing census data from the 1950s. At one point I observed them working at a feverish pace, with an air of great determination, in an attempt to make a deadline that was a few days off. Little could any of us know at that point that the poll would still not have been conducted four years later.

While Kirkuk is the most famous disputed area in Iraq, there are smaller communities all along the internal border between Kurdistan and the rest of Iraq. Some, like the small town of Aqre, have been functioning as part of Kurdistan since 1991, when Aqre was effectively annexed to the Dohuk Governorate by Kurdish authorities. Since the annexation was unofficial, there were many problems associated with this that affected average people living there. I spoke with members of a family in Aqre in the years prior to 2003 who told me that they were unable to access the legal records pertaining to the property they owned, because it was in Mosul and they could not go to Mosul for political reasons. Most of Aqre's population changed allegiance from the GOI to the KDP in 1991. It remains a small, picturesque town with ancient houses stretching up its rocky slopes. Population gain has led to a building boom on the surrounding plains.

PHOTO 5.1 Men sit and visit overlooking the town of Aqre, 2002. (Photo by the author.)

Visits to Aqre, which I have made many times, do not reveal anything out of the ordinary. However, Aqre's official status remains "disputed," a status with which its inhabitants must still deal on an everyday basis.

The border between Kurdistan and the rest of Iraq was a military face-off line between GOI forces and the peshmerga until the United States and Britain went to war against the regime in 2003. The Kurdish line of control was pushed out by the peshmerga. In some of the areas into which the peshmerga triumphantly rushed, the population was mainly Kurdish and welcomed them profusely; indeed, their arrival was the culmination of a long-held dream. In other areas, this was the feeling initially, but with the passage of time, sentiments have become more mixed. In a few places, the peshmerga who arrived starting in 2003 are reviled by local non-Kurds, who have sometimes been vocal about wanting them to leave. Meanwhile, other nationalist movements such as Assyrian and Turkoman, are active, asking for their own recognized "homeland" within Iraq. Their activists push for their identity to become inscribed on the land in much the same way that Kurdish identity has in the undisputed parts of Iraqi Kurdistan since 1991. For these nationalists, places have ethnic or national identities. Places *should* have such identities, to the exclusion of other identities, and these identities are then passed on. The status quo is for those identities to be passed on by men through their sons and sons' sons, and so on.

Since 2003, I have traveled through the disputed areas several times and found the atmosphere to be tense both on the ground and in the air. In the summer of 2008 I saw, though my taxi window to the south, several U.S. aircraft, including helicopters and fixed-wing aircraft that appeared to be drones, hovering and circling around a particular spot, apparently in pursuit of someone or something. Although I craned my neck to watch them as we went by, I noticed that no one else in the shared taxi in which I was riding seemed to care. As for the ground, I saw virtually no evidence of the U.S. occupation, but the Kurdish-controlled checkpoints were, as Nahela put it during another trip I took with her between Zakho and Hewler in 2008, "serious" checkpoints. This was in contrast to the many peshmerga checkpoints throughout undisputed Kurdistan that are relaxed and friendly. Indeed, we were often questioned in a gruff manner but never detained, as we saw that people in some other cars were. On my last taxi ride through those areas on the way to the airport, the driver turned and grinned after we had successfully passed through the tense area. "I told the guards you are Kurdish," he said, beaming because it had worked. The driver made even me an unintended, inadvertent player in the Kurdish claim to territory, and to the claim that territory has identity and that identity should be territorialized.

Must emplacement be tied to patrilines, and passed only through sons? I regard this question as one of the most important questions before the people of the Middle East and North Africa. When the state allows only men to pass on citizenship, its citizenry is effectively comprised of state-defined patrilineages. The man who first acquired citizenship in the state, which typically took place in the early to mid-twentieth century, is the founder of a citizenship patrilineage. In oil states, those patrilineages hold patrimony that represents significant wealth. Some signs suggest that this rigid state of affairs may be changing in Iraq. In Merdan's office, I watched his staff putting together the documentation related to Article 140 and Kirkuk. Here is part of a conversation I had with him about their work:

MERDAN: We are using the 1957 census to register people in Kirkuk for the voting that will take place once Article 140 is implemented. We are considering anyone descended from someone counted in the census as a legitimate voter.

DIANE: What do you mean by "descended from?" Usually that only means people descended through males.

MERDAN: We are counting people through their mothers, too.

DIANE: So, just to make sure I understand, if there was a woman in Kirkuk in 1957, and she married a man from Mosul and they had children, you are considering those children Kirkukis?

MERDAN: Yes, we are trying to argue that.

DIANE: This means that the children can claim to be both from Mosul and Kirkuk, right?

MERDAN: Yes, that's right, they could.

DIANE: Are you arguing this, or is it accepted?

MERDAN: We are arguing it. Everything is up in the air right now, so we will see what happens!

Merdan was promoting a nonpatrilineal definition of "Kirkuki" identity—arguing that *any* descendant, not just patrilineal descendants, of someone living in Kirkuk when the last census was taken in 1957 could now return to Kirkuk and be issued a voting card. Because what he was saying was such a departure from the entrenched modern citizenship patterns in the Middle East, I wanted to be sure I understood, so I repeated back to him a more detailed version of what I thought he was saying:

DIANE: So, a Kirkuki woman is living in Kirkuk in 1957. She marries a non-Kirkuki, and moves away to another city. Their children are not considered Kirkuki, because their father is not. By now there are several additional generations. Are you saying that all people who are her children and grandchildren and great-grandchildren can claim to be Kirkuki?

MERDAN: Yes. All of them.

The efforts by the KRG that the project in Merdan's office represented were in the initial stages when I had this conversation in 2008. No one knew then that the referendum would go on to be postponed repeatedly. Whether or not other politicians in Iraq will accept this unconventional, bilateral form of descent reckoning remains to be seen. If they do, this would be a very significant alteration of the concept of ethnic transmission in Iraq. Also if so, this attempt to expand the definition of Kirkuki could well be taken to be "cheating" by other groups, such as the ethnic Turkoman, who have long had a significant presence in Kirkuk and have probably not deviated from a patrilineal definition of Kirkukiness. Bilateral descent reckoning in this case means that thousands more people can claim Kirkuki status than before, and since this new definition is coming from within the Kurdistan Regional Government, the people who would learn about and act on the new definition would be disproportionately Kurdish.

But another outcome of this altered concept of a claim to place, if it succeeds, could actually have the unintended consequence of making claims to place *less* potent, because it means people have more than one place that is "theirs." No longer is a person's father's village necessarily "their" village, even if they have never been there. In this model, a person can claim affinity with a mother's village, father's village, and conceivably four grandparents' villages, eight great-grandparents' villages, and so on. (High rates of village and lineage endogamy would make it unlikely that someone would have eight great-grandparents from eight different villages, but it is still possible in theory.)

Another ethnographic example from 2008 comes from a different source. I met a young man in Hewler who was a convert from Sunni Islam to Protestant Christianity. We spoke about issues of identity, and the problem of identity change with which any convert is confronted in Iraq and the broader Middle East. He steered the conversation toward the legal dimensions of conversion, specifically the fact that Iraqis, as other Middle Easterners, stand before the state as members of patrilineally transmitted confessional groups that are noted on their citizenship documents, the national ID card, and other government records. The young man told me that he knew some people who had appealed to the government to have their religious identity changed in their official state documentation. Then he went on to say that there was a growing consensus among his small group of friends who had converted that the whole system needed to change. He told me that he wanted something that I had also heard others say they desired: a state that did not keep track of the religious identities of its citizens. He made it clear that he wanted this not just for the Kurdistan Region, but for Iraq as a whole.

The effort sounded as though it was in its infancy. However, it represents a very interesting step toward allowing more flexibility in the patrilineal system that renders place, ethnicity, and religion as inflexible and given within the modern Iraqi state and the Kurdistan Region.

Patron-Client Politicking in Kurdistan

Iraq has been in a political state of flux since the fall of the Saddam Hussein regime in 2003. The United States' military is gone, although many of its diplomats and contractors remain. Conflict between those who make up the state has so far not been violent, although attacks by Islamist insurgents continue in those parts of Iraq outside Kurdistan. The Iraqi government is prevented from making some decisions because its members cannot agree. Many issues that need to be dealt with, such as security and hydrocarbon law and policy, are stalled, or only moving slowly.

In Kurdistan, however, the political system is much more established and the environment is one in which politicking is open to virtually anyone ranging from a bureaucrat like Merdan to a religious convert who wants a different type of citizenship. Women are now involved as well; for several years the Kurdistan parliament has had a quota of 30 percent women. Kurdistan regional elections took place in 2005 following a thirteen-year hiatus, and again in 2009. The KDP was holding its Thirteenth Congress during my field trip in December 2010. There seemed to be a political buzz in the air. The congress was the topic of many conversations analyzed both by cynics who argued that the process did not allow for genuine participation by all, and by people, most of them party members, who seemed to believe in the process.

In elections held in Iraq (including Kurdistan) in 2005 after the ouster of the Ba'thist government, nearly 7,000 candidates stood for election to 275 seats in the Iraqi parliament (BBC News 2005). Some people protested in the media, and one protested to me about a specific incident she saw, that fraudulent voting occurred in the election. Overall, however, the Iraqi population seemed to embrace the experience of being able to vote, and to believe that although the election occurred under occupation, it was largely fair. Iraq had another successful election cycle in 2010. Kurdistan is well represented in the Iraqi parliament, and at many junctures along the way since 2003, Kurds have been brokers who have, it can be argued, kept the Iraqi state together. The state appeared very fragile especially during the conflict between Sunni Arabs and Shi'i Arabs from 2006 to 2008 that some called a "civil war."

As the authors contributing to the volume edited by Ernest Gellner and John Waterbury (1977) have shown, the patron-client relationship has long been integral to the political and social makeup of Mediterranean and Middle Eastern societies. Kurdistan and Iraq are no exception, and much political jockeying there involves the formation, attempted formation, or maintenance of a patron-client relationship. A patron is someone who has something, a good or an opportunity, to dispense. A client is someone who receives that good or opportunity in exchange for loyalty and service. The Kurdistan Region is the site of vigorous connecting between prospective or actual patrons and clients. In the new global milieu, this jockeying is more complex than in the past. Everyone, even a very powerful person, is a client of someone. As I have noted, many politicians belong to notable patrilineages whose members have operated as leaders and patrons in political realms ranging from the tribe to region to state (colonial, inde-pendent, or occupied). A politician, or aspiring politician, tries to amass clients by behaving like a patron. Patrons must have something before they can give it away to others to gain their loyalty, so they busily cultivate their own patrons higher up the ladder within the region and state, and abroad. Rich, varied, and creative connecting is the result. Much of the interacting that takes place in the office or diwan of the politician or tribal leader can also be seen as an effort by the visitor to enlist the leader as a patron. The persons who makes a visit to an office or diwan may well receive what they have come to ask for, and expectations will be placed on them in return. Those expectations may be overtly expressed, such as in the case of a sharecropping arrangement that is very specific. More probably they will be unexpressed at the time. The person will go away happy that his or her needs have been met, but with a sense of obligation to be loyal.

In one political office I visited, that of a minister in the KRG, the min-ister followed the convention of allowing the general public to visit on a specific day of the week. Anyone could come and see the minister during specified hours. The requests were sometimes related to the area of purview of the ministry, but sometimes they were not. In some cases, people simply said they were poor and needed money, and the minister's office would give them a sum of money, enough, perhaps, to buy a few days' worth of food. In other cases the request would be more substantial, such as for a development project to be initiated in the person's neighborhood or village. In such cases the petitioner was likely to leave without a definitive answer, but satisfied that he or she had been heard and that the effort might later yield some results.

The possibility of patronage is also present in diplomatic visits by leaders in Kurdistan to people with more power and authority, such as Sami Abdul Rahman's visit to Saddam Hussein. Perhaps he emerged from that meeting with some kind of bargain. For example, perhaps the KDP or KRG agreed to allow trade to flow through the Ibrahim Khalil border and on to the government-controlled area in exchange for a guarantee that the government would not attack. While I do not know any details, bargains of this nature must have been struck at some point, since the trade did flow, and the government did not attack other than in a limited way, such as when it entered Hewler briefly in 1996. Much of this trade went against the international sanctions levied against Iraq following its attack on Kuwait in 1991, and was therefore technically smuggling, even though much of it took place out in the open. In any case, such meetings between a more powerful person and a person with less power but who is also influential in his or her own sphere can be seen not simply as diplomacy but as an effort to ratchet the relationship around until a patron-client bargain is struck. Clients usually provide loyalty in exchange for security, and in the case of a highly charged political situation such as the one between Iraq, the Kurds, and the international community between 1991 and 2003, many of the details of such a patron-client relationship would have been clandestine and not necessarily visible to the public.

Many of Kurdistan's leaders in both state and nonstate roles belong to shaikhly lineages. They are descended through males from prominent sufi leaders, and the men in such lineages are often addressed as "Shaikh," even though many no longer practice sufism. Martin van Bruinessen describes Kurdish hereditary (patrilineal) shaikhly positions in a passage that is worth quoting in full:

> There has been a tendency in Kurdistan for the position of shaykhs
> to be hereditary. All Qadiri shaykhs in southern Kurdistan belong to

only two families, the Barzinji and the Talabani. The Naqshbandi order expanded rapidly in the early 19th century, partly at the expense of the Qadiriyya, precisely because many persons who were not the sons of shaykhs were given ijazas. The highly charismatic Mawlana Khalid, a Kurd from the Sulaymaniya region, who had studied with one of the greatest Indian Naqshbandi teachers, trained a large number of disciples and appointed well over thirty shaykhs to various parts of Kurdistan. In the following generations, however, the tendency towards hereditary shaykhhood showed itself also among Kurdish Naqshbandis. As a result, certain branches of the orders developed almost into tribes. The Barzanis constitute perhaps the most radical example of this process. The shaykhs of Barzan attracted followers from various origins, some of them tribal but most of them non-tribal peasants, who already lived in or near the shaykhs' village of Barzan or later settled there. The community distinguished itself by a strong sense of egalitarianism and willingness to accept outsiders as members, but in the course of conflicts with the surrounding tribes it came to behave very much like a tribe itself. The Haqqa community mentioned above constitutes another case. (Bruinessen 2000:50)

One man whom I came to know in the early 2000s belonged to a Qadiri shaikh lineage and worked in a professional role for a local United Nations office. People rarely used his name, but called him "the Shaikh." It seemed clear to me that descent from a prestigious sufi leader was a major facet of his personal identity. However, when I asked him about his own practice of Islam and sufism, he told me that while he did pray sometimes, that act was the extent of his religious observance. One day he told me that he felt very financially stretched and could barely pay his bills. He did not appear to be living a lavish lifestyle, and I knew that the UN paid high salaries. So, I pressed him as to how it was possible that he had difficulty paying his bills. He told me that the main reason was that he had a number of personal employees who performed domestic labor, were drivers, and worked in other positions. He paid them quite well for what amounted to very little work. As he spoke, it seemed he felt burdened by this, so I suggested that he scale back. "I cannot," he said. "It is expected of me as a shaikh that I will have people under me whom I take care of and who depend on me for their livelihood. This has always been the role of a shaikh and it is my role today." The shaikh had re-created the patron role of an earlier kind of shaikh in a completely secular way, and he had done it using his salary from a global source, the United Nations, rather than the tribute that the followers of religious shaikhs used to give them (which is still the case with a few practicing sufi leaders). This example speaks to how enduring the roles of patron and client can be, and it suggests that they are highly adaptable to new economic forms.

Patron-Client Relationships in a Modernizing State

As Shmuel Eisenstadt and Luis Roniger (1984) note, citing Amal Vinogradov (1974) and Amal Rassam (1977), patron-client relationships in Iraq have changed since land reform in the mid-twentieth century took away the ability of large landowners to exploit the peasants under them. However, as I have also stated elsewhere in this book, they note that even though such relationships may be less coercive, former peasants still have relationships with their former landlords that still have a client-patron quality, and while landowners no longer exploit the peasantry for their own extravagant gain, many of the people living in Kurdish villages still live a lifestyle very similar to their forebears. "Over a period of time," Eisenstadt and Roniger note, "this relationship has changed from an all-comprehensive, religiously sanctioned dependency. It has become more specific and instrumental and commitments are more tenuous, involving a freer selection of patrons and intercessors" (1984:89).

The village guard system in Turkey, which employed approximately 50,000 people in the southeast of the country by the late 1990s (Vermot-Mangold and Council of Europe Parliamentary Assembly Committee on Migration Refugees and Demography 1998) can be likened to the chete system in Iraq. In the village guard system, Kurdish villagers living in areas of Turkey where the PKK is active are paid and armed by the central government to fight the PKK. In the chete system, the Iraqi government paid Kurds in Iraq to fight the KDP and PUK. However, there was a fundamental difference between the two systems: the Iraqi government funneled chete payments through aghas, thus creating patrons and strengthening their hand in relationship to the peasantry at a time in Iraqi history when that relationship was otherwise being weakened due to land reform. The aghas carried on as leaders of tribes, and the peasants continued as tribal members who were called upon by the aghas to show their loyalty, sometimes by fighting other tribes. Some arrangements of this kind may persist between some tribal chiefs and the KRG, when those chiefs supply fighters to the peshmerga. Such an arrangement was insinuated to me in a conversation with a tribal chief. The Turkish government, on the other hand, pays the village guards directly, and thus does not further the patron-client system. Without a middleman, the government is the direct patron.

In my observation the KRG is now creating such relationships itself, and mainly with people who are in need, such as IDPs and divorced women. To its credit, it has gone to great lengths to take care of the people within its boundaries who are in need, including thousands of people from other parts of Iraq who have sought refuge, some of whom I describe in the next chapter. This is much of the reason that Kurdistan is a place of refuge within Iraq, a place to which people flee, rather than from which they flee. In the process, older forms of patronage and clientage are being replaced with newer forms. For example, women have been, and remain, a way for families to transform themselves, over time, from one level of the patron-client hierarchy to another, whether up or down. As Stanley Brandes (1987:132) has written, "By elevating female chastity to a symbolic virtue, women could readily become pawns in the struggle for family honor. Chaste women were transformed into a resource, which could be exchanged for wealth, power, and prestige." Thus the typical high-status lineage keeps its women and girls above reproach in order to ensure the continuation of the family's high status, and an urban lineage of social climbers does the same to increase the chances that its younger generation marries well, thus increasing their status. As illustrated by the prime minister's tweet that I cited at the beginning of chapter 1, the KRG has been actively changing the laws of the region to reflect values that it considers to be more "modern." In so doing, it is taking on roles that once belonged to households and lineages. Some of these laws stand to bring significant changes to the kinship and gender system if they are widely applied (which is not yet the case). For example, the law now stipulates that the government will provide for a divorced woman:

> (4) The [Kurdistan] Regional Government shall be committed to taking care of divorceswoman [*sic*] who has no monthly income and it allocates a monthly income for her until she finds a job or remarries. (Kurdistan Regional Government 2008)

Long-standing patrilineal and Muslim customs call upon a divorced woman's parents to take her in and to provide for her economically if they are alive and well, and her brothers if they are not. With this law, the KRG becomes her patron and she its client. Women activists in Kurdistan have lately begun to protest for better distribution of resources, demonstrating that activism on behalf of women can also take the form of activism for a broader constituency of disaffected citizens (Al-Ali and Pratt 2011).

Little has been written about patron-client relationships in anthropology since the decline around 1990 of a vigorous anthropological literature on the topic. However, it has been taken up by scholars in other disciplines, especially in political studies and related fields. The tone of this literature can be quite moralizing. For these authors, patron-client relationships overlap heavily with, or are even synonymous with, "corruption." "Patron-client relationships have dominated and influenced formal bodies. . . . (that) distance local people from decision-making . . . local people do not believe in the power of state institutions, but in the power of patrons," writes Cevat Tosun (1998:602) about a particular case in the Turkish tourism industry. The new patron-client relationships may further the interests of the wealthy. While the poor and the middle class do not benefit, or at least do not benefit significantly, they are still caught up in the promise of the relationships, which rests on a dream that if one can just get to the right position within the vertical patron-client system, then one can reap all of its benefits. In Iraqi Kurdistan I have heard many complaints from people who observe others profiting from patron-client relationships, and would like to secure such an arrangement themselves. I have argued (King 2005) that complaints of this nature in the 1990s and early 2000s after the Government of Iraq's patronage relationship with most Kurds was severed may have contributed to the desire of many people to out-migrate to the West. Michiel Leezenberg (2006) makes the argument that patron-client networks in Kurdistan have proven very adaptable to urban contexts, leading to increases in wealth and power for those who have wielded them successfully. It seems they are a major component in the economy of the new Kurdistan and Iraq.

Kurds as a Middle Eastern Counterpublic

Kurdish nationalism has been built on a discourse of "freedom," not from distant Western powers as has been the case with many nationalist movements elsewhere, but from domination by the surrounding states, each of which has a majority of people belonging to a non-Kurdish ethnic group with whom the Kurds have a long history of mutual antipathy. In the Middle East beyond Iraqi Kurdistan, publics and elites alike often express feelings of enmity toward the West, as I have witnessed in Turkey, Syria, and Lebanon. The Pew Global Attitudes Survey's work has yielded convincing survey data showing at least widespread exasperation with American foreign policy by a majority of people in the Middle East, and outright contempt for the United States by significant numbers (Pew Global Attitudes Project 2007). This is not the case in Kurdistan, where the population and leadership alike has long been pro-American.

Kurdistan has been the recipient of a different kind of imperialism than that referred to in speeches by leaders elsewhere in the Middle East. The Kurdish population coalesced into a nation only in a frail way and unsuccessfully, since that process did not lead to an independent state, during the formative years of the late nineteenth and early twentieth centuries. Elsewhere, the demise of the Ottoman Empire gave rise to nationalist movements, especially Arab and Turkish, which then became associated with states. The Kurds were stateless during the same period that their neighbors—specifically the elites dominating those neighbors—were state building. Unlike many of the nationalist discourses heard in neighboring states, collective identity making and nationalism by Iraqi Kurds have not been predicated on anticolonialist discourse. Since the creation of the Iraqi state, Iraqi Kurds have more often than not been in conflict with the Arab-controlled Baghdad government, which has used its considerably greater power against them. Iraqi Kurdish leaders were killed, silenced, and/or in exile during the period between the collapse of the Kurdish nationalist movement in 1975 and the uprising in 1991. Compared to the surrounding Turkish, Iranian, and Arab national movements in which elite liberal classes vied (and still vie) for state control, Iraqi Kurdish leaders have been for the most part noncosmopolitan. Although the Kurdish national movements of the twentieth century did have some leaders who were educated in the West, many others were not. There was no institution in Kurdistan like the American University of Beirut, which in the twentieth century simultaneously taught Arab young people in American ways while serving as a focal point for Arab rebellion against Western control. The leaders of the Kurds' ethnic neighbors formulated their nationalisms in part by railing against the West—the very West that had, in many cases, equipped them and placed them in power. But in Iraqi Kurdistan little such hybridity existed prior to 1991, and little anti-Western discourse emerged. Until the 1990s, even Iraqi Kurds living in the West were cut off from Iraqi Kurdistan and could exert barely any influence there.

Clandestinely and from their exile in neighboring countries before 1991, and within the Iraqi Kurdish public sphere since 1991, Iraqi Kurdish leaders have promoted a vision of azadî (independence/freedom) vis-à-vis a local other, mainly Iraqi Arabs. I regard the azadî discourse as occupying a similar niche in state building as anti-Western discourse in neighboring states. It has served as a key source of elite legitimacy, serving to rally diverse constituencies to the cause. It thus has an outcome vis-à-vis their local publics similar to the outcome of anti-Western discourse in neighboring states, but with the added benefit that Western governments are not alienated and are usually supportive. The Kurds are famously stateless. Kurdish nationalism remains only partly successful. In the Kurdistan Region, it operates in a fuzzily defined category of sovereignty that, despite recent gains, still does not have the status of a new state like East Timor, Kosovo, or South Sudan. It does not have a flag on the street outside the UN building in New York.

Politicking on behalf of the Kurdish nation in Iraq continues. It now operates at many levels, including the global, on which I will have more to say in the next chapter. In a dusty village, a chief still receives guests and tries to solve their problems. In a gleaming high-rise building in Hewler, a man who is both a business and political leader makes deals that will make both him and some of the people around him wealthier. Planes land outside, carrying oil executives. KRG president Mes'ud Barzani and Iraqi prime minister Maliki regularly politick over oil revenues. Politicking in Kurdistan may have risen to its highest economic level ever in 2012, when the KRG and Exxon Mobil came to an agreement. The Kurdistan Region now plays host to the world's largest company pumping the world's favorite commodity.

6

Refuge Seeking, Patriliny, and the Global

Emrevîn. (We fled.)

–Phrase repeated in countless conversations and interviews

I am a guest for lunch at the home of a family living in the Barushki neighborhood of Dohuk. The conversation turns to the Anfal campaign, in which the Iraqi government led by Saddam Hussein attacked people in Kurdish villages from the air, dropping chemical weapons on them. Suzan, a relative of the family who is also a lunch guest, tells her personal story of fleeing the government's helicopters in 1988. She managed to get away with her life, but did not escape injury; in various places on her body, some of which she shows us, are large areas of scarred skin. She and her family fled to Diyarbakir, Turkey, staying there for four years, but both her husband and son died there. Suzan begins to cry as she recounts her story, going on to tell how her village in the mountains behind Dohuk had been destroyed by the government four times since the 1960s. Her story is like countless others I have heard from people in Iraq and from Iraqi Kurdistan.

Kurdistan's recorded history is consistently bloody. It lies at the meeting point of three old imperial territories, Persian, Turkish, and Russian. It came under British attack in World War I and became a British Mandate after the war. The violence produced by these encounters can be called "large scale" and seen as a precursor to the globalized violence that was to follow it, because these were big powers. Kurdistan has also had, and still has, many sources of "small scale" localized collective violence as well. Most Kurdish people belong to a tribe, and tribes sometimes get into conflicts with one another. Like tribes, patrilineages sometimes also get into conflict and split over land, women, access to a resource, or other causes. Between the large and the small scale, increasingly the source of violence is the modern or modernizing state, such as the Ba'thist Iraqi state that waged such horrible attacks on its own citizens in the decades leading to 2003. Collective violence can be said to come in waves, and inconsistently. Evidence suggests that it never stops.

Each wave of violence in Kurdistan, whether small, medium, or large scale, has prompted people to flee in search of safety. A century ago, most Kurds who migrated did so only "internally," within Kurdistan. The vast majority of refuge seeking events were highly local, within a small area of a few to tens of kilometers, such as from the realm of one local leader to another. For example, a refuge seeker might flee to the neighboring tribal chief's territory, where he or she would be granted asylum and allowed to remain indefinitely. The reason for flight might stem from perpetration, victimhood, or both (depending on the point of view of the person or entity assigning such a label). Or, the refuge seeker might have killed someone accidentally, and the victim's lineage mates might be out for blood.

A person who has or is an enemy and does not have enough allies around himself or herself to remain in place needs safety granted elsewhere, and quickly. Refuge seeking and refuge granting are still possible, and indeed are frequently implemented in Kurdistan. Now, however, such flight and refuge episodes may come to the attention of authorities representing far larger spheres of power than a tribal chief, such as the regional government, state government, and international agencies. While refuge seeking used to involve mainly local social connections, it now invokes and involves connections at the state and global levels.

Kurdistan is a very rich site for exploring refuge at the crossroads of the local and the global, traditional structures such as patrilineages and tribes and the modernizing state. Anywhere in the world, people who flee "internally," within the boundaries of the state, are likely to come to the attention of state authorities. Those who cross a border usually come to the attention of authorities belonging to a different government, and often of the global refugee and asylum regime consisting of interstate agreements and international agencies like the United Nations High Commissioner for Refugees (UNHCR). Refuge seeking is now embedded in the modern (or purportedly modern) state, which is itself embedded in a global milieu of public awareness and accountability structures such as laws and treaties and media. In the global legal regime, a "refugee" is a person who has crossed an international border into a second country, applied for refugee status through UNHCR, and is waiting to be resettled in a third country. An "asylum seeker" is a person who has crossed an international border into his or her intended resettlement country, where he or she has applied directly to the government for asylum. An internally displaced person (IDP) has fled without leaving the state in which he or she normally resides. Refuge now takes place within and between states, which are part of a global system of states that (for the most part) recognize one another as sovereign authorities. Refuge, no matter on what scale, is now globalized.

Here is a United Nations summary of the global numbers of refugees and IDPs: "In 2004, there were more than 17.5 million people in the broader category of 'persons of concern' to UNHCR, including internally displaced persons, returned refugees and 'stateless persons,' in addition to refugees and asylum seekers. This figure, though down from a peak of 27.4 million in 1994, only encompasses a small minority of the world's internally displaced persons as it is restricted to those receiving assistance or protection from UNHCR. While nearly 5.6 million internally displaced persons were 'of concern' to UNHCR in 2004, the total number of internally displaced persons worldwide was estimated at 25 million—more than twice the number of recognized refugees" (UNHCR 2006:17).

All human migrants enter a new social milieu at their destination. In the past, the act of migrating within Kurdistan may have resulted in one's descendants acquiring a slight dialect change and a new set of primordial allegiances. Contemporary Kurdish migrations complicate both primordial/local, and modern/global refuge and asylum regimes. On the one hand, "old-fashioned" types of migrating, such as from the protective zone of one tribal chief to that of another, now takes place within a state. Both the chief and the refuge seeker are, in all likelihood, citizens who are accountable to the laws of the land. If the refuge seeker has murdered someone and is fleeing because the victim's relatives are out for revenge, then law enforcement personnel may become involved to enforce a law against murder. The murderer's space of refuge will be a prison. At the other end of the spectrum, the production of violence, in particular

violence that Kurds flee, is now also global. The contest between Iraq and
the United States that began in 1990 drew in many governments and several militaries from around the world. The Cold War was over, and this was
the new lone superpower's first big contest. Iraq was occupied by the U.S.
military for much of the following two decades. The occupation was constant in Iraq's airspace from 1991 to 2011, and it was instated on the ground
from 1991 to 1996, and 2003 to 2011. Just as the weapons are modern and
products of the global economy, the range of choices is global too. It is
often claimed (e.g., United Nations Development Programme 2004) that
globalization makes people aware of their options. A person in need of
refuge a century ago, or contemplating his or her options while a prisoner
of war, might have only been aware of a small sphere of political actors.
Now the sphere encompasses Europe and America, as well as other locations. Malaysia, for example, has long offered entry to Iraqi passport holders without a visa, and in recent years I have met several young people in
Iraqi Kurdistan who had returned after studying in Malaysian universities.

Refuge from and in Deshta Village

It is December 2010 and I am in Deshta, the village that passed down
Hawer Agha's patrilineage to the Haweri lineage members as described in
chapter 3. In one direction is a plain, sloping gently to the southeast, on
which dry-land farming yields wheat, lentils, melons, and other crops.
Behind it is a mountain, its lower alluvials often dotted with grazing animals and its upper reaches craggy and stalwart. The village is picturesque,
although less so during the parched summer months. The confluence of
the Tigris and Khabur rivers is nearby. The village is in many ways a very
desirable piece of land. It is small; when I first visited it in 1998, it had only
ten households, and only a few structures have been built since then. The
village's smallness, however, belies the fact that it is also a very global
place, a place in which both the dramas of the modernizing state, the older
structures it contains such as patrilineages and tribes, and an increasingly
interconnected world are played out.

Deshta has by no means been a place of social stability during at least
the past several decades. The plain on which it sits is heavily contested
territory within the Iraqi state headquartered in Baghdad. That state was

founded in the early twentieth century by British colonizers following the end of several hundred years of Turkish rule, and with a mandate from the Allied winners of World War I. Especially after the British were expelled in the revolution of 1958, Iraq increasingly came to see itself, despite its undeniable ethnic diversity, as essentially and ontologically "Arab." This process reflected trends in the broader region of Arab-majority states and in the global rise of the modern state that imagined itself to be a *nation*-state, the rightful home of one (ideally *only* one) ethnic nation.

The people who have shared the broader area surrounding Deshta are ethnically diverse, including Kurds, Neo-Aramaic-speaking Christians, Arabs, Turks, Armenians, and (until the 1950s) Jews. Modern Deshta's immediate surroundings, however, are heavily Kurdish, and it is within the area long informally recognized as "Kurdistan." The village was founded by Sunni Muslim Kurds in the early twentieth century led by a tribal chief, a descendant of Hawer Agha, whose descendants still own the village land and who first took me there. A significant number of Yezidi Kurdish villages are nearby.

For most of the period in living memory, until the 2003 invasion by the United States and Britain that changed the Iraqi government, Iraq's Sunni Arab–dominated government was in conflict with the Kurdish minority. Since the government had greater population numbers on its side and heavy military machinery and weapons purchased with oil revenue, the warring parties were extremely mismatched, with the Kurds incurring heavy losses. As I recounted in chapter 2, the conflict culminated in 1988 in a concerted genocidal campaign, known as "Anfal" after a Quranic reference to spoils of war, to eliminate the Kurds once and for all. Millions suffered and hundreds of thousands were killed. Several thousand village houses were destroyed, many after having been rebuilt following earlier attacks. In the town of Halabja, at least 5,000 people were killed and thousands more injured in the most concentrated attack of Anfal (see Hiltermann 2007 for details). In some parts of Kurdistan, a visitor can choose practically anyone in sight, ask him or her about past losses, and hear some of the most horrifying accounts imaginable. To cite one of many examples: A man I met in the village of Shkafta in the Barzan Valley told me that nearly all of his male relatives, his father, brother, and uncles, were "taken," *girtin*, by Iraqi government forces in the 1980s, never to be heard from again. Everyone else, including himself, was forcibly relocated to southern Iraq. He had returned, he told me, in 1997, six years after the Kurdish uprising had made return possible. He appeared to have been very young during the government's gendercidal attack, which I imagined had saved his life. His story is just one of many thousands like it in Kurdistan.

As a part of the conflict, the Kurdish occupants of Deshta were forcibly removed by government forces in the 1960s, and Arab families were made to live there instead. The Kurdish families fled, most of them heading to the nearby town of Zakho and a few to the larger city of Mosul, where they rebuilt their lives. With a low level of literacy and few marketable skills, many struggled with poverty and uncertain futures. One man, Loqman, a villager who had long been a client of the Haweri lineage as a sharecropper and fighter, recounted his and his family's comings and goings from Deshta from the 1960s to the 1990s: "We left the village and went to Mosul for four years. Then I joined Mohammed Agha's chete fighters, and our household was in Zakho for three years because the government wanted us Kurds to return to our area. Then in 1974 we returned to Deshta, and remained six years. Then, the Iraqi government kicked us out. We fled to the mountains with Khalid, another chete leader from the Haweri lineage, and stayed for one year. Then we moved to Zakho, and again to Deshta in the 1990s." Loqman and his family now live in Zakho.

In 1991, during the Kurdish uprising, the Arab families fled and the Kurds rushed to reclaim their land. Like Arab nationalism, this event was not merely local in any sense. It was in many ways a product of the war between the United States and its allies and Saddam Hussein's government following the latter's invasion of Kuwait. Kuwait was desirable to Iraq because of its wealth in oil, a global commodity if there ever was one. In part, the Kurdish freedom fighters rose up when they did because they were encouraged to do so by U.S. president George H. W. Bush in a Voice of America broadcast. Highly local flight and return patterns were influenced by a distant power on the other side of the globe.

The Deshta villagers returning in 1991 found that the village had been destroyed, its houses leveled to the ground by bombs dropped by Iraqi government aircraft. Some of the bomb casings from those attacks are still in the village, being put to use as boundary markers for children's soccer games, containers, stools, and other implements. With the help of a

European NGO, the families rebuilt their houses and resumed farming. When I arrived in 1998, I found many of those families living in their recently rebuilt houses. Some maintained their houses in Zakho and lived in the village only part time, and others had returned to live there full time. Sheep and goats belonging to the villagers were once again corralled beside the houses at night and taken to the grazing slopes during the day. Villagers sharecropped with the landlords. A sign at the village's entrance trumpeted that the houses were the work of the NGO. Additional work was being done to bring electricity to the village and on the water supply for homes and irrigation.

Again, in this case, we can see large-scale processes at work that belong more to the global than the local milieu in refuge-seeking and return-migration events. Why did the United States invade Iraq with ground troops in 1991, and why did it establish the no-fly zone over the north (and also the south, which is not our subject here)? The causes of the war were a source of much debate in the United States. Some, mainly those on the political right, said that the war was a just and overdue response to a brutal dictator, and others, mainly those on the political left, took the

PHOTO 6.1 A bomb casing lies in a field near a village. It was dropped on the village in the years prior to the 1991 uprising. When photographed in 2002, it was one of many strewn about the area. Since then, many have been recovered and put to various household uses, such as dried flower vases. (Photo by the author.)

view that the war was a quest for oil, and revenge by President George W. Bush against President Saddam Hussein for allegedly attempting to assassinate his father in Kuwait in 1993. While the causes of the war will be debated by historians for years to come, it is undeniable that Iraq is extremely rich in hydrocarbons, which the world economy needs and over which Saddam Hussein's government sought to retain and expand its control. One compelling way to see Iraq's internal struggles and struggles with other states, and therefore the need of people affected by those struggles to seek refuge, is through the prism of the global thirst for oil.

For several years following the 1991 flight of the Arab families who had been placed in the village, and the return of the original Kurdish families, the village again appeared to be thriving. On one visit in the late 1990s I did an analysis of the meals that the family that was hosting me and I consumed during one day. Everything we ate, except for a few minor items like salt, had been produced within the village—from the wheat that became the flour in our freshly baked bread, to eggs and meat from chickens and geese, to onions and tomatoes and many other vegetables. One day we prepared and ate a freshly killed porcupine that one of the men had shot

PHOTO 6.2 A girl removes freshly baked bread from an earth oven in a village in the Simel District in 2010. Baking bread is one of the most important practices learned by adolescent girls living in rural settings. (Photo by the author.)

that morning. The surplus food that the village produced was sold in town. By the age-old standards of village life, the village was functioning well.

By the 2000s, however, village living had started to become less attractive, and families began to move back to town. I tracked down members of each household, or at least talked to people who knew the circumstances of each household, and tried to understand why they had left. I found that modernization and globalization were transforming Iraqi Kurdistan's towns at a faster pace than they were transforming its villages. Anywhere in the world, capital penetrates urban areas first. Kurdistani village life involved heavier labor, lacked reliable electricity and water, and involved a commute for secondary education that was impractical for most families. In town, one could work at a job that was cleaner and involved less exertion, children could receive more years of education, the electricity was more reliable and powered, among other devices, satellite dishes and televisions that connected one to the world through hundreds of channels in many languages. By the time I visited in 2008, only a few of Deshta's original occupants remained, and most said they were preparing to leave. Members of the chiefly family, the village's owners, were farming, but they usually did not sleep in the village, instead commuting from town.

I was surprised, then, to find in 2008 that the village had some new occupants: families who had fled violence in Mosul, which had become particularly bad since the beginning of the second American-led war in 2003 that removed Saddam Hussein's government in Baghdad, and the ensuing occupation. The refugees were a ragged, diverse lot. One was an Arab widow with several children, one of them severely disabled, who had fled a neighborhood reeling from several terrorist attacks. One Kurdish family had fled a blood feud in the Mosul area, and although that case might have seemed on the surface to be only "small-scale" collective violence, many people told me that year that the larger-scale conflict in Iraq, mainly between U.S. forces and a shadowy resistance led by Al-Qaeda, had provided cover for the settling of many personal and small-scale scores, some decades old. So, it can be argued that their story, too, fits a model of local refuge seeking that now had much broader connectedness. Another Kurdish family had come from elsewhere in the Kurdistan Region with their herds because the drought, which was affecting the whole area, had affected their own grazing areas more than it had Deshta's.

In December 2010 I found still more momentous changes in village personnel. All but one of the previous households had left the village. However, the village was teeming with people. Twenty-two new families had arrived and were crammed into approximately half that number of houses. All were members of the same Yezidi patrilineage from Shingal (called "Sinjar" in Arabic), a heavily Yezidi area to the southwest, and had fled a blood feud with members of another branch of the lineage. One person on their side was dead, and three were dead on the other side. Several members of each group were in jail.

In tribal feuding custom, a debt is collective, not individual, and hierarchies within the group are taken into account. Martin van Bruinessen found many reports of "protracted feuds" in his travels through Kurdistan in the 1970s. His informants volunteered accounts of feuds that had continued for many years and had resulted in up to 100 deaths. He notes that "neither in the Koran nor in the stories I was told is there any suggestion that the murderer himself should be killed for revenge: in the tribal milieu a murder is not primarily an individual affair, but one between groups. . . . If a tribal chieftain were killed by a non-tribal, subjected serf and the chieftain's relatives' only revenge would be to kill that serf, they would in fact be lowering the chieftain to the rank of a serf. But the idea that a serf would kill a lord just on his own account is incongruous to a tribesman. They would immediately suspect another chieftain of instigating the murder, and therefore seek revenge at that level" (1992a:65–66). I too have heard many accounts of feuds in Kurdistan. Some feuds have affected people I know well, including Nahela, whose father was killed in an apparent feud murder in the 1960s.

I interviewed the group's leader. "We still want to kill each other," he told me. "They cannot come here, because they will not be allowed across the regional border. We cannot go back there, because they will kill us. So we feel safe here." Authorities from the Iraqi government, the Kurdistan regional authorities, tribal leaders, the highest Yezidi religious authority, and NGOs from abroad (all of them Western, it was implied) had been involved in assisting them and attempting to broker peace, but their problem was very complex and remained unsolved. We joked that I might have a new idea for them, but I left as puzzled as anyone as to how the two branches of the lineage could ever be reconciled short of making a willful decision to forgive, which did not appear to be under consideration. On other occasions, I had heard about, and even witnessed in one instance, the successful brokering of peace between feuding parties by a third, "neutral" party. One such party may yet achieve success in this case.

Refuge Seeking, Connectedness, and the State

The case of Deshta implicates the global system of sovereign states and global consumption regimes, in which we are all participants. If we keep this in mind, we can easily draw a line of connectedness from a Deshta villager to an American pilot patrolling the skies over Iraq during the period of American domination of Iraqi airspace from 1991 to 2011. The villager lives in the now-official Kurdistan Region, which was preceded by a rebellious Iraqi Kurdistan whose autonomy went unrecognized by Baghdad between 1991 and 2003. Although the United States was distant and uninvolved when the Kurds suffered the height of the attempted genocide in 1988, it intervened in 1991, patrolling the skies over Deshta and for twelve years holding the hostile Iraqi government at bay. The U.S. military occupation of Iraq from 2003 to 2011 had tragic results in most areas of Iraq other than Kurdistan, as an insurgency fought back against both the occupier and the civilian population. In Kurdistan, however, the occupation was interpreted by the vast majority of people as a rescue. In Deshta, a place that was itself occupied by Arab settlers (who may very well have dwelt there reluctantly), Kurdish life resumed under flyovers by American pilots. They flew petroleum-fueled planes.

Following World War II, Hannah Arendt observed that even though the concept of asylum had a "long and sacred history," following the mass movement of stateless people during the war, while states tended to protect their citizens who were abroad, they were reluctant to make asylum official by ratifying it in law and policy (Arendt 1951:356–357). A state looked after its own, in other words, but was seemingly reluctant to acknowledge another state's failings by granting that state's citizens protection within its own borders. Over sixty years later, this is no longer the case, and many states now have asylum policies, though how generous these policies are varies through time and from place to place. But Arendt's early worry can be seen as a precursor to those of Manuel Castells and others: that the state was often unable or unwilling to involve itself in forced migrants' situations.

Some have claimed that the end of the nation-state is coming or is perhaps already here (Jáuregui Bereciartu 1994). Manuel Castells has made a well-known assertion that state power is decentralizing. As a result, he argues, minorities, groups other than the majorities that define the nation, are increasingly turning to their own communities and "non-governmental structures of self-reliance" (Castells 2010:339). In this line of thinking, refuge seekers, whether seeking safety inside or outside of their own states, would find themselves "on their own" on an increasing basis, without state oversight or management.

The case of refuge seeking in and from Iraqi Kurdistan allows for a counterargument to the thesis of Arendt, Castells, and others that the state is retreating from the business of managing and granting refuge and asylum. Whether migrating locally or crossing international boundaries, Kurdish refuge seeking is seemingly obsessed over by states. In Kurdistan's four main states and adjacent states, the state even concerns itself with whole patrilineages of refuge seekers, not just individuals, because it assigns people to categories that are ultimately patrilineal and it offers or denies refuge based on those categories. At the Western end of a migration quest, a looser "family reunification" concept may apply. Refuge-seeking migrants are documented, instructed, employed or referred for employment, housed and fed by "friendly" states or agencies permitted or deputized by the state to work. They are documented, instructed, hunted, arrested, abandoned, and threatened with torture and death by "unfriendly" states, often "their own."

Moreover, patriliny allows the state even greater reach than it might otherwise be able to claim. As I have argued, patriliny is an important "glue" holding Kurdistani society together. It makes for a middle level of social structure and a framework for interrelations that lies somewhere between the overarching umbrella of the large state entity and its various expressions in everyday life. It can be argued that the state keeps track of lineages to an even greater extent than it keeps track of individuals. In many of the state's practices of "making legible" (Scott 1998) the lives and life processes of its citizenry, it interacts with citizens as descendants of successive generations, and of males to a greater extent than other ancestors. Most basically, this is manifested in the law that states that citizenship is acquired only through descent (*jus sanguinis*), and more specifically, that only a man can pass on citizenship. It had appeared that this aspect of Iraqi law was set to change following the overthrow of the Ba'thist government by the United States in 2003, but the issue remained unresolved for several more years (Abdullah 2010). The latest version of the nationality law, passed in 2006, allowed both parents to pass on Iraqi citizenship. In October 2011, the Iraqi parliament voted to lift Iraq's reservation to Article 9 of the Convention on the Elimination of All Forms of Discrimination against Women (CEDAW) (Human Rights Watch 2012:564), thus fully lifting the ban forbidding female Iraqi citizens to pass on citizenship to their children. It remains to be seen whether, by whom, and for whom this change will be implemented within the Iraqi legal system. Over time, however, if the law remains in effect, it will have far-reaching implications regarding who comprises the Iraqi citizenry.

On the Iraqi Personal Identification Card, a green-colored card commonly carried by Iraqis throughout Iraq, including the Kurdistan Region, the names of the individual's father and mother are listed, along with his or her father's father and mother's father. Out of four grandparents, in other words, only the names of the males are disclosed, the most recent nodes in an individual's father's patriline, and mother's patriline. More generally, as I have seen on numerous occasions, individuals are often called upon to disclose at least their most immediate patrilineal details, the names of their father and father's father, in interactions with the state.

The flip side of state interaction with citizens on a patrilineal basis is that the state may interact with a patriline (or branch of one) and not the individuals within it. This is often seen in property ownership, for example. Let us say a man owns a plot of land, and he has a wife and several children. When he dies, the ownership automatically passes to his children.[1] His sons have the responsibility of making sure their mother's needs are met for the rest of her life. If the family is poor, even if they are very young, they may be forced into being breadwinners while children. Because the process of inheritance from the deceased man to his children is automatic, many families do not take any legal action when a landowner dies, but simply continue to hold the land in common. Only if they were to decide to divide it between the multiple individual owners would they need to initiate a legal process. Over time, the individual nature of that ownership can become quite complex as the spouse(es) and descendants of the original owner are born and die. By default, it is the group that owns the land to a greater extent than the individuals.

When people seek refuge within the Kurdistan Region of the Iraqi state, they do so in a thoroughly patrilineal context in which the reputed bond between place and patriline has been disrupted. Refuge seeking in Iraqi Kurdistan and by people from there is therefore highly gendered. It is gendered not simply because both women and men flee, and their experiences may differ, but because collective identity itself, organized as it is through patrilines, is gendered. More often than not, when people seek refuge with other people, they do so in patrilineally delineated groups. (People do sometimes flee as individuals, and here patriliny is relevant too. For example, sometimes a lone female is in flight from her family because she fears becoming a victim of an honor killing, which I argue in chapter 4 is a patrilineal practice.)

The story of Evin, a young woman I met in 2002, illustrates the role patriliny can play in the way refuge seeking is understood. Born in Iran, she related to me this explanation of her identity and displacement shortly after we met:

> I am from Silemani originally, but I grew up in Iran because that is where my family fled after the Kurdish movement collapsed in the 1970s. We came back from Iran in the early 1990s and I spent two years in Silemani. But because we were aligned with the Kurdistan Democratic Party, we had to flee again after the conflict started between the parties. So we are IDPs [she used the acronym for Internally Displaced Persons] here in Erbil. I completed my university study here, and I don't know how much longer we will have to stay here. Although things are improving between the parties, we still cannot go home to Silemani with the current political situation.

Despite having a university degree and living very near her "home," Evin lives in limbo, refraining from really starting her life. She has spent only two years in her "home." What makes it "home"? Not her birth, which she had clearly stated took place elsewhere. Our conversation took place in English, but when people in Kurdistan use the term "origin" in English, it is usually a translation from the term *'esil*, which is a reference to where their *patriline* originated or is from, not where an *individual* may be from. One's *'esil* encompasses one's ultimate "correct" place of residence. Silemani, like Erbil, is in the part of Kurdistan where the majority of people speak the Sorani dialect. By many standards, the woman was now living "at home" after an extended stay in another country with her family. But Silemani remained Evin's reference point, and her life, except for two years of it, seemed to be on hold.

Refuge and Memory

How did Evin's family come to have 'esil in the place she now calls "home"? Refuge seeking by her original patrilineal forebear may well be part of the story. Nineteenth-century observers of life in Kurdistan recorded many instances of abuse by shaikhs, the leaders of tribes, and the Kurdish princes. When those same leaders are described today, however, there is often no trace in the description of activities that today might be regarded as negative. Instead, one hears accounts by their own patrilineal descendants, as well as descendants of people associated with them, that emphasize heroics and downplay other aspects of their memory. Patrilineal memory becomes myth in de Certeau's sense, "an allusive and fragmentary story whose gaps mesh with the social practices it symbolizes" (de Certeau 1984:102).

For example, "Bedir Khan Beg" is a name that is very well known across all quadrants of Kurdistan. He has many descendants, most of whom now live outside Kurdistan, and some of whom I have met. Active in the early to mid nineteenth century, he was the last prince of the Botan Principality and ruled territory that is today mainly in Turkey, with a small part of it in Iraq. I have heard people speak of Bedir Khan Beg and his sons with great respect, and he is remembered as an important figure in early Kurdish nationalism. Anglican missionary George Percy Badger, writing about the Kurds he encountered between Mosul and Diyarbakir in 1842, describes Bedir Khan as leading a revolt on behalf of peasants who had complaints such as this: "Our inability to satisfy the demands of our rapacious masters is looked upon as a crime, and in revenge our villages are razed, our very beds and implements of husbandry are taken from us, some of our people

are murdered" (Badger 1852:46–47). It is clear that conditions for the peasantry were dire, and they must have welcomed having a leader who would
help them to resist Ottoman oppression.

But Bedir Khan was not only a liberator. Many historical accounts
agree that Bedir Khan perpetrated tremendous violence, massacring thousands of people, violence that today can be classified as "genocide" (Travis
2010). Badger, for example, goes on to describe a series of horrific mas-
sacres of Nestorian Christians by Bedir Khan and his men (1852:370–374),
asserts that Bedir Khan imprisoned, beat, and killed Yezidis in order to
force them to convert to Islam (133), and that he enslaved the Christian
workers who built fortresses for him in the mountains (184).

Bedir Khan Beg's sons went on to provide leadership to the Kurdish
nationalist movement in ways that are laudable, such as by codifying the
Kurdish language and promoting an awareness of Kurdish nationalist
claims in Europe. But today's patrilineal descendants carry the name of the
violent and abusive father, not his sons. I once asked a proud member of
the Bedir Khan lineage, a person well versed in the lineage's history, "What
were Bedir Khan Beg's accomplishments?" I received this reply: "He tried to
modernize the Cizre, and to be a fair ruler, and they had factories for making carpets, guns, and other things. He was for learning, for culture, for
schools. You can see this in his sons, because after the fall of his principality, all his sons were educated. . . . He was not like a feudal ruler, you
know?" In this statement, which is all my respondent had to say in answer
to my question despite my further probes, Bedir Khan comes off as simply
a modernizing figure and not a mass killer.

Bedir Khan must of course be seen in the context of his time, which
was a period of tremendous political upheaval in Kurdistan. I have had
similar conversations with other people who claim descent—and today
garner respect because of that descent—from other men who perpetrated
mass violence in the nineteenth century. The stories they tell are similarly
sanitized. What I find noteworthy about these accounts is not that history
is remembered selectively, for it always is. Rather, memory is sanitized *as it
travels down patrilines*. The teller of such an account is much more likely
to be, say, a son's son's son's son or daughter than, say, a daughter's
son's daughter's son's daughter. Some nonpatrilineal descendants of these
famous figures may not even know that they are descendants, because no

one has kept the memory alive through generations of descendants who are female or are descended through one or more females.

I find another angle of this type of memory keeping, or rather its lack, to be interesting: people whose forebears may well have fled these men's violence are likely to have received no memory whatsoever through the patrilineal links that preceded them. Instead, their own patrilines only go back a few generations, until memory stops. Their apical ancestor may not have a very long list of remembered accomplishments. On the whole, more prestigious lineages are traced back further in time, and less prestigious ones only a few generations. People who belong to less prestigious lineages' claim of 'esil is based on a man commencing to make memory in a certain place, but in many cases no one knows how he came to live in that place. To read some of the accounts of nineteenth-century Kurdistan, and listen to people talk about lineage originators who lived during the same period, is to do a study in contrasts. Kurdistan was a violent, desperate place from the 1830s on, but for the most part this does not come through in the patrilineal narratives I hear from Kurdish interlocutors.

Contextualizing Refuge Seeking from Kurdistan

A chronicle of modern out-migration from Iraqi Kurdistan would not rightly begin with Muslim Kurds. Members of the Christian population of Kurdistan have been going to the West at a greater rate than the Kurds, and for a longer period. The Chaldean patriarch of Mosul, Mar Shimun XXI, was educated in England in the 1920s (Luke 2004 [1925]:103). People in the area told me that they refer to the city of Detroit in the United States as "New Tel Kayf" after the majority-Christian town of that name because Detroit is now home to thousands of Christians from Tel Kayf and the surrounding area.

The Kurdish diaspora began with a trickle toward the West in the early part of the twentieth century, but the beginnings of large-scale Kurdish out-migration can largely be traced to the collapse in 1975 of the Kurdish rebellion in Iraq led by Mulla Mustafa Barzani. Although Barzani had led his followers to Iran to found the short-lived Mahabad Republic in 1946, many of whom went on to refuge in the Soviet Union, those migrations were ultimately temporary. The mid-1970s rebels, on the other hand, fled to Turkey and Iran, and many were accepted as refugees in the West after a time in refugee camps. The vast majority remain in the West today. The largest Kurdish community in the United States, in Nashville, started with a small group of these refugees. Due to political oppression and fear of oppression in Iraqi Kurdistan, many of the resettled refugees lacked communication with home. They were afraid to write letters, and what telephone service there was to the outside world was expensive, and one would wonder if agents of the Iraqi government were listening. Consequently, many of the exiles chose to remain out of touch, and families back in Iraqi Kurdistan did not know if their sons (refugees were mostly young males) were alive or dead until after 1991, when communication became widely possible for the first time.

Of the approximately one million people who identify themselves as "Kurdish" living in Europe, most are from, or were born to, people who migrated from Iraq and Turkey. Of the estimated 40,000 in the United States, the vast majority are from Iraq. Many, perhaps most, Kurdish migrants arrived in a new location, whether near or far, through a process of "chain migration," in which migrants choose their destination based on the presence there of people already in their social networks. In Dohuk, I learned that Walid, one of the original members of the Nashville community and now a highly successful professional in his field, was in town on a several-week visit, and he agreed to be interviewed. He told of being a teenager fighting with the Kurdish resistance in the 1970s when the revolt collapsed and the fighters fled to Iran. Waiting in an official refugee camp, he and several friends applied and were accepted for resettlement in the United States. "My departure date was the 24th of April, 1976," he told me nostalgically. "I had no concept of the United States, except that it was a place of opportunity. The officials asked me and my friends which city we wanted to go to. None of us could name a single American city! So, they put us where they wanted to, and this was Nashville. We were the very first Kurdish people to arrive. After us, when more people were asked where they wanted to go, they named Nashville because we were there. Now thousands have followed us."

In the 1990s, out-migration to the West from the Kurdistan Region of Iraq resulted in thousands of asylum seekers entering Europe with traffickers, where they applied for and usually received political asylum. In that decade, more Kurdish people left Kurdistan as a whole than during any other decade in recorded history, with the largest numbers leaving Turkish and Iraqi Kurdistan for Western Europe. The flow from Turkey, primarily to Germany, began in the 1960s. The first emigrants were drawn to employment opportunities that promised a better life than the difficult one experienced by some in Turkish Kurdistan (Rajagopalan 2008). Flows of refuge seekers followed, beginning from both Turkey and Iraq in the 1970s. A "Kurdish refugee" imaginary is now found in discourses of nationalism, states and statelessness, and migration produced by scholars, governments, and NGOs. When I entered the phrase "Kurdish refugees" into the Google search engine in October 2011, it returned 174,000 results on the main Google page, and 2,040 results in Google Scholar. At the height of the imaginary in the late 1990s, the Kurds represented the quintessential asylum seeker in Western Europe. Rickety boats of huddled Kurdish asylum seekers were intercepted by marine authorities off Italy. Kurds paid smugglers to ferry them across Turkey and into Europe through the forests of Bulgaria, by wading across the Maritsa River into Greece, and by other illegal means. The flow of Kurdish migrants to Europe has been analyzed, studied, and fretted over by policy makers and commentators from across the political spectrum. For many scholars, migrants such as Kurdish refuge seekers incur "losses" that mark an age of "forced or voluntary migrations, massive transfers of population, and traveling and transplanted cultures . . . born of crisis and change"; they "suffer" and are "precariously positioned at the interstices of different spaces, histories, and languages" (Seyhan 2001:4). Imposing the frames of this imaginary on Kurdish migrants even though they represent a famous problematic of statelessness, however, obscures a more holistic view of migration and movement by people in and from the Kurdish homeland.

Jørgen Carling (2002) contends that aspirations to migrate "are formed by the interplay between individual characteristics and the specific historical and cultural environment" (23). The social environment of Kurdistan, specifically a patrilineal way of understanding the kin group and by extension the specific historical and cultural environment, powerfully shapes the way refuge seeking is practiced and understood. As people in Iraqi Kurdistan have recounted their memories of flight and refuge seeking to me since the mid-1990s, some patterns have emerged. A typical recounting often starts with ancestral forebears, who came to produce a homeplace by their sustained presence in a specific place, usually a village. The person then goes on to describe episodes of flight and refuge seeking. They narrate the events leading to each episode, state reasons for it, and describe their feelings and reminiscences. They describe identity categories such as tribe, and talk about the relationships of these categories to place. Their stories reflect the kinds of tragedy that are to be expected in narratives about fleeing for one's life, including the full range of human experiences, motives, and emotions. Their accounts bespeak tremendous resilience and are often offered with humor and creativity, marking them as agents who refuse to be cast as mere victims.

In recent decades, as the world has globalized, migration flows have not only not abated, but by many measures they have grown. Even "internal" migration patterns, in which migrants do not cross from one state to another, often prompt and draw on global processes and institutions. Consequently, theorists of migration and identity have appealed for an "unbinding" of migration categorizations. The old "push-pull" models of international migration theories starting in the 1960s gave way to more fluid ideas encompassing complex motivations and identity construction. Foci in migration anthropology began to include "flows, boundaries, and hybrids" (Hannerz 2002), as well as diaspora, internationalism, and public culture (O'Neal 1999). Each of these concepts in some way addressed a lessening of the rupture between migrants' point of origin and their destination.

Linda Basch, and her colleagues (1994) argue that many migrants remain deeply invested in nations on whose putative territory they are no longer living and propose that such people be regarded as "transnationals" rather than as deserving of more fixed categorizations such as "immigrants." Liisa Malkki (1995) engages in a "critical mapping of the construction-in-progress of refugees and displacement" (495) in which she calls for a "denaturalizing, questioning stance toward the national order of things" (517). By taking into account contextual factors such as patriliny and refraining from privileging certain kinds of borders, such as those demarcating states, over others such as those demarcating tribes, I hope to reveal, as Pamela Ballinger does for another violence-saturated place (the Balkans), "the (always unstable) constitution of locality and peripherality in a region profoundly shaped by displacement" (Ballinger 2002, following Stewart 1996).

By now, many Kurds are citizens of the Western countries to which they migrated. In the 1990s and around the turn of the present century, Kurdish migrants constituted a flow of such significance that the Kurds' role as asylum seekers was a frequent topic of conversation by UN and NGO staff, up to the highest levels of government, especially in Western Europe. This encompassed often-shrill arguments as to the "reasons" for Kurdish out-migration: was it "merely economic," or was the Kurds' claim that their homeland was too dangerous a place to live credible, and therefore "legitimate"? Judith Kumin summarized the debate in UNHCR's *Refugees* magazine (1999), decrying recent reductions in European governments' acceptance of asylum claims, while many participants in European political debates called for tighter immigration controls.

Migrants and would-be migrants from Iraqi Kurdistan were resolute. A survey demonstrated that "26,873 out of 27,028 interviewed Iraqi Kurds living in the shelters [in Turkey] had the intention of resettling in the West" (Kirişçi 1995, cited in Içduygu 2003:71). They went despite the significant expense and many dangers along the way. In a 2002 article, migration analyst Nicholas Busch accused Turkish government authorities of "dirty jobs" such as assassinating Kurdish businesspeople and complying in human trafficking, and concluded that Iraqi Kurdish asylum seekers in Europe were in "genuine need of protection" and were not merely "economic migrants" as some asserted (Busch 2002).

Answers to the question as to whether the migrants' claims are "economic" or "legitimate" are elusive, even for those governments that try doggedly to obtain an answer. Many Kurdish people contemplating migration to the West have told me that they feel pushed by memories of dictatorship and attempted genocide as well as shifting tiers of local political power (King 2005). Some seem to feel pulled by a powerful fetishization of "America" and the West, among many other motives. Sheer economics certainly have been a factor. A man who worked as a schoolteacher told me that before 1991, he was paid what amounted to $270 per month, which was plenty to live on. After the Gulf War, however, teaching was essentially reduced to volunteer work, and his salary dropped to $21 per month. In recent years the salary for teachers has improved tremendously. It is again possible to support a household on a teacher's salary, albeit not at all lavishly, since the cost of living has also climbed.

Moreover, migration events in individual lives take place within the context of the life course. A person may be a refuge seeker at one point in life, an economic migrant at a later point, and a returnee late in life. Despite this diversity, in personal histories narrated by Kurdish interviewees who have migrated multiple times over the course of their lifetimes, I have heard countless stories of migration impelled by fear of violence. Violence seems to be a consistent feature of life in Iraqi Kurdistan, even though rates of it have dropped precipitously in recent years.

Elusive Refuge

Refuge can be elusive, however. I present here the story of one migrant who had returned from years in Iran as a prisoner of war, only to find his "home" unsatisfactory and depart again, this time for Europe. I found a small incident that took place during my interview with him to be more indicative of the trauma he had experienced than even some of the horror he was recounting.

The war between Iraq and Iran, which lasted from 1980 to 1988, was a source of terrible suffering for Iraqis. Many Kurdish men served in the Iraqi military and suffered and died fighting Iran, a fact that is perhaps counterintuitive because the government's genocidal attacks against the Kurds were in part a product of the war. During the late 1990s, Iran and Iraq agreed to exchange prisoners of war who had been in their custody since the war ended. Some of the released men were Kurdish and from the area where I was carrying out research.

One day in the weeks following one of the prisoner releases, my friend Amina came to see me with a request. Her relative, a middle-aged man named Mustafa, had just arrived home from prison in Iran, where he had been held since the war. He was thrilled to have found refuge in his own home. He had over ten years' worth of events to catch up on, and his family members had been sitting with him for hours, telling stories. My friend told him about my research, and soon he told her that he wanted to be interviewed himself. Would I come to his house with her to interview him? she asked.

I was reluctant for two reasons. First, I feared that he had high hopes for the interview that I could not fulfill. Perhaps he thought I was a journalist who would help him immediately get the word out to the world about the injustice he had experienced, or he wanted me to help him in some way that was not possible. I feared I would let him down. Second, with the Iraqi Ba'thist government still in power and Iran rumored to have secret agents in Iraqi Kurdistan, I feared that as an American my citizenship in a country that was the enemy of both regimes might mean that meeting, much less sitting and taking notes in his home with several of his relatives present, would put both of us in danger once word got out. I had told people I was primarily studying culture, not politics. Would this interview put my research in a different light for local people, one that could endanger us both?

Amina listened to these concerns, but was undeterred. "Mustafa is not afraid. He begged me to bring you to him. He understands. Do not worry!" So, I went, agreeing to do the interview only as long as no one would know about it apart from my friend and the members of Mustafa's household.

The interview lasted three hours. I barely got a word in edgewise as Mustafa told his story in a rapid-fire chronological narrative. He had been tortured, moved from place to place, and, perhaps most painfully, twice falsely told that his release was scheduled but it was then retracted, his hopes dashed. As the interview began, he seemed lucid, but his state as a traumatized person struggling to adjust to his new circumstances became more apparent as the interview went on.

During the interview one of Mustafa's relatives brought each of us a can of Coke and a straw. While he had been in prison, a new form of aluminum pop-top had been invented, the kind that stays with the can instead of coming completely off. Accessing the beverage requires a back and forth leveraging motion rather than a simple motion of pulling up the tab as with the previous design. Moments after I had opened my own can of Coke, put the straw in it and taken a sip, I noticed that Mustafa was still struggling to open his. He was pulling up, as one would have done before he entered prison. It appeared that this was the first time he had tried to open a beverage can since entering captivity in the 1980s. I tried to tell him how I had opened my can, but he interrupted me, rejecting my help. He kept trying by pulling and twisting, but with muted movements, as though he did not want me and his niece to notice his struggle. Finally the lever came off, rendering the can unopenable. At that, he slowly took it and put it on the table next to him, but toward the back, placing it nearly outside the area of his peripheral vision. It was as if he were trying, however unconvincingly after such a dogged struggle to open it, to indicate that he did not want to drink any Coke after all. Or perhaps he did not want to be able to see the offending can. As he reached to abandon it, I again started to reach for it to help him, but sensing his desire to deflect attention from the whole incident, I pulled back. Looking up, I saw a deeply humiliated look on his face.

There are several ways to read Mustafa's struggle with and ultimate banishment of the Coke can. One is with globalization in mind; who in the world but very isolated people such as prisoners of war had not made the transition from the old type of Coke can to the new? In another reading, the can represents years lost to Kurdistan and Iraq's violence. Thousands of men, women, and children had disappeared in and from Iraqi Kurdistan in the preceding decades. Most never returned home. The years in which a new kind of Coke can was invented were also the years during which Mustafa's children had been growing up without him, and his wife had waited for him, wondering about his fate. These were years of local and far-reaching news.

Mustafa continued telling the story of his captivity with purpose and passion. I listened intently, never taking another sip from the straw of my own can of Coke. I do not remember Amina taking a sip of hers, either.

In the months following the interview, I occasionally saw Amina, and she continued to report that Mustafa was well. One day several months later, however, she told me that he had gone to Europe to seek asylum. I was astonished because I had failed to see this coming. To me, he was a homecomer. When I had interviewed him, my impression had been that he saw himself this way as well. He had spoken as one who had arrived, not as a person who was giving thought to departing! But as Amina reported, he began to grow increasingly unhappy at home, to see it as an insecure place where he could not build a future. When he learned that many other people were leaving for Europe, he decided to join them. He had become a person for whom the possibilities for refuge and a better life had expanded to a far place, a place elsewhere on the globe.

Patrilineal Ethnicity

In Iraq and the broader Middle East, ethnic identity is emphasized to a great degree by many individuals and in a variety of ways by modern states. Especially since the pan-Arabist movement of the twentieth century, ethnicity seems to have an enduring, potent role in everyday relations between people and in the way states relate to, manipulate, and categorize their citizens. The potency and meaning of ethnic emphasis varies from place to place and time to time, and has long been influenced by external forces such as colonialism, occupation, and war. Whatever its causes and context, the record is clear: the playing up of ethnic identity has led to tremendous bloodshed in Iraq, and, as of this writing, threatens to do so still further. Iraq has not been a place where alterity was celebrated, but rather where it has sometimes led to zero-sum contests. Bloodshed based on ethnicity or ethnoreligious identity by no means began with the invasion by the United States and Britain in 2003, even though their presence certainly unleashed, and for a time did little to quash, widespread ethnosectarian conflict. Rather, it has a long history. What gives ethnicity its power in Iraq, and for that matter across the Middle East region? I believe that one important factor is the way in which identity is passed from parents to children, and then ratified and manipulated by the modern state. Despite the diversity found in Iraq, the members of every kin, tribal, religious, and ethnic group in Iraq of which I am aware agree on patrilineal identity construction: fathers pass on identity categories. With only one parent, not two, passing on identity, identity can be made, and remains, potent from generation to generation. When patrilineal logic is allowed to trump other logics that would encourage fluidity in identity claims, identity is never halved. It is never made complex and hybrid through *two*. This is patriliny, a concept that gives rise to a diverse and complex set of practices and logics, at its simplest. Patriliny begets ethnic difference, and ethnic difference is a convenient way of organizing people for contests over resources such as oil or state power. Refuge seekers flee contests that have become, or threaten to become, violent. A patrilineal framework can therefore be useful in an analysis of refuge seeking in, to, and from Iraqi Kurdistan.

One important traditional method of storing wealth in Kurdistan is on a woman. At marriage, a Kurdish bride, like brides of other ethnic identities in Kurdistan's part of the world, receives a marriage payment of gold jewelry from her husband and his family. (Marriage payments typically consist of more than gold, and may include cash, fabric, clothing, and other household items.) Kurdish friends have emphasized to me multiple times that the gold belongs to her personally and not to the family, although I have also heard stories of coercive husbands who later force their wives to sell their gold. For the most part, however, I have observed that gold is indeed an enduring form of wealth storage. Many women wear at least some of the gold components of the marriage payment regularly, sometimes displaying on their bodies a collection of jewelry worth many thousands of dollars. Where she goes, her gold goes. Upon first seeing this, I asked if anyone knew of a woman losing her gold to a thief who had removed it from her body. "Never!" I was told by more than one person, who conveyed that such an act was unthinkable.

Like her wealth, a woman herself is, in one way at least, more portable than a man. The postmarital residence conventions that fit neatly with patriliny throughout the Middle East dictate that brides move at marriage. Grooms stay either in their natal household or set up a new household nearby, most often in the same neighborhood. In a village setting, a couple that sets up a new household usually builds a house right next door to the groom's parents' home. A genetic study found evidence of these postmarital settlement patterns in gene distributions in Turkey, indicating that much of the genetic diversity of the area could be accounted for by women's movement as opposed to men's (Gokcumen et al. 2011). A man's wealth is, or at least has been traditionally, in land, the least portable commodity there is. He stays on the land of his father, and his father, and his father—an ideal that flight and refuge seeking disrupts. A married man in flight does well to flee with his wife who is wearing all of her gold. If it is already on her and the situation prompting flight is acute, she is more likely to escape with it than if she has to retrieve it from somewhere in the house. Many women wear at least their gold bangles on their wrists on a daily basis. (If they own larger pieces, they may store them because of their bulkiness.) In a conflict situation, a woman is not seen as a combatant, so she can often slip through to a greater degree than a man can, and, with the household's wealth on her body, her passage is vital to the family's economic future. Such a couple is better prepared for a new life away from

PHOTO 6.3 Shush, a village near Hewler, in 2005. (Photo by the author.)

"his" land. In Kurdish communities in the United States, many couples who arrived with the wife's gold were able to sell some of it to ease the economic pain of starting a new life. I heard people gossip about who had brought her gold and who had not, how much each person had, who had decided to sell and who had not, and so on.

Although some forms of Judaism place more emphasis on identity succession through the mother than the father, there is no evidence that Kurdistani Jews did this. Rather, they were patrilineal like all of the other groups around them. For example, Zaken (2007) lists several patrilineal forebears of Kurdistani Jewish leader Hacham Mordechai, presumably in order to clarify his full identity. Mordechai was head of the Jewish town of Sandur, which expanded its population in the early twentieth century by receiving Jewish refuge seekers from the surrounding area. He himself was descended from refuge seekers who fled there after killing a Gentile (131). This account shows how patrilineal identity and refuge seeking can converge and shape each other, as a refuge seeker later becomes a refuge-granter. Kurdistan's Jews are now entirely gone. Most left for Israel in the 1950s along with the vast majority of the Iraqi Jewish population. The Jewish departure from Iraqi Kurdistan is a story in itself, one that radically reshaped Kurdistani towns like Zakho and Amadiya, where the Jews had outnumbered all other groups combined.[2]

The "Diaspora" with a capital "D" has a homeland that is defined by a particular interpretation of a sacred text, the Jewish scriptures. A "diaspora," with a small "d," is also textually defined, but its text is the modern state and all of the ways in which modern stateness is inscribed in late modernity—on globes and maps, and on billions of pages of documents that are legal, political, and historical. A constitution may be revered just as a sacred text is, or it may even make a claim to sacredness, as in Iran. The constitutions of most Middle Eastern states ratify patriliny as it is expressed in everyday practice, and migrants take patriliny's cultural logic to different settings. In one of the Kurdish households that I regularly visit on the West Coast of the United States, a little girl is growing up. By American reasoning, she is "half Kurdish," her father's category, and "half Hispanic," her mother's category. Her parents were very young, and unmarried, when they conceived her in 2005, and soon a question of custody came before the court system. My friend Asiya, the girl's Kurdish grandmother and father's mother, stepped in. The girl was already living in Asiya and her husband's household, and she succeeded in making the custody official. During my several visits in the few years after she was born, her grandmother Asiya emphasized to me repeatedly that she is Kurdish. The little girl speaks Kurdish well, better than English or Spanish. I know from my conversations with Asiya that she is well aware of the way Americans talk about identity as bequeathable both by mothers and fathers, but, she tells me, she refuses to think this way. Instead, Asiya seems determined to inculcate in the girl a strong sense of Kurdish identity as a bulwark against such logic.

Patriliny is upheld at an even higher level of policy and law than the state. The United Nations still follows many states in tracing refugeeness, the recognized state of being a refugee, patrilineally, through fathers alone. Joseph Massad writes of the Palestinian case, in which refugee status (and thus a claim of membership in the Palestinian nation) is determined by the United Nations: "It is being born to a Palestinian father that now functions as the prerequisite for Palestinianness ... this definition carries itself to future generations, whereby it is the sons of these fathers who will continue the reproduction of the Palestinian people" (Massad

1995:472). Writing of a similarly protracted displacement situation, Tasoulla Hadjiyanni (2000:30) notes that the Greek Cypriots displaced in the 1974 invasion but who remain on the island have a special legal status as *displaced persons*, and that this status was extended by the government of Cyprus in 1975 to include children whose father was a displaced person. Hadjiyanni notes that this policy is "the result of gender bias in the transfer of the displaced title. By recognizing only the descendants of refugee fathers as displaced, children whose mother is a displaced person but whose father is not cannot officially use the *displaced* title" (31). The United Nations' ratification of patriliny lends it special power not only in states, but over those people caught in the interstices of the modern state system.

Out-Migration in the 1990s–2000s

One family in the Haweri patrilineage is typical of Kurdish households with adults who were of age by the early 1990s. Their household in the border town of Zakho consists of a man, Umar, his wife, Halima, and their four children, as well as Umar's sister Nahela. Previously another sister, Sabeha, lived with them. (I introduce Sabeha and Nahela in chapter 3.) Umar, Nahela and Sabeha's mother Khanum, who was widowed in the 1960s, lived in the house before she died around the turn of the millennium, and a brother and his wife and their children did for a brief period as well. The family now lives in a house owned by Umar, Sabeha and Nahela's close lineagemates, their father's brother's children. In 1996, Khanum, Umar and Halima and their children, and Sabeha were living in Mosul, which is about an hour's drive from Zakho. (Nahela had grown up there but by 1996 had begun to split her time between Mosul and Zakho because she had recently graduated from Mosul University and started working as a teacher in Zakho.) At the time, Mosul was under the control of the Baghdad government of Saddam Hussein. Although life could be difficult for Kurds living on the government-controlled side, the family had been living there for several decades and had chosen to remain there with their businesses and schools, and for the better opportunities the city offered over the Kurdish-controlled area. But then one night in 1996 they got a call from a family member on the Kurdistan side, letting them know that their lives might be in danger because of the newly exposed clandestine activities of one of their relatives. The Government of Iraq was known to hold whole kin groups responsible for the actions of one member, and sometimes this meant being arrested, tortured, imprisoned, killed, and/or disappeared. In the 1990s, it had held Khanum in jail for several weeks because one of her sons was fighting with the peshmerga. This time, they knew the government meant business. The caller told them that if they hurried, they could participate in an evacuation to the United States. The U.S. military had arranged for buses to leave the main Kurdish cities and take evacuees to Turkey, from where they would be flown to the United States.

The night was a long one. The phone call itself had put them in danger, since the government was well known to listen in on some calls. They made a plan to flee to the Kurdistan side. They could not flee that night, however, because the roads between the Kurdish and government-controlled areas were closed during the night. Finally, they left hurriedly in the morning, taking only what they could bring in the car. As I recounted in chapter 2, the Clinton administration had agreed to evacuate 6,500 people when its effort to unseat the Saddam Hussein regime collapsed and the Iraqi military had entered the Kurdish-controlled area and carried out targeted assassinations. Afterward, Saddam Hussein had appeared on television and threatened to kill any American or any Iraqi who had associated with Americans. The 6,500 people were employees and their families of American NGOs as well as USAID and the military, which had kept a very small ground force in Zakho following the 1991 Gulf War. As close family members of an employee of an American organization, they qualified for the evacuation.

By the dim light of the early morning, the family successfully made its way along the road from Mosul to Zakho, passing out of the last Iraqi checkpoint, into the first Kurdish one, and into the border area where they hoped to participate in the evacuation. But they had arrived too late. The last bus had left for Turkey. Dejected, they went to the empty home of their father's brother's children, who had also been on the list but had reached the bus in time. There they remained, and now, over a decade and a half later, they are still living in their cousins' house. Their cousins have built new lives in the United States. I am happy to report that this arrangement will soon come to an end, since they are currently building their own new house across town. Soon, their cousins in America will have a vacant house back home and will need to decide what to do with it. Some of them visited recently to help plan their future.

After some time had passed, the family expected to be able to return to Mosul to retrieve their belongings, but as it turned out they were victims of treachery. When they left in 1996 they had hastily entrusted their things to a neighbor but learned later that the neighbor had absconded with everything. Sabeha told me over and over, "My gold jewelry! I left my gold there. What was I thinking? I left it locked up. But they took it. They took all of it! It had taken me years to assemble that collection. It represented most of what I owned in this world! All of it is gone, all of it!" She told me that the total weight of the gold was an impressive three kilograms. The family's cash reserve, hidden in the house, was gone as well. On one occasion, during a conversation while she was working busily at her sewing machine making a dress, Sabeha illustrated the wealth she had left behind. "I had one hundred pairs of underwear and sixty bras. I had too many shoes to count, and many, many dresses!" as though the act of sewing had prompted her to measure the loss in clothing. The house, too, was gone. When attempting to buy a house in Mosul decades earlier, they had been told that as Kurds, and especially as Kurds with a close family member fighting in the resistance movement, house ownership would not be allowed. So they had made an arrangement with an Arab friend to put the house in his name, but they would pay for it and it would be understood that they were the rightful owners. But it was theirs no longer. The man had not only not saved it for them, he had drastically remodeled it to the point that it was almost unrecognizable. In 2004, Nahela and I went to Mosul and saw the house, she for the first time in eight years and I for the first time. We could only see it while riding by, but the sight of the altered structure made her gasp, and she expressed her deep sense of anger at the betrayal.

The Haweri lineage to which this set of adult siblings belongs has a long history in Zakho and the surrounding area. The area is considered, both by them and by people in the community, to be their "home," even though they had actually been living in Mosul for several decades. As they settled into their departed cousins' house and reluctantly began a new life in Zakho after missing the evacuation bus in 1996, it did not occur to them—which became clear as the story was recounted to me later—to approach the local government or the United Nations for classification as Internally Displaced Persons. The Kurdistan Regional Government now has a long history of working with UN agencies and NGOs to provide land and other benefits for IDPs, so such classification could have been of great benefit. It did not occur to anyone in the local government to classify them that way. I am very familiar with this problem because, especially during the early years, I sat in on many discussions about their "situation" as residents in their cousins' house, not their own.

Why did it not occur to anyone to classify this sibling unit and the rest of their family as IDPs when their story, as people who fled government thugs in fear for their lives, rings similar to those of IDPs all over the world? My interpretation is patrilineal. Because their lineage's origin, its 'esil (as described in chapter 3) is in Zakho, they are considered to belong to Zakho even though they no longer kept a residence there or had lived there for several decades. In Iraq, people become IDPs when they are away from "their own" area, which is defined as the area where their patriline has history and is acknowledged to "belong." Patrilineal categories include not only lineages, but religions and ethnic categories and tribes. All of the patrilineal descendants of a man who was a Sunni Muslim, spoke Kurdish as his first language, and lived in the Doski tribal territory are by definition Sunni Muslim Kurdish members of the Doski tribe. Of course, this rigidity can be manipulated. What about religious conversion? What about locational change? These are questions I address in chapter 2. But the patrilineal ideal, of the fixity of patrilineal identity as it is passed down male generations through time, is alive and operative in everyday life as people live, migrate, and define themselves and others. As I show in chapter 7, at the other end of the spectrum—the global—the Kurdish diaspora that has resulted from the large rate of out-migration, is now an important connector of Kurds in the homeland to life in the outside world. Many people and members of their patrilineages are abroad now, living in the global village.

7

Kurdistan in the World

Şam şekir e bes welat şîrintir e. (Damascus is sweet but the homeland is sweeter.)

-Common Kurdish proverb

The Kurdistan Region of Iraq is now a participant in the world's system of states, even though it is, technically, only a "region" within a federated state. It conducts its own foreign policy business without going through Baghdad. Iraqi Kurdistan has long been called "autonomous" within Iraq, but it in many ways now exercises autonomy in the world, too.

Isolated, desperate, and fighting a decades-old insurgency prior to 1991, the population of Iraq's Kurdistan Region lived with very little awareness of what people there call "the outside"—the area beyond Iraq. They endured attacks by the Iraqi government that some, such as David McDowall (1997), have labeled "genocide" and attempted to break away from Iraq in 1991 in the wake of the Gulf War. Kurdistan's inhabitants had been busy for decades fighting an insurgency against a(n) (Sunni) Arab other. They were walled off by forbidding mountains and official borders outside their control, hemmed in by media that was only local as well as totalitarian, and denied regular travel abroad. Despite their status as belonging to a significantly large ethnic group of twenty million or more, no elites represented them in the world's power circles. No academic departments or chairs in Western universities took "Kurdish" as their defining category. No airport runways in their region received planes from abroad. Little global literature made its way to their location or was translated into their languages.

When the Kurds assumed control over Iraqi Kurdistan in 1991, the authoritarian and abusive government of Iraq suddenly had much less influence over them. Only then were the people of Iraqi Kurdistan able to connect with the rest of the world and to participate vigorously in global-ization. Seemingly overnight, after they succeeded setting up their own administrative zone following the Iraqi government's withdrawal from the area, Kurdistanis started connecting with the outside world. They started to become a part of what Hannerz (1989) calls "the global ecumene." Their emergent state became a "connected" place, a zone with a significant international presence in which a populace was increasingly aware of, and influenced by, knowledge, trends, and possibilities from the world beyond its borders. As I have recounted in this book, starting in the 1990s Iraqi Kurdistan became an outpost for many of the world's major international relief and development agencies while a significant diaspora took shape simultaneously. Following the overthrow of the Ba'thist Iraqi government by the United States and its allies in 2003, it became a recognized region in a federal Iraqi system, connecting still further with the world. It now has many of the features of a place that is globally plugged in, and Kurdish nationalism is coming into its own in a highly globalized context. Lord Acton wrote in the mid-nineteenth century, "Exile is the nursery of nation-ality, as oppression is the school of liberalism" (Dalberg-Acton 1907:286). A nationality born of exile is strongly evident. Liberal politics are in formation as well, even though, as I emphasized in chapter 5, they take their place alongside other forms of politicking.

While much of the rest of Iraq remains dangerous and relatively cut off from the world, the Kurdistan region is becoming a kind of Kurdish hub. "Kurdistan," the imagined, longed-for state that is home to the Kurdish nation, the *whole* Kurdish nation, has at least partially arrived in the form of the Kurdistan Region of Iraq. It now has a significant number of Kurdish residents who have relocated there from Iran, Syria, and Turkey in addition to returnees from the Western diaspora communities. Diasporic Kurdish nationalism now blends with homeland nationalism (Houston 2008; Wahlbeck 1999). Satellite television, significant flows of people and goods, mobile phones and the Internet are all features of daily life. New options for gender and kin relations, new institutional forms, and new citizenship possibilities present themselves. Significant wealth from oil revenues is having an impact on the overall economy, and much more significant economic growth is ahead if conflict can continue to be averted.

Iraqi Kurdistan displays a kind of globalized modern, a modern that is fashioned locally, like all moderns, and encompasses its own vernacular particulars (e.g., Deeb 2006; Hirschkind 2006; Özyürek 2006), but that takes place in a zone of high global attention paid by the United Nations, NGOs, nonlocal media, world powers such as the United States and Europe, major industry (mainly in the form of hydrocarbon extraction), and rights groups such as Amnesty International. The global finance industry may be the newest arrival; for example, in July 2009, the Kurdistan Regional Government hired the global finance firm PricewaterhouseCoopers to carry out an audit and advise it on government finance.

Field Note, 7 December 2010, Frankfurt airport, boarding a direct flight for the Kurdistan Region:

There was a shuttle bus from the terminal to the plane, on which we passengers had to wait for about fifteen minutes before it started to move. During that time I noticed a number of people who were not traveling together recognize and greet each other in Kurdish. It was as though we had all just emerged from the crowded airport through a funnel, and what was left on the shuttle bus was a Kurdish community. There had been a short period of silence once we had taken our places on the bus, but soon three or four little reunions were underway. How is the family? How long has it been since your last trip? went the conversations. I noticed people who did not seem to know each other start to speak too. An older Sorani-speaking couple greeted [a] young family, who answered in Kurmanji. "Is that your son?" asked the older woman. "Yes," beamed the young man. She congratulated him. Then the middle-aged man sitting behind the older couple started talking to them. "I haven't been to Kurdistan in ten years," he said. I looked up and noticed his eyes were welling up with tears. In the shuttle was Kurdistan, reconnecting.

Diasporans, like the people in the shuttle at the Frankfurt airport, are a very important part of the Kurdish body politic. They are important when they stay home in their adopted countries, since they create Kurdish social fields there, and they are important when they return and bring new ways and expectations as well as capital back to the homeland. Visiting a

Kurdish family on the West Coast of the United States in July 2012 whom I have known since the mid-1990s, I noted that they were still very "plugged in" to things Kurdish, despite having lived in the United States for nearly a generation. They visit and are visited by other Kurdish families on a regular basis, and keep up with the news from Kurdistan. Their younger generation is in the process of pairing off with life partners who are either Iraqi Kurds or, as the mother of the family told me, "must be." She was referring to her son, who had had several non-Kurdish and non-Muslim girlfriends. "I don't care what he is doing now," she told me. "I only care whom he marries." Later she insinuated that marrying a non-Kurd who was a Muslim would be OK. It was clear, however, that her preference was another Iraqi Kurd.

Movement by diasporans can have its ironies. Those who travel to a country that has a more widely accepted passport than an Iraqi one can exercise high degrees of mobility, as in this field note that I wrote about my friend Zahera, who was nineteen at the time:

Field Note, 14 February 2002:

"I arrived yesterday through Syria. I came by myself!" gushed Zahera. I confirmed that this was completely alone, without any other assistance. "Yes, I really came alone. It was fine. I have the support of my family—my brother doesn't mind because he trusts me. It's not difficult. I have come back three times since I and my mother first went out [to the United States as refugees] in 1999!" Then she added, "Diane, you must write about how there is more freedom here now. When you were here before I would never have dreamed of coming alone."

A few days later, Zahera traveled the several-hour journey from Dohuk to Silemani by herself using public transportation, later telling me that she did so just because she wanted to see the city for the first time. She stayed in a hotel, looked around, and returned home to Dohuk. A mutual friend of ours told me that she saw this as pushing the boundaries of propriety. When I mentioned that Zahera had come by herself through Syria, our friend stuck to her point. "Coming through Syria is a completely different thing. Here she is known and can bring her family shame. In Syria, no one knows her so that is not a big deal." Mobility does not become an option for everyone at the same time, or in an even fashion. My sense is that the majority of nineteen-year-old women, and quite a few men, would not be allowed to make either of the journeys that Zahera made, whether across the ocean or across Iraqi Kurdistan. Within Kurdistan, thousands of women move as individuals every year, but they do so within the context of a particular institution: marriage. Every subculture and tribe local to Kurdistan practices patrilocal residence by default. The patrilineally related patterns of keeping track of male lines of descent, preferred FBD marriage, bridewealth (as opposed to dowry),[1] and patrilocal residence are found across all of Kurdistan, and have long been avenues along which girls and women have traveled. Now, girls and women are starting to consider, and a few are starting to practice, mobility on occasions other than their marriage.

The flying of aircraft is a highly governed activity. Permission for an international flight must be granted by one state to take off, by another if flight occurs over foreign territory, and by another to land. Permission must also be given by the international aviation bodies to which the states are accountable and whose rules they follow. The only aircraft that flew into or out of Kurdistan from 1991 to 2003 were those belonging to the international coalition enforcing the no-fly zones north of the 36th parallel and south of the 33rd parallel in Iraq. When those of us on the ground in Kurdistan saw or heard an aircraft, we knew it belonged to Turkey, France, Britain, or the United States, whose planes were flying over Iraqi airspace against Baghdad's will. Neither the group of "recognized" states that numbers around 200 worldwide, nor the central Iraqi government, acknowledged openly that the Kurdistani administration, rather than an administration representing the Iraqi state, was governing Kurdistan below those planes. The anthropology of globalization is a genre struggling to reconcile anthropology's well-known attention to the everyday with a new world that is now "fragmented" and "decentered" (Lewellen 2002). The anthropology of the state, an area of growing concern (e.g., Sharma and Gupta 2006), builds on a rich anthropology of the nation that is ongoing (Abu-Lughod 2005; Chatterjee 1993). In Kurdistan, global connectedness and state sovereignties are shown to be completely interdependent. Of course they are interdependent everywhere, but Kurdistan's changing fortunes render their interconnectedness more visible than elsewhere. Now Kurdistan has two major international airports, and its government

announced in 2012 that it would build a third outside Dohuk, a city that
has never had even a small airport, much less a major one. According to
the South Korean company contracted to oversee the project, it is expected
to serve half a million passengers per year (Welling 2012). My former
traveling companions in Frankfurt and I may well comprise some of them.

From the start, I found that people in Kurdistan more than lived up to
a long-standing positive stereotype of the Middle East, that it is a place of
rich hospitality. In a word, they connected with me. In Kurdistan, social
connections are the stuff of great energy exertion, within homes, and
within networks of kin and friends. They can be cursory, such as when a
man with a large gun at a checkpoint smiles and asks you how you are
before saying anything required by his role, as I have seen many times. He
may even call me "sister," and I will call him "brother" before our brief
encounter comes to a close. This is not to say that connecting in Kurdistan
is always easy. There is a lot of mistrust in Iraqi Kurdistan, and in my experience a lot of lying. But I have seen people push through the difficulties
that an environment of mistrust can engender to extend a hand and to
trust again and again. I marvel at Kurdistanis' appetite for and ability
to make social connections.

What I see many people as doing, now that Kurdistan is globalizing, is
taking their practiced ability to make social connections to a whole new
level, a level that operates on a global scale. The decidedly noncosmopolitan people I met in the early years of my research knew exactly what to do
when they met me: they received me, a social researcher from the other
side of the world, by offering me tea, then a meal, then accommodations
with their family. Negotiation and exchange drive hospitality. Like others
in Kurdistan, when I am there I am caught up in a rich tapestry of giving,
taking, and remembering each time I carry out fieldwork. The conventions
of this type of interaction foster deep social relationships, relationships
steeped in generous amounts of time spent together. For example, I
learned that if you want something from someone, it is not proper to ask
them for it immediately. Instead, it is appropriate to sit and trade news
and stories first. Sometimes I go to a home or office planning to ask someone there if I can interview him or her, and I end up in an extended visit,
sometimes of several hours, before I sense that it is appropriate to broach
the question of a structured interview in which I have my computer out

and voice recorder running. No matter the fate of the structured interview (if there is still time for one assuming consent has been granted), at minimum, multiple rounds of tea or Turkish coffee will have been served, but very likely a meal and a heaping bowl of fruit as well. In the process my interlocutors and I may have become fast friends if we were not already.

Now, many previously local businessmen use the skills that previous generations used only locally, in negotiations at the lineage or tribal level, to forge deals with representatives of international companies and governments. It is likely that the typical Western man on my flight to Vienna whom I described in chapter 1 had just come from seeking and probably making deals with those local people. If I had been able to take a poll on the plane, I probably would have learned that many passengers were sleep deprived, having stayed up late drinking tea and telling stories with their Kurdish hosts. Deals were inked in the morning. Money would be made by all. There would be future visits, and more meals, and tea, and fruit, and if all was going well, more deals.

Connections between Kurdistan and the outside world used to be mainly to the West. Now, however, they are to anywhere and everywhere. Headlines such as this one regularly appear in the media: "Students Present Kurdish Culture at Indian University" (Niheli 2012). There has been a tremendous increase in low-wage workers coming from countries that previously had no connection to Kurdistan. These workers have few protections, and if they run into problems with their employers, they have little recourse. For example, in 2008 I came to know a woman from Ethiopia, Abeba, who was working as a housemaid in the home of a young family in Hewler that consisted of a wife, husband, and their toddler daughter. Abeba told me that she was in the last year of a three-year contract. My sense was that she was not happy with her job or living situation, although I had no reason to believe she was being mistreated other than receiving very low pay, which she told me was around $150 per month. When I returned to Kurdistan later in the year, I asked about her. A close friend of the family told me that her employment with the family had abruptly ended. My friend told me that Abeba had spread rumors in the community that the parents were mistreating their daughter. Worst of all, their daughter was chronically ill despite having seen several doctors, and they had come to believe that Abeba was practicing witchcraft against her and causing the illness. Abeba had, they said, written curses against their daughter on pieces of paper and hidden them around the house, in mattresses and other tucked-away places. They felt Abeba's actions explained why their daughter was sick. The couple was so angry that the husband paid $2,000 for her to be flown back to Ethiopia, even though her contract was not up. "They were so desperate to get rid of her that they just paid her plane fare, shipped her home, and that was that," I was told.

There are, of course, many ways to analyze this story. An important aspect of its context is that housemaids in the Middle East tend to be paid very little and are often abused (e.g., Varia and Human Rights Watch 2010). In this particular case, Abeba told me that only rarely was she able to see her friends who were also from Ethiopia and worked in other houses. "I stay in all the time, just working," she told me. I wondered whether she had received payment for all of the days she had worked, or whether her employers justified not paying her due to the accusations they made against her. This whole incident, it seemed to me, represented some of the challenges of Kurdistan's new status as a receiver of laborers rather than a sender. A woman who had traveled far from home was paid exploitatively low wages, came to be seen as malign, and was cast out. She represents the tip of the iceberg. As Kurdistan's fortunes increase, so will the exploitation of people from impoverished countries. Hers is just one story among many I have heard so far.

Iraqi Kurdistan at the Center

The Kurdistan Region of Iraq has become a center for Kurdish nationalism in a broad sense. It is a place where dissidents taking refuge from neighboring governments meet, and where linguists are refining the Kurdish language and authors are producing copious amounts of literature in it. Thousands of people fleeing the fighting in Syria have been given refuge there since 2011. Now that it is largely at peace after decades of war and suffering, the Kurdistan Region serves as a kind of "homeland" both for Kurds who are from the rest of Kurdistan, and those who belong to the Kurdish diaspora, the million-strong community of Kurds living outside the Middle East. The Kurdistan Region is a connector of Kurds worldwide and the new geographic heart of what it means to be Kurdish. Without it, Kurdish identity in the world would be going in the direction of extinction, as Michael Chyet (2003) predicted. With it, Kurds connect in Kurdistan, and in turn, to the world. In this sense, its growth is not simply another case of capitalist frenzy drunk on petroleum like Oman, of which Mandana Limbert writes, "Within ten years, Oman went from being one of the most isolated states in the world (in league with Albania, Nepal, or North Korea at various moments in the twentieth century) to being an internationally recognized and economically connected petro-state" (Limbert 2010:6). Kurdistan is experiencing a similar pace of economic development, but with the added fact of being an ethnic center. Arabs do not look to Oman as the center of Arab identity and culture, but Kurds in diverse locations everywhere now look to Iraqi Kurdistan as the place from which Kurdishness emanates in its freest and purest form.

The Kurdistan Region of Iraq is a place where the local and the global converge in a particularly rich fashion, and where some of the world's and Middle East's most vexing and problematic issues are being debated and their consequences played out. Iraqi Kurdistan represents a site for experimentation with the modern in which questions belonging to both classical modernity and globalized late modernity are being posed simultaneously. Issues that give rise to questions include gender and kinship relations, migration (impelled and voluntary, local and transnational), modern institution and state building, global petrodollars and economic forces, outside military intervention and postconflict recovery, citizenship and religio-ethnic identity categories, and the role of global institutions such as the United Nations and nongovernmental relief and development agencies. Many inhabitants of Iraqi Kurdistan are now addressing a number of questions germane to building a postdictatorship civil society. The question "Is an independent state the rightful culmination of a nationalist movement?" was posed a century earlier in many other places, but Iraqi Kurds have only recently been able to act on and answer in the affirmative (Olson 2005). "Does the citizen stand before the state as a member of particular ethnic and religious categories, or as an individual whose rights of affiliation are not the concern of the state?" Currently, Iraq answers in the affirmative to the former. I have met Kurdish activists who told me they were lobbying to change this situation, claiming that religious categories should not be listed on the state identification card that each individual carries.

Old social categories and forces are alive and well. It seems to me that many are not diluted by the new global scale of relating, but are instead shored up. For example, the Kurdistan Region connects to the world, in part, through people with patrilineal pedigrees. It has diplomatic offices in many of the world's capitals that function very similarly to embassies. The two most important and prestigious such offices are in the United States and Britain. In Britain, Bayan Sami Abdul Rahman is the KRG high representative to the UK. She is the daughter of Sami Abdul Rahman, one of the main political architects of the region and the former deputy prime minister who was killed in 2004. In Washington, Qubad Talabani is the KRG representative to the United States. He is the son of Jalal Talabani, founder and leader of the PUK and the current president of Iraq.

Another example comes from an important Kurdistani leader, Ferhad, who was the main force behind an important educational institution. I met him early in my fieldwork and have long observed the workings of his institution. In my observation, it is organized in a very top-down fashion, with layers of patronage and clientage, as institutions in Iraq have long been. It has strong patron-client relationships beyond the local area as well. One day Ferhad told me, "I am constantly looking for assistance from the outside. I do not care where the support comes from. I look to the Islamic fundamentalists in Saudi Arabia, to evangelical Christians in America. . . . It doesn't bother me that these two groups support me for very different reasons! I know that the fundamentalists want us to become more Islamic. So, for them we will bend a little toward Islam. Of course, the Christians want us to become Christians. So, for them we will bend a little in that direction. I don't believe any of it—I just want their support. They want to give it, so we are all happy. As a result there are new facilities being built—a computer lab for Islamic study, books being donated from the West." In this example, modernity's accoutrements are donated by interest groups, but the result is that a local patron is able to build his institution and increase his favor with his clients, which patrons have done throughout the world and in the Middle East since long before the advent of modernity.

And yet, possibilities for change are in the air. Kurdistan is both a place of intense self-reflection and influence. The Erbil International Hotel (EIH) is one of the venues where vigorous conversations about the composition and future of the Kurdistan Region take place. While staying there for several days in October 2008, I came to see the hotel's lobby as perhaps one of the most interesting places in the world in terms of the variety and consequences of the social connections taking place there. The hotel's restaurant is one of the main places where Kurdistani elites gather, and the hotel is a logical place for visitors from outside the region to stay. The hotel is owned by the Middle East Consortium for Reconstruction and Investment (MECRI), Kurdistan's largest company. MECRI has significant KRG ownership, so the KRG puts up many of its own guests there. I myself was a guest of the government on that trip, invited to speak at universities about my research.

What struck me about the people in the hotel lobby was not so much that they were from both local and far-flung places, but that Hewler functioned for them as a kind of hub. Kurdistan, even its largest city Hewler, used to feel entirely peripheral to me. Especially with the tremendous influx of capital that has followed the discovery of oil in Kurdistan, it has now transformed into a "center of things" kind of place. In the EIH lobby I met several prominent Kurdish leaders from Turkey. One had spent time in prison. He became my Facebook friend after we met in the hotel. A few weeks later, he was back in prison and I was swept up in a Facebook campaign to get him released, which he later was. What was he doing in Hewler, and in particular in EIH? He did not say, but it seemed likely to me that he and the others with whom he was traveling were guests of the KRG and were using their time in the region to further Kurdish causes in Turkey.

Another guest I met in the hotel's restaurant was Nayla, a Lebanese woman from Beirut who had recently been hired to manage a new health club for women. She spoke in a highly animated fashion about how excited she was to introduce local women "to the idea of fitness and taking care of their bodies." "I am so excited about the changes this will bring to the society here!" she gushed. I thought of a hypothetical local woman who had spent much of her early life engaged in village labor, who may have spent time on the run during the years prior to 1991, and who had finally and happily settled into a sedentary middle age in the city. Did she need to exercise for her health? Certainly, but did she want to, given all that she had experienced in life, and given that the preferred bodily aesthetic for a woman her age was anything but thin? Kurdistan faces tremendous public health challenges. Among other conditions, diabetes and obesity are rampant, especially among women. Nalya also mentioned her desire to introduce local women to "treatments to make themselves more beautiful." I thought about the many ways I had seen Lebanese women in Beirut altering their appearance. Beirut is a major cosmetic surgery center, and many of its women place a tremendous emphasis on, and devote great resources of time and money, to such treatments. Did Kurdistan need that, I wondered as I listened to Nayla? Evidence from not only Lebanon but other societies in the region suggested that as material prosperity grew, women's style choices changed, and they would place increasing emphasis on their appearance. On the streets of Hewler and other cities in Kurdistan, this trend is already in evidence. Kurdistan's connections to the world are producing new forms of the self and the presentation of the self. I thought that Nayla's zeal must surely be hastening the process. Anthropologist Mark Allen Peterson came to the conclusion that he and his students at the American University in Cairo had a different understanding of the modern. His had to do, among other things, with inequalities and political economies. But for his students, the modern was more about "*style*: how you spoke, what you ate, what movies you'd seen, what you wore, where you bought it, and where you were seen wearing it" (Peterson 2011:5–6). I imagine that Nayla and other style missionaries will be very successful in the Kurdistan Region.

If Lebanese people are influencing life in the Kurdistan Region, as thousands are, conversely, Kurdistan is having a new and possibly highly consequential influence in Syria. As I write this in 2013, the Ba'thist Syrian state led by Bashar al-Assad is losing control of its population, and rebels control much of the country. Several of the dissident groups are comprised mainly of Kurds. The most significant Kurdish groups are the Party of Unity and Democracy (PYD) and the Kurdish National Council of Syria (KNC). The PYD, founded in 2003, has a history of being pro-regime. The KNC, founded in 2011, opposes both the PKK and the regime. In July 2012, representatives of both parties met in Hewler and forged an alliance through the brokerage of Region president Mes'ud Barzani. Their members began to control territory in northern Syria, in areas where the population is majority Kurdish. The Kurdistan Region of Iraq suddenly finds itself in a strong position from which its leaders can offer a hand of patronage to the Syrian Kurdish resistance. The peshmerga of Iraq have been training Syrian Kurdish fighters. I have read shrill accounts in the media, especially from Turkish, Israeli, and Iranian sources in addition to the predictable Ba'thist alarmism, and many commentators wonder what will come of the KRG's assistance to Syrian Kurds. I wonder as well, but I regard the possibility of unity across the Syria-Iraq that results in a unified Kurdish state as unlikely. More likely, the KRG area will continue to serve as a place for Syrian Kurdish fighters to plan and train, even though Hewler will never be the capital of a Kurdistan that stretches to the Mediterranean. Hewler's hotel lobbies and restaurants will continue to be very important venues for planning the future of Syria's northern Kurdish zones and quite possibly the future of Syria itself.

Modern Changes

For the most part, the advent of a more "Western" way of life seems to be welcomed by leaders and average people alike. A high-ranking KDP official told me the following in Hewler in May 2008, adding that he was speaking personally and not for the party:

> In the Middle East, in the Orient, especially the Arabs, they are proud of their past. And their position to globalization, well, America is the symbol of globalization, you know? Economically, culturally—especially culturally. We Kurds, we say, people who do not have a big or dominant culture or a style of life, playing a big role in the region, we don't need to be afraid of globalization or the American way of life. We only will gain from it. We will not lose because we have nothing. . . . Therefore, as a person, I have to be free. I personally joined in that. [While living in Europe] I went with my wife to the swimming pool, we rode bicycles, we wore shorts, and there was nothing bad in that.

For this man, lifestyle changes brought about by globalization are a good thing. A different view, however, came out in an email exchange I had with Lolan Sipan, who founded the Kurdish Textile Museum in Hewler in 2004. These remarks in July 2008 are representative of the strong and detailed sentiments he expressed against influences from the outside that produce change: "[M]ost of the Kurdish people want to be westernized as soon as possible and leave all the cultural heritage and values behind without knowing HOW to develop and to improve the future life of the Kurds." In addition to its traditional Kurdish textile collection, Sipan's museum has a tent made of black goat hair into which visitors are invited. This style of tent is thousands of years old, and was once seen dotted across the landscape of Kurdistan and neighboring areas of the Middle East. I have visited the museum several times and have marveled as local people, many wearing Western-style dress, approach the tent with an air of novelty. Many sit in it and have their photograph taken. As an anthropologist traveling in the widest possible social circles in the region, I have been in such tents in nomadic settings on numerous occasions, but it is usually clear that the visitors have not. A familiar object that is thousands of years old has become a museum piece in a very short period.

Arjun Appadurai and Carol Breckenridge argue that "the politics of desire and imagination are always in contest with the politics of heritage and nostalgia. While the engines of private enterprise (by and large) fuel the former, the apparatuses of nation-states thrive on the latter" (1989:iii).

PHOTO 7.1 Black goat-hair tent, used for transhumant herding in the spring and summer. 2001. (Photo by the author.)

In the Kurdistan Region, there is no shortage of nostalgia that is being maintained and generated by the state, but it is not yet broad based. The regional government is very busy building monuments and holding commemorations, very much on its own terms. It seeks to communicate to its populace and to outside observers that the people of Kurdistan have suffered and do not deserve further suffering, and it seeks to promote the heroic deeds of its fighters and nation builders. Sipan's museum, while it may receive some government support, was not opened on the initiative of the state. It was his personal project, using textiles he had personally collected over a period of decades. It is probably the most-visited museum or gallery in the Kurdistan Region.

I have long heard both female and male Kurdish friends express the wish that there would be more places to gather in Kurdistan that are less charged with gendered identity. Most public spaces are still heavily male. However, new types of eating establishments have been opening that eschew the old design of a men's area and a "family" area for parties that include women, and they have a completely "modern" architecture and atmosphere. The first such place not only in Iraqi Kurdistan, but in Iraq as a whole, was the restaurant in the Mazi Supermarket complex in Dohuk. When friends first took me there in 2001, they were giddy with excitement over how "modern" it was in comparison to the traditional bazaar. As evidence of its modernity, they pointed to its well-lit aisles, check-out counters with belts to move the items along, and its escalator, all of which were "just like in America or Europe." People even came from as far away as Baghdad to visit the supermarket and adjacent theme park, which local people often noted with pride. Dohuk as a cosmopolitan place! It hardly seemed possible, since Dohuk had long been known as the most provincial of Kurdistan's governorates. Best of all, female friends told me, people loved how a girl or woman could go there and sit wherever she wanted, and no one would "bother" (sexually harass) her. Indeed, we sat there without any male chaperones and no one bothered us. Of course, my female friends would not dream of going there alone, but going with other friends of the same sex—and with no brother, nephew, or husband along as a chaperone—was now conceivable. That said, Mazi was also a place where either sex could go to discreetly check out the other. It sent a mixed message: It was modern, and therefore not sexualized. It was modern, and therefore a place to see the opposite sex in public in a way that was inconceivable in other local public spaces.

When the modern state becomes more powerful, and nonstate powers within the nation such as tribes are subdued, the state assumes a greater role in personal security. During the past few years, I have noticed a dramatic decline in the number of firearms that are visible on the streets. When I first went to Kurdistan, it was practically impossible to go anywhere without seeing a man carrying a machine gun. Most of the men who carried guns were members of the peshmerga, but many would continue to carry their weapons even when they were off-duty. The Kalashnikov rifle was often associated with traditional Kurdish dress. Men who were wearing more Western clothing tended to carry a pistol. It was common to catch a glimpse of a pistol wedged into a man's pants in the small of his back, or, less commonly, in a holster.

An encounter I had in 2010 illustrates the "old ways" of firearm carrying. I was at the Stars Hotel Restaurant in the town of Shaqlawa, a picturesque resort that sits at a strategic intersection on the Hamilton Road. The Stars Restaurant has long been Shaqlawa's "place to be," although it now has competition. At another table I noticed an elderly man wearing

PHOTO 7.2 A man walks a trail on the mountain behind his village, 2005. (Photo by the author.)

traditional dress and sitting alone at the table. He had a bodyguard with him. I have often seen guards looking relaxed and sitting and eating with those they are charged with protecting, but this one was thoroughly on his guard. They sat quietly and eventually left in silence. Afterward I asked the waiter if he knew who the man was. He readily identified the man as one of the main chiefs of a certain large tribe. The reason for the guard's tenseness became apparent to me. We were several tribal territories away from that tribe's area. As recently as a few years ago, that tribe had supplied many peshmerga to the KDP, and Shaqlawa had been controlled by the PUK. It was likely the chief suspected he had enemies in the area, or maybe he knew he did. He was a man away from his land, and a young bodyguard carrying a large gun was in order.

On that same visit to Kurdistan, however, I was struck by how far fewer guns were visible than in the past. There was a marked decrease in the number that one could see on the streets. One day a friend's driver came to pick me up in Hewler to take me to her house. I knew that, normally, the hired driver of an important person, which this friend is, carried at least one gun. Most drove a large SUV and kept a loaded machine gun mounted in the front, and many would have a pistol on their person as well. This time, however, I noticed the absence of a visible weapon, so it was clear there was no machine gun. I imagined the driver must have a pistol though, and asked him about that. He grinned and said, "When [my boss] wanted to hire me, she said, 'Where is your gun?' I said, 'I don't have a gun. I am a driver without a gun.' She thought this was very strange, but then she liked the idea and she hired me. I am a driver, without a gun! See? I have no gun!" he said, recounting the story with a tone of great novelty, as though he were proud to be pioneering a new local motif.

A decrease in the number of guns visible in public is a strong sign of the increasing power of the state Kurdistan. A modern state has, or ideally has, a lock on the legitimate use of violence. Nonstate violence, whether individualistic or based on a collective such as a patrilineage or tribe, is not legitimate. Although a time in which the Kurdistan Region is a place where guns are tightly controlled seems a long way off, it is also clear that the regional government is assuming a much greater role in security than it or the Iraqi government had done before. It is also clear that average people feel more relaxed about their personal security, a welcome change from just a few years ago. In this respect, the Kurdistan Region is starting to feel much more like the Western countries that are in many ways its model.

As Max Weber noted nearly a century ago, in modern bureaucratic rule, "It is not the person who is obeyed by virtue of his own right but the enacted rule, which is therefore decisive for who obeys the rule and to what extent" (Weber and Whimster 2004:133). Weber goes on to contrast this type of rule with "traditional rule," the purest type of which is "patriarchal rule" (135), and "charismatic rule," which is "on the basis of affectual surrender" (138). Rereading through these familiar categories in Weber's overall theory of modernity and its others, I experience the temptation, yielded to by so many for so long, to see modernity's others as its antecedents. Yet Kurdistan stands as a place where all three of Weber's types of legitimate rule are present, and not only present, but found working both in concert and in tension.

Homi K. Bhabha (1994) regards the colonizing project as communicating to the colonized a set of binaries mitigating against the agency of the colonial subject. He rejects these binaries for their masking of hybridity and insistence on cultural boundedness. During my research, my Kurdish interlocutors have spoken often of binaries: of patron and client, East and West, for example. But these binaries did not render them passive subjects. Rather, I have seen many people ultimately convert such binaries as "here" (Iraqi Kurdistan, which I conflate with Bhabha's "colonized') and "there" (the West, which I conflate with Bhabha's "colonizer") into cultural hybridity by undergoing processes of incorporating their two worlds into one way of life. By going about the globalization process in much the same way as they would incorporate a new friend into their social network or in terms similar to the quotidian structure of local patron-client power relations, they at least partially denied some of the potentially more difficult concomitants of the globalization experience such as living with difference and confronting "assimilation." Their own belief in binaries thus gave rise to agency. As such, it is the kind of agency described by Herzfeld (2005:188) that "only becomes apparent through the essentializing practices that give it form," or more specifically, an essentializing power structure motivating an essentializing practice, one of the "movements or processes that are produced in the articulation of cultural differences" (Bhabha 1994:1).

The Kurds', and in particular Iraqi Kurds', status as "postcolonial" is complex and in some ways unique. The standard colonial experience meant being (to whatever extent) governed by Europeans starting at some point during or after the fifteenth century, and having a rebellion and throwing off the colonial oppressors during the nineteenth or twentieth century. Especially in the Middle East, after the revolution came dictatorship. The problem of the colonized became the problem of the oppressed, who suffered the humiliation of oppression by one of "their own." Iraqi Kurds had a different experience. They were colonized first by the Turks, and then in rapid succession by the British followed by Arab Iraqis. In comparison, the United States, perhaps the strongest cultural and economic influence in Iraqi Kurdistan that is not an immediate neighbor, has seemed to many people to be more like an ally than a colonizer (several noteworthy betrayals notwithstanding, such as in 1975 when the United States found it expedient to abandon the Kurdish rebellion that it had been supporting). Can the KRG, with fewer reasons to lash out against the societies from which many of the world's technological and institutional models currently emanate, build a society that is less reactionary and therefore less oppressive than those of the postcolonial states of the twentieth-century Middle East, of which Iraq was a tragic exhibit? It is my hope that it can.

PHOTO 7.3 Many Kurdistanis now live in urban settings, such as the planned community near the city of Hewler called "American Village," shown here in a promotional brochure from 2010.

"Never Forget"

When I started my research in Kurdistan in 1995, I had a strong sense that I was doing "salvage ethnography." I looked around and saw a population of haunted people who told me stories of having been hunted "like animals," as people repeatedly described the experience, by the military of the Iraqi state. My first host household, that of Layla and her many teenaged and young-adult children, had moved from place to place over a period of several years as they were forcibly relocated by the government to one of its collective settlements (*mujamma'at*, also translated "collective towns" or even "concentration camps"), and as they fled a once comfortable urban life in Mosul for a wretched existence in the mountains among people who only begrudgingly accepted them. They lived in six cities, towns, and villages from 1978 until I met them in 1995, moving in most cases as impelled internal migrants rather than people making free choices regarding their location. It was clear as they recounted this that in addition to the trauma they had experienced and fled, they felt uprooted and out of place, even though they had ended up near where the family had begun in the 1960s. From them, and later from many other people, I got the sense that the horrific events of the recent past might not be over. I sensed that I might simply have been doing my fieldwork between waves of genocide, not at the end of them. The possibilities for human cruelty had operated in Iraq in grossly exaggerated form, just as in the Inquisition, or the Holocaust, or as they later did in Srebrenica. Who was to say, and what was to indicate, that it had come to an end?

Although I did operate under a cloud of fear in the early years, and I did have to deal with the effects of conflict in several forms as I describe in the beginning of this book, in hindsight, I arrived in my field site of Iraqi Kurdistan as a remarkable period of stability was beginning that is still in existence as of this writing. A whole generation has now grown up with the Kurdistan Regional Government in control and vigorously pursuing visions of modernity and prosperity (for better or for worse) in an environment of relative political calm and low levels of violence. It has come of age under a government that is turning torture chambers into libraries and government security facilities into parks.

A horrific past still haunts the dreams of many older people. For some people of all ages, the present still yields troubles on a smaller scale.

Amnesty International warns that torture still takes place in the Kurdistan Region (Amnesty International 2009). Journalists are occasionally murdered, their deaths unexplained. Human rights advancement and journalistic freedom can entail one step forward, two steps back. In 2007, Khandan Hama Jaza released the results of systematic research on prostitution in Kurdistan. Interviewing "296 prostitutes, 93 sex-buyers and 72 organizers" (Qaradaghi 2007) she argued in her coauthored book *Oqiyanusêk le Tawan* (*Ocean of Crimes*) (Îbrahîm et al. 2008) that prostitution in Iraqi Kurdistan is pervasive and, in the vast majority of cases, coercive. She was granted an award by the regional government for her work (Qaradaghi 2007). By 2010, however, she had fled to Germany after she was attacked three times, her husband was kidnapped, and her daughter was threatened with kidnapping (Chawrtayi 2010). The Kurdistan Region is a place of tremendous paradoxes, but contrasts with the past are still stark. The present is simply better.

I close this book with some paradoxical recollections of an elderly woman, Morshida, whom I interviewed in March 2002 in Dohuk along with her son-in-law Rashid. Morshida described to me moments of both elation and terror as the Iraqi military bore down on her neighborhood of Girebasi (where I later lived as well) during the Kurdish uprising in 1991. She and her neighbors and kin fled. In her account, local social connections bring advantages, but danger also lurks.

MORSHIDA: In 1991, KDP peshmerga surrounded the city. This time, the people rose up. . . . They cleaned the city from Saddam Hussein's army. The KDP came into the city. We went outside and we were waiting for the peshmerga to come into the city . . . we were clapping for the peshmerga when they came into the city. We were hiding in the basement. We were afraid to go outside, but we heard people say, "Come out . . ." Because the peshmerga came from the mountains, and they instigated the people . . . there was resistance by Iraqi troops, there was fighting between the two, that's why we went to the basement. We heard the sounds of gunfire being exchanged. It was a day and a half before they cleaned the city of the troops. We heard everything, but one night, the Iraqi government bombed our relatives' house. We saw lots of dead bodies in the alley, our same alley here in Girebasi. Members of Saddam's security forces, the Amn al Amm, were dead. We went outside and we saw them. When the Iraqi government bombed the

house, no one was hurt. Iraq bombed the whole city. When the peshmerga came down from the mountain, the people joined them, and it
was the people and the peshmerga together against the Iraqi troops.

DIANE: Do you remember the date?

MORSHIDA: The date was today! On the 5th of March! We stayed until the
21st of the month [the Newroz holiday]. We were very happy with the
peshmerga. Then the army came back. We celebrated Newroz, then
two or three days after Newroz the army came back. It was the biggest
celebration of Newroz ever! Of course it was forbidden to celebrate
during the government era. Then two days later, Iraqi forces came
back, they bombarded the city. We saw helicopters, and the government, on their way, they killed people on their way. I did not see this
with my eyes, but we heard that Iraq killed some people. . . . [Then] we
asked our neighbors to take us in their truck . . .

DIANE: Why did you ask that neighbor?

MORSHIDA: We had no car, and we had to leave! We knew them! We were
one people, *mirovêt êk bîn*, through marriage to my husband's relatives. If they were not our relatives, they would not have taken us . . .
we asked them to take us and they said yes.

DIANE: Exactly how are you related to this person?

MORSHIDA: . . . a long time ago, they married from us and we married
from them.

DIANE: So it's not a close relative?

MORSHIDA: No. When we asked them to take us, they said yes, and the
man, the owner of the truck, even told his wife to respect us. He told
her that we are relatives.

DIANE: How many other people were in the truck?

MORSHIDA: Six *'a'ila* [households or lineages]. There were three brothers,
each one of them had a truck, and they took people . . . who were in
our same alleyway. Some people asked and they refused. The people in
the truck were just neighbors, not relatives. There were people they
refused to take because they hated them. One of the families, they put
their things in the truck, but they told them, "You have to unload
them," because they did not like them.

DIANE: What did he tell them?

MORSHIDA: [in a jovial tone] He said "There is no place, no room"
[laughter, both Morshida and Rashid].

DIANE: But it was really because he did not like them?

MORSHIDA: Yes.

DIANE: So in the truck were neighbors that he liked, and relatives.

MORSHIDA: Yes, people who were good neighbors, they loved each other, they were friends. But that woman was a gossip! Long tongued (*zimanê dirêj*), ooooo! [Morshida laughter] She was gossiping, and after we left, she went to some people's houses and looted things, but not our house.

DIANE: How far up did the truck go?

MORSHIDA: The first stop was in Qala Diza, during the day. The second stop was in Diyana. We kept going because people said the government was chasing us. The government was in Amadiya so we went on to Diyana. We stayed two or three days in Diyana.

DIANE: Where did you sleep?

MORSHIDA: We slept in a lady's house, Safiya. People there saw the arriving families from Dohuk. She looked at us and she realized that we had met each other in the past through mutual friends. So, she invited us to stay with her.

DIANE: After Diyana?

MORSHIDA: The first stop was in Haj 'Imran. The Iraqi government was chasing us. After that we went to Khane, an Iranian town.

DIANE: Did the Iranians allow you to cross the border?

MORSHIDA: People were blocking the border. But the Iranian border police allowed us to cross. We stayed there in Khane. There were some Kurdish people in Khane who came and said, "Please come with us." So we stayed with them. Then we found our relatives there, who have a small house there. [The lineage of] my father's father's brother—with the same mother but not father.

DIANE: Did everyone in the truck stay with them?

MORSHIDA: Everyone else in the truck stayed in tents from the government. We were lucky that we knew someone near where the Iranian government told everyone to go, to Dera'a. We went to get tents, but suddenly we ran into our relatives, and they said, "Come with us!" Our relatives were already there in a refugee camp. They had been there since 1975 [when an earlier Kurdish uprising was crushed by the Iraqi government]. They had houses, because they had been there a long time. We stayed in Zewa for about a month . . ..

DIANE: So you discovered your relatives, you did not plan to go there?

MORSHIDA: We had no idea [that we would find them there]! [Then] we got news that everything had been looted, and we were anxious to go back to our house as soon as possible. We found that people had looted our house, a lot of things had been taken. My husband had a car shop, for spare parts. When we came back we found that people had taken everything from the shop. After we returned home, he sold the shop. After the shop had been looted by people, my son started working in the exchange market in Dohuk. Then the currency fell, and my son had bought a lot of dollars for a very high price, but suddenly the UN came with Oil for Food [the humanitarian program that began in 1996] and he lost over a million dinars.

Morshida's account illustrates the rich social connections in Kurdistani social life, connections based on kinship and marriage, on place, and on shared history. When people need help, they turn to the people with whom they have spent time forging connectedness. Morshida and her family were able to draw on their social networks for help in a dramatic flight that took them to a neighboring country. Even though they were unable to plan for the journey, they kept running into people whom they knew and who treated them favorably as a result. After a terrifying journey through the mountains of Iraq, they were even able to find their relatives on the other side of the border in Iran.

Morshida's account also illustrates the potential danger in relying on kin and friends, especially in the face of a state-sponsored military bent on eliminating you. What about the woman who was left behind for being a gossip? What was her fate? After the official interview ended, I remember pressing Morshida as to what happened to the woman and her family. I learned that they had survived. I also pressed Morshida as to whether the woman's life had really been in danger. She told me in a matter-of-fact tone that of course it had been. Morshida, who in the years since I interviewed her has died, initially came across to me as a kind, jovial, disarming person. And yet, in this account she narrated with what I could only see as chilling callousness how her neighbor had consigned a family to what could have been their deaths. They could have squeezed a few more people into the truck, so this was no case of "lifeboat ethics," but simple cruelty, payback to someone she and other neighbors did not like. Mark Levene (1998) has called the broader area where Morshida lived, the area of and around Eastern Anatolia, a "zone of genocide." Genocide can happen in the form of chemicals dropped from helicopters by states, as the Iraqi government did, but it can also have a more face-to-face quality. In the middle of an attempt at genocidal killing such as the one Morshida's account illustrates, people can turn on you and fail to help you, and this can be just as fatal as a mass attack itself.

Finally, in many ways Morshida's account illustrates the days during which the Iraqi Kurdish nation was born, a community of people who from that point forward began to function as one political entity, however fractured and defined in multiple ways. The experience of being hunted shapes a person. When you are hunted, you need people to help you. The people who will help you are the people with whom you have history and preferably kin connections. Of course, each person is shaped differently by trauma and the threat of trauma, but it is safe to say that everyone is shaped. As the people of the Kurdistan Region march forward into a seemingly gleaming and materially prosperous future, all but the young also carry with them the experiences of 1991 and earlier. The birth of the Iraqi Kurdish political entity and the life of its people during its first few decades is a breathtaking, yet fraught and even dangerous story, and one that can only partially yet be told.

NOTES

1. How should ethnicity be rendered linguistically, as a noun ("Kurd") or an adjective ("Kurdish")? A noun can be understood to make an ontological statement about someone's very being, and implies fixity. An adjective assigns to a person a trait, and implies flexibility. My preference would be to use the more flexible term, the adjective. However, during my time in Iraq I have come to see how deeply ontological ethnic identity is for many people, especially given that ethnicity has been the basis on which many have been victimized and killed. So, even though the English language seems to be moving away from ontological statements about ethnicity, and in English describing a person as "Kurdish" is becoming more common than describing someone as "a Kurd," I would not feel comfortable doing so all the time. What would that take away from people for whom claiming to be "a Kurd" is a right that they have not always had and insist on, going forward? In the Kurdish spoken in Iraq, I still hear people saying "I am a Kurd" (*Ez Kurd im*) on a regular basis. (In Turkey, I have heard this less frequently. People will more often make a reference to speaking the Kurmanji dialect than to "being" Kurdish.) In this book, to both show respect for my friends and to convey the constructed nature of identity, I switch off between "Kurd" and "Kurdish." A related term, "Kurdistani," refers to people belonging to the population of Kurdistan without specifying ethnicity.

2. "Hewler" is the city's name in Kurdish. It is known as "Erbil" in Arabic, a name that is sometimes used in Kurdish as well. "Arbela" is the city's historic name in English-language literature.

3. Armenians were the majority in Eastern Anatolia, which from a Kurdish point of view is "northern Kurdistan." Armenian and Turkish nationalists eschew the term "Kurdistan." After the Ottoman regime of Sultan Abdulhamid II, followed by the Young Turks, massacred and attempted genocide against Armenians in the late nineteenth and early twentieth centuries, Kurds became the majority.

4. Ismet Sheriff Vanly's geographical and historical overview of Iraqi Kurdistan (1993) is a good source on population figures to the early 1990s.

5. As I point out in this book, identity categories in Iraq such as ethnicity and religion are constructed along patrilineal lines. Ethnicity may be passed on by a

father, imposed by the state, or acquired in some other way. Religion may be passed on by a parent (nearly always a father in Iraq) or chosen by a convert. Therefore, I offer these categories with the caution that they might not apply at the individual level. For example, a person born into a Muslim family may be an atheist, even though the "Muslim" label is applied to him or her socially.

6. There are now a number of fine studies of Yezidi life in Iraq, including Christine Allison's (2001) work on oral tradition and Nelida Fuccaro's study of colonial Iraq (1999).

7. These are my own population estimates, based on familiarity with the estimates repeated with the Kurdish community. There are no systematically gathered data of which I am aware on the Kurdish population in any country.

8. The region has gone by several different names. Starting in the 1970s it was known as the "Kurdish Autonomous Region" after the Kurdish resistance reached what turned out to be a short-lived autonomy agreement with the central Iraqi government. In the 1990s, following the 1991 uprising, the term "Iraqi Kurdistan" came into common use. "Northern Iraq" is frequently used as a reference to the Kurdish majority, excluding the city of Mosul or areas to its west that are also clearly in the northern portion of Iraq. In Turkey, this term is preferred because "Kurdistan" has long been taboo and even illegal. "Northern Iraq" is also widely used by Western diplomats and among NGOs to refer to the Kurdish-majority area. Finally, in 2005 the area defined in 1991, and additional adjacent areas that came under Kurdish control following the deposing of the Iraqi regime by the United States and its allies, acquired an official name, the "Kurdistan Region." A few other terms are in use as well.

9. However, I agree with Christopher Houston (2009:21), who expresses concern that these translations may represent the neo-Orientalism against which Edward Said cautioned (Said 1979:322). Houston sees them as part of a larger publishing trend in Turkey and elsewhere in which "Western colonialism and its associated ideologies [are] the major interlocutor for indigenous or 'non-Western' politics" and expresses concern about the discernment of the "varied audiences" of these texts (2009:22).

10. Amal Rassam and Amal Vinogradov are the same person.

11. One additional anthropologist should receive mention here. Henry Field was primarily a physical anthropologist who wrote a multivolume work called *The Anthropology of Iraq* (1940) He was a prolific researcher, primarlily in anthropometry, and he worked for the U.S. government on a covert project commissioned by President Franklin D. Roosevelt (University of Miami Special Collections 2011). Both anthropometry and links to intelligence agencies are frowned on in mainstream anthropology today (e.g., González 2009). My hope is that a latter-day George Stocking will train a new and critical eye on Field's work. During its 2003–2011 occupation, the U.S. military hired some people with training in anthropology to gather intelligence in the war theater.

It would be interesting to do an in-depth comparison of present and past uses of anthropology by the United States in gathering intelligence in Iraq.

12. Hosham Dawod (2012) uses "house" in reference to Saddam Hussein's patrilineage and that of his mother.

13. My project here is not to analyze global markets' reach into Kurdistan (though they now have an extensive reach), to highlight Kurdistan as an extractive economy (although it definitely is), to show Kurdistan's connection to neoliberalism and post-Fordism (which it certainly has, mainly through petroleum), or to analyze Kurdistan's role in the United States' and Britain's controversial Iraq War (it and its diasporans' role was substantial), despite the worthiness of these projects.

14. This point may threaten to invoke a now-discredited modernization narrative from the 1950s and 1960s (e.g., Lerner 1958) that prematurely announced that sweeping "change" was transforming the Middle East, when people's lives there continued to be dominated by authoritarian governments and many forms of *desired* change remained elusive. I take the risk of this assertion because during the course of my visits there I have witnessed changes too stunning to play down.

15. "Hala" is a pseudonym, as are all names of living individuals in this book, with the exception of public figures, whom I name with a forename and a surname, and the man named "Osama."

16. That is, unless the only person at home was of the opposite sex and not someone subject to the incest taboo such as a sibling, parent, grandparent, aunt (nonaffinal) or uncle (nonaffinal). In such an instance, convention would call for the person to apologetically turn you away at the gate.

17. Based on eighteen months of fieldwork in a Kurmanji-speaking village, Lale Yalçin-Heckmann's book (1991) is the most in-depth ethnography of a single Kurdish community. Hakkari and the Kurmanji part of Iraq used to belong to the same sociopolitical area. Some tribes, such as the Doski, were even split by the international border in the 1920s. Yalçin-Heckmann's book deals richly with aspects of social connecting similar to those I examine in this book, and in an area with great cultural and historical overlap.

18. Mark Levene (1998) notes that Iraqi Kurdistan (as part of a broader area stretching northward) "since the 1890s has been repeatedly plagued by genocidal killings" (393). I agree, but I would start the period for which he makes this assertion a few decades earlier.

19. The author was probably William L. Eagleton, a U.S. diplomat who wrote several publications on the Kurds.

20. Austrian Airlines, the first European airline to operate passenger service to Iraq since 1991, began flying to the Kurdistan Region in 2006, but did not begin service to Baghdad until 2011. American passenger carriers have not resumed flying to Iraq following the cessation of flights leading up to the 1991 Gulf War. As of January 2013, they are not prohibited from operating in the Kurdistan Region (United States Federal Aviation Administration 2012).

21. Aihwa Ong (1999) identifies a process within globalization that this seems to exemplify: "[G]overnments cede more of the instrumentalities connected with development as a technical project to global enterprises but maintain strategic controls over resources, population, sovereignty" (21).

22. Taylor 2005.

23. A pseudonym.

24. "Turkish" is both an ethnic designator and a term referring to a citizen of Turkey. Since Turkey is ethnically diverse, many people are the latter but not the former—Turkish citizens, but not Turks. I do not know whether Gunter used the term for the ethnicity or the citizenship category, but I imagine he meant citizens of Turkey, whatever their ethnicity. "Lebanese" is not an ethnic term, and refers simply to citizens of Lebanon.

25. Seeing signs of Lebanese investment seemed a bit surreal to me at first. I thought back to my experiences in Beirut in 2002 and 2003, when thousands of people marched in protest against the possible, and later real, war by the United States and Britain and their allies to unseat the Saddam Hussein regime. Back then, I had emailed that same KDP official and mentioned the local sentiments against the Iraq War, which sharply contrasted with the pro-war feeling over in Kurdistan. I thought he would be interested to know about the contrast, since he had lived in Lebanon earlier in his life. "Just wait," he said at the time. "After things quiet down over here they will all be here starting businesses." I imagine that the marchers and business-starters were probably not the same people, but his remarks still seemed prescient five years later.

26. Storytelling and other forms of in-person entertainment have been threatened by the rise of the television in Kurdistan just as they have been anywhere in the world, although I would add that there are different ways to watch television. In Kurdistan, I have observed that the television is often left on in a room in which the main activity is conversation. The tendency in the West seems to be to have the television off, or at least the volume turned down, during the course of a gathering that is mainly considered a social event. Still, the roles of the story-teller (*çîrokbêj*) and bard (*dengbêj*) are declining. Some important scholarly work on Kurdish oral tradition has been done (e.g., Blau 1975; Kreyenbroek and Marzolph 2010; MacKenzie 1962a,b), but much more is needed.

CHAPTER 2   FIELDWORK IN A DANGER ZONE

1. For more detail, see Nezan 1996, Robson and Refuee Service Center 1996, and Yavuz 1998.

2. A pseudonym.

3. For an in-depth study of the PKK's history and ideology, see Marcus 2007.

4. While this sort of immersion has a long history in anthropology, I think it is becoming rarer with the rise of urban life around the world. A middle-class lifestyle in one country can have more in common with a middle-class lifestyle

in another country than with an impoverished, rural, or peasant lifestyle in the same country. Embodied research that involves significant adjustments to a middle-class researcher's lifestyle is becoming less automatic in Kurdistan, too. As the standard of living rises, many people now eat a more diverse diet, sleep on a bed with a frame, and have modern heating and cooling systems in their homes. I have, in the course of doing embodied research, learned to chop tomatoes at floor rather than counter level, and thoroughly enjoy sleeping on the roof in the summer. Now many local people, however, are chopping on counters and have abandoned sleeping on the roof in favor of indoor air conditioning. Very soon, if Kurdistan continues on the current upward economic trajectory, embodied research for a middle-class person such as myself may mean "studying up."

5. Skin color is a topic of frequent conversation in Kurdistan, and light skin is generally valued over dark skin. On more than one occasion I have heard a parent with two children of differing skin shades say, right in front of the children, something like, "Isn't this one beautiful because of his [or her] light skin, and isn't this dark one so ugly?" In addition, blue eyes are highly prized, and green eyes almost as much. For example, men may profusely congratulate a man whose newborn child has blue eyes, and mothers may ensure the child is protected against the evil eye with amulets on the child's clothing.

6. Diyarbakir's Kurdish name is "Amed." During my time there in the 1990s I heard people call it "Diyarbakir" more often, but this appellation has shifted since then as the Kurdish movement in he area has assumed a new boldness.

7. Nagengast (1994) has extensive documentation of sentiments in Turkey that are similar to what I heard, if perhaps not quite as potent (judging from her article, at least).

8. A growing number of universities in Turkey now permit research on Kurdish life despite the overall negative environment for Kurdish studies there. Ramazan Aras teaches at the new Mardin Artuklu Üniversitesi, which may make him the first sociocultural anthropologist to reside and work in Kurdistan on a full-time basis.

CHAPTER 3 A MAN ON THE LAND: LINEAGES, IDENTITY, AND PLACE

1. Among Arabs, a tribal leader is called a *shaikh* (Kurdish *şêx*). In Kurdish use, this term refers to a Muslim sufi leader or a male of the midlevel Yezidi caste.

2. I did not ask about other patrilineal descendants Hassan may have had.

3. This is probably a reference to local air pollution from cooking fires fueled with locally collected wood and other items such as tires, rather than a reference to the oil fires burning in southern Iraq during the Gulf War.

4. I write here of Christians who belong to Iraq's long-present Christian churches, such as the Assyrian Church of the East and the Chaldean Catholic Church. I am not referring to new converts to Protestant Christianity, who are also present in Iraq and whom I mention in chapter 7.

5. See Varisco (1995) for a thorough and interesting analysis of the Prophet Mohammed's genealogy. Some claims to sayyid status, such as the one made by Saddam Hussein (Dawod 2012:103), are a bit spurious.

6. I have heard it pointed out many times, both by scholars and nonscholars, that "the Kurds have never had a state of their own." This statement often carries the insinuation that Kurdish nationalism has been a pointless exercise or, that for Kurds, having a state is not "natural." This statement is problematic on a number of levels. What does it mean for an ethnic group to "have" a state? Does it mean dominating the state, or simply constituting the majority of its citizens? For the several hundred years before the European colonial powers created state boundaries throughout the Middle East in the early twentieth century, no ethnic group other than the Turks and Persians "had" (dominated; constituted the majority in) a state. Only the Ottoman Turks and the Persians can be said to have created their own modern states as their long-standing empires came to take on many modern characteristics and were then replaced by successor regimes. However, a number of different ethnic groups, including the Kurds and Arabs, "had" small-scale polities with dynastic leadership governing under loose Ottoman control. These are usually referred to as "principalities." One could also call them vassal states. My point is that they were at least very statelike, and at some points in their history had a great deal of autonomy. Kurds therefore may have "had" more states than many of their ethnic neighbors.

7. E. B. Soane's book on the tribes of "Southern" (today mainly Iraqi) Kurdistan (1918) is also helpful and interesting in this regard, containing many charts showing the patrilineal descent patterns of chiefly Kurdish lineages.

8. Azhar Shemdin, Hazim's daughter, wrote the following to me in an email on 23 January 2002: "Hanna Batatu was my professor at AUB when he was doing the research for that . . . book. I gave him my father's photo that is in that book. Batatu has put the wrong name on it. It should read 'Hazim Shemdin Agha.' Also, the reference to the land holdings in the study is by Hazim Shemdin Agha, and not 'Shamdin Agha.'"

9. American missionary Fredrick Coan describes Rashid Beg as having a relationship with the Turkish government as well. His account is not kind: "[T]he attractive valley of Berwer . . . contains six Christian villages. In Berwer one emerges from the *asheret* (free) region to that of the *rayat* (subject) and sees again the outrageous tyranny of the Turk and Kurd. . . . Berwer was in the hands of as villainous and cruel a Kurd as ever went unhanged. . . . Reshid Beg paid a certain sum of money to the Turkish government for the privilege of collecting taxes. If he paid the Turks ten pounds sterling for each village, it is perfectly safe to say he collected two hundred for himself" (Coan 1939:186–187).

10. The violence of the late twentieth century that resulted in the deaths of hundreds of thousands of people in Kurdistan also caused people to delay marriages and to have fewer children. See Beth Osborne Daponte, and

colleagues (1997) for some interesting theorizing on Kurdish population growth between 1977 and 1990.

11. The area administered by and recognized as coming under the Kurdistan Regional Government in today's Iraq is smaller, excluding most of the area of the governorates of Ninewa and Tameem/Kirkuk. However, population figures from the beginning of the twentieth century tended to be calculated for the whole area of the former Mosul vilayet. I have been unable to find population statistics from that period that would allow a comparison between today's Iraqi Kurdistan and the same approximate land area in the early twentieth century, hence the comparison between the Mosul vilayet and five contemporary governorates rather than the three (Dohuk, Hewler/Erbil, and Silemani) that mainly comprise Kurdistan. OCHA, the UN's Office for the Coordination of Humanitarian Affairs, gives the following figures for each governorate: Dahuk 616,600; Erbil 1,845,200; Ninewa 2,473,700; Sulaymaniyah 2,159,800; Tameem 839,100.

CHAPTER 4   GENDERED CHALLENGES: WOMEN NAVIGATING PATRILINY

1. Henny Harald Hansen's (1960, 1961) studies of Kurdish women's lives based on a four-month stay near Silemani offer rich description of aspects of the lives of Kurdish women in both rural and urban settings, which she described as labor heavy and relatively restricted. Hansen predicted that, just as women had elsewhere in the world, Kurdish women would soon be faced with new social patterns brought about by changes in technology (1961:185). These changes began in earnest during the lifetimes of many of the same women with whom she worked.

2. Nahela was referring to the high rate of traffic accidents in Kurdistan, which Nakshabandi (2007) has documented. I have seen horrific accidents myself, and I have known several people who were killed on the roads. In 2007 Nahela herself survived a crash that killed her aunt, her father's sister, who had been sitting next to her in the back of a taxi when they collided with another car.

3. Leszek Dziegiel (e.g., 1981) visited the Dohuk area four times between 1977 and 1980 with a Polish agricultural research team. To my knowledge he and I are the only sociocultural anthropologists to have carried out ethnographic work in the Kurmanji-speaking area of Iraq.

4. The subject of religiosity and the influence of religion in Kurdistan is a vast one, to which I cannot do justice here.

5. David Romano (2007) has published the most comprehensive overview of Islamism in Iraqi Kurdistan of which I am aware.

6. Our conversation took place in English. Had he been speaking in Kurdish, he would not have used the term "virgin" for males, since that word, *kich*, also means girl.

7. In most anthropological literature on the subject, the abbreviation is "FBD," for "father's brother's daughter." I prefer to call it FBS/D, for "father's brother's

son/daughter." As Suad Joseph notes, "The interest of most scholars has been on the *male* relationships of that marriage system" (1999:274) (italics in original). Joseph's suggested gender-inclusive abbreviation is "FaBrDa/So." Furthermore, Korotayev (2000:395) argues that "Islamization, along with an area's inclusion in the eighth-century Arab-Islamic khalifate (and its persistence within the Islamic world) is a strong and significant predictor of parallel-cousin (FBD) marriage."

8. The terms "honor violence" and honor-based violence (HBV) are also used. I use "honor killing" since it seems clear in the vast majority of cases that the victim's death is the goal of the perpetrator, even if death is not the outcome. "Honor murder" is another commonly used term. An "honor suicide" takes place when the victim is forced to kill herself by the people who would otherwise do the deed, for example by telling her that if she does not shoot herself, they will torture her and then kill her. She chooses to kill herself rather than be subjected to additional suffering.

9. Human Rights Watch has produced a comprehensive report on FGC in Kurdistan (Khalife and Human Rights Watch 2010).

CHAPTER 5   POLITICKING

1. McDowall (2004) and Bruinessen (1992a,b) are the best English-language sources on modern Kurdish history.

CHAPTER 6   REFUGE SEEKING, PATRILINY, AND THE GLOBAL

1. Iraq's Personal Status Law, which governs inheritance, is an interesting combination of shari'a and secular, "modern" values. While in most forms of shari'a sons receive twice the ownership share of daughters, Iraqi law has allowed for equal portions since the 1950s. There are loopholes, however, that permit sons to receive more in some cases. See Juan Cole (2009) for an account of how in 2004 Iraq's Personal Status Law was nearly abrogated in favor of each religious group in Iraq practicing its own canon law.

2. Ariel Sabar's book, *My Father's Paradise* (2009), is a poignant memoir by a member of the second generation of Kurdistani Jewish diasporans. The reader is introduced to Jewish Zakho through Sabar's struggle to understand his father's considerable nostalgia.

CHAPTER 7   KURDISTAN IN THE WORLD

1. "Bridewealth" refers to goods and currency transferred at or around the time of marriage from the groom and/or his family, to the bride and/or her family. "Dowry" refers to such transfers from the bride and/or her family to the groom and/or his family.

GLOSSARY AND ACRONYMS

agha	landlord, tribal chief, and patron
'a'ila	patrilineage
azadî	independence, freedom
beg	a title similar to agha
chete	tribal mercenary
diwan	council chamber
djinn	an invisible spirit that can possess a person
donum	one donum = 0.618 acre
doşek	floor cushion
'eşîret	tribe
'esil	pedigree of attested patrilineal origin
fellah	peasant; plural fellahin
haram	forbidden
jandarma	Turkish gendarmerie
khanum	"lady"; a high-status female
liwa	governorates that comprise a vilayet; province
mal	patrilineage
miskîn	well behaved, gentle
mudir	governmental administrator
mujamma'at	government-controlled collective settlements
mukhabarat	secret police
muxtar	mayor
nahiya	borough
namûs	honor; patrilineal sovereignty
peshmerga	Iraqi Kurdish resistance fighters ("those who face death")
qadha	district

sayyid	a status that claims patrilineal descent from Prophet Mohammed
şerim (eyb)	emotion prompted by a community's perceived scornful gaze
serspî	an older woman ("white head")
shah	"sovereign" in Persian
shaikh	a Kurdish Muslim sufi religious leader
shari'a	Islamic law
sîk, souq	a Middle Eastern or north African bazaar
umma	the worldwide Muslim community
vilayet	Ottoman administrative unit
waqf	an Islamic endowment

EIH	Erbil International Hotel
FBS/D	father's brother's son or daughter
FGC	female genital cutting
GOI	Government of Iraq
IDP	Internally Displaced Person
KDP	Kurdistan Democratic Party
KNC	Kurdish National Council of Syria
KRG	Kurdistan Regional Government
MECRI	Middle East Consortium for Reconstruction and Investment
NGO	Nongovernmental Organization
PKK	Kurdistan Workers' Party
PSL	Personal Status Law (Iraq and neighboring countries)
PUK	Patriotic Union of Kurdistan
PYD	Party of Unity and Democracy
UNHCR	United Nations High Commissioner for Refugees
USAID	United States Agency for International Development

REFERENCES

Abdullah, Sara Burhan. 2010. "IRAQ: Citizenship and Women's Rights under the Iraqi Constitution." *JURIST Legal News & Research*.

Abu-Lughod, Lila. 1999. *Veiled Sentiments: Honor and Poetry in a Bedouin Society*. Berkeley: University of California Press.

———. 2005. *Dramas of Nationhood: The Politics of Television in Egypt*. The Lewis Henry Morgan Lectures, 2001. Chicago: University of Chicago Press.

Adelkhah, Fariba. 2000. *Being Modern in Iran*. New York: Columbia University Press.

Adib-Moghaddam, Arshin. 2006. "The Whole Range of Saddam Hussein's War Crimes." *Middle East Report* 239:30–35.

Agence France-Presse. 2000. Rival Kurdish Groups Pledge to Work Together.

Al-Ali, Nadje. 2007. *Iraqi Women: Untold Stories from 1948 to the Present*. London: Zed Books.

Al-Ali, Nadje, and Nicola Pratt. 2011. "Between Nationalism and Women's Rights: The Kurdish Women's Movement in Iraq." *Middle East Journal of Culture and Communication* 4 (3):339–355.

Al-Hamash, Khalil, Adnan J. Radhi, Aziz Y. Al-Muttalibi, Ra'ad Ahmad, Samir Abdul Rahim Al-Chalabi, Khudhayir S. Al-Khazraji, and Iraq Ministry of Education. Wizārat al-Tarbiyah. 1993. *The New English Course for Iraq*. Baghdad: Maṭba 'at al-Sālimī / Republic of Iraq Ministry of Education.

Al-Hamash, Khalil, Adnan J. Radhi, Khudheyer S. Ali, and Iraq Ministry of Education. Wizārat al-Tarbiyah. 1998. *The New English Course for Iraq*. Baghdad: Maṭba 'at al-Sālimī / Republic of Iraq Ministry of Education.

Al-Khayyat, Sana. 1990. *Honour and Shame: Women in Modern Iraq*. London: Saqi Books.

Allison, Christine. 2001. *The Yezidi Oral Tradition in Iraqi Kurdistan*. Richmond, Surrey, U.K.: Curzon.

American Board of Commissioners for Foreign Missions. 1837. *The Missionary Herald*. Boston: Crocker and Brewster.

Amnesty International. 2009. "Hope and Fear: Human Rights in the Kurdistan Region of Iraq". http://www.amnesty.org/en/library/asset/MDE14/006/2009/en/c2e5ae23-b204–4b46-b7f5–06dc1501f62f/mde140062009en.pdf.

Anderson, J.N.D. 1960. "A Law of Personal Status for Iraq." *International & Comparative Law Quarterly* 9 (04):542–563.

Appadurai, Arjun. 1990. "Disjuncture and Difference in the Global Cultural Economy." *Public Culture* 2 (2):1–24.

Appadurai, Arjun, and Carol A. Breckenridge. 1989. "Editors' Comment." *Public Culture* 2 (1):i–iv.

Arendt, Hannah. 1951. *The Origins of Totalitarianism.* New York: Harcourt, Brace and Company.

Atran, Scott. 1985. "Managing Arab Kinship and Marriage." *Social Science Information* 24 (4):659–696.

Baban, Hemin. 2010. "Sex-Related Diseases Increase in Iraq's Kurdistan." *Rudaw,* http://www.rudaw.net/english/kurds/3257.html.

Badger, George Percy. 1852. *The Nestorians and Their Rituals: With the Narrative of a Mission to Mesopotamia and Coordistan in 1842–1844, and of a Late Visit to Those Countries in 1850: also, Researches into the Present Condition of the Syrian Jacobites, Papal Syrians, and Chaldeans and an Inquiry into the Religious Tenets of the Yezeedees.* Vol. 1. London: Joseph Masters.

Ballinger, Pamela. 2002. *History in Exile: Memory and Identity at the Borders of the Balkans.* Princeton, N.J.: Princeton University Press.

Barth, Fredrik. 1954. "Father's Brother's Daughter Marriage in Kurdistan." *Southwestern Journal of Anthropology* 10 (2):164–171.

———. 1979 [1953]. *Principles of Social Organization in Southern Kurdistan.* New York: AMS Press.

Basch, Linda, Nina Glick Schiller, and Cristina Szanton Blanc. 1994. *Nations Unbound: Transnational Projects, Postcolonial Predicaments, and Deterritorialized Nation-States.* London: Routledge.

Batatu, Hanna. 2004. *The Old Social Classes and the Revolutionary Movements of Iraq: A Study of Iraq's Old Landed and Commercial Classes and of Its Communists, Ba'thists, and Free Officers.* London: Saqi Books.

Bayly, C. A., and Leila Tarazi Fawaz. 2002. "Introduction: The Connected World of Empires." In *Modernity and Culture: From the Mediterranean to the Indian Ocean,* edited by Leila Tarazi Fawaz and C. A. Bayly, 1–27. New York: Columbia University Press.

BBC News. 2005. "UN Rules Out Iraqi Election Rerun." *BBC News,* http://news.bbc.co.uk/2/hi/middle_east/4555850.stm.

Bell, Gertrude Lowthian. 1911. *Amurath to Amurath.* London: William Heinemann.

Bhabha, Homi K. 1994. *The Location of Culture.* London: Routledge.

Bird, Isabella L. 2010 [1891]. *Journeys in Persia and Kurdistan: Including a Summer in the Upper Karun Region and a Visit to the Nestorian Rayahs.* Cambridge: Cambridge University Press.

Blau, Joyce. 1975. *Le Kurde de 'Amādiya et de Djabal Sindjār: Analyse Linguistique, Textes Folkloriques, Glossaires.* Paris: C. Klincksieck.

Bohannan, Paul. 1954. "The Migration and Expansion of the Tiv." *Africa: Journal of the International African Institute* 24 (1):2–16.

Bourdieu, Pierre. 1990. *The Logic of Practice.* Stanford, Calif.: Stanford University Press.

Bozarslan, Hamit. 2000. "MERIA Research Guide: Kurdish Studies." *Middle East Review of International Affairs (MERIA): A Magazine on Middle East Studies* 4 (2). http:// meria.idc.ac.il/news/2000/00news3.html#Kurds.

Braidwood, Robert J., and Bruce Howe. 1960. *Prehistoric Investigations in Iraqi Kurdistan.* Chicago: University of Chicago Press.

Brandes, Stanley. 1987. "Reflections on Honor and Shame in the Mediterranean." In *Honor and Shame and the Unity of the Mediterranean*, edited by David D. Gilmore, 121–134. Washington, D.C.: American Anthropological Association.

Brenneman, Robert L. 2007. *As Strong as the Mountains: A Kurdish Cultural Journey.* Prospect Heights, Ill.: Waveland Press.

Brereton, Derek P. 2005. "House Society and Practice Theories Illuminate American Campsteads." *Anthropological Theory* 5 (2):135–153.

Brown, Wendy. 1992. "Finding the Man in the State." *Feminist Studies* 18 (1):7–34.

Brubaker, Rogers. 1996. *Nationalism Reframed: Nationhood and the National Question in the New Europe.* Cambridge: Cambridge University Press.

Bruinessen, Martin van. 1992a. *Agha, Shaikh, and State: The Social and Political Structures of Kurdistan.* London: Zed Books.

———. 1992b. "Kurdish Society, Ethnicity, Nationalism and Refugee Problems." In *The Kurds: A Contemporary Overview*, edited by Philip Kreyenbroek and Stefan Sperl, 33–67. London: Routledge.

———. 2000. *Mullas, Sufis and Heretics: The Role of Religion in Kurdish Society.* Vol. 44, *Analecta Isisiana.* Istanbul: The Isis Press.

Busch, Nicholas 2002. "'Economic Migrants?'—The Causes of the Kurdish Exodus." *Fortress Europe? Circular Letter*, http://www.fecl.org/circular/5312. htm.

Carling, Jørgen. 2002. "Migration in the Age of Involuntary Immobility: Theoretical Reflections and Cape Verdean Experiences." *Journal of Ethnic and Migration Studies* 28 (1):5–42.

Carsten, Janet. 2000. *Cultures of Relatedness: New Approaches to the Study of Kinship.* Cambridge: Cambridge University Press.

———. 2004. *After Kinship.* Cambridge: Cambridge University Press.

Castells, Manuel. 2010. *The Power of Identity.* 2d ed. *The Information Age: Economy, Society, and Culture.* Malden, Mass.: Wiley-Blackwell.

Chatterjee, Partha. 1993. *The Nation and Its Fragments: Colonial and Postcolonial Histories.* Princeton Studies in Culture/Power/History. Princeton, N.J.: Princeton University Press.

Chawrtayi, Mustafa 2010. "Upon Writing Book on Prostitution, Kurdish Writer Forced to Flee to Germany". *Rudaw*, http://www.rudaw.net/english/culture_art/3244.html.

Chyet, Michael L. 2003. *Kurdish-English Dictionary.* New Haven: Yale University Press.

Clarke, Morgan. 2007. "Closeness in the Age of Mechanical Reproduction: Debating Kinship and Biomedicine in Lebanon and the Middle East." *Anthropological Quarterly* 80 (2):379–402.

———. 2008. "New Kinship, Islam, and the Liberal Tradition: Sexual Morality and New Reproductive Technology in Lebanon." *Journal of the Royal Anthropological Institute* 14 (1):153–169.

———. 2011. *Islam and New Kinship: Reproductive Technology and the Shariah in Lebanon.* New York: Berghahn Books.

Coan, Frederick. 1939. *Yesterdays in Persia and Kurdistan.* Claremont, Calif.: Saunders Studio Press.

Cole, Juan. 2009. "Struggles over Personal Status and Family Law in Post-Baathist Iraq." In *Family, Gender, and Law in a Globalizing Middle East and South Asia*, edited by Kenneth M. Cuno and Manisha Desai, 105–125. Syracuse, N.Y.: Syracuse University Press.

Collier, Jane Fishburne. 1974. "Women in Politics." In *Woman, Culture, and Society*, edited by Michelle Zimbalist Rosaldo and Louise Lamphere, 89–96. Stanford, Calif.: Stanford University Press.

Collier, Jane Fishburne, and Sylvia Junko Yanagisako. 1987. *Gender and Kinship: Essays toward a Unified Analysis.* Stanford, Calif.: Stanford University Press.

Cooper, John. 2008. *Raphael Lemkin and the Struggle for the Genocide Convention.* New York: Palgrave Macmillan.

Dalberg-Acton, John Emerich Edward (Lord Acton). 1907. "Nationality." In *The History of Freedom: And Other Essays*, edited by John Neville Figgis and Reginald Vere Laurence, 270–300. London: Macmillan.

Daponte, Beth Osborne, Joseph B. Kadane, and Lara J. Wolfson. 1997. "Bayesian Demography: Projecting the Iraqi Kurdish Population, 1977–1990." *Journal of the American Statistical Association* 92 (440):1256–1267.

Davis, Eric. 2005. *Memories of State: Politics, History, and Collective Identity in Modern Iraq.* Berkeley: University of California Press.

Dawod, Hosham 2012. "Tribalism and Power in Iraq: Saddam Hussein's 'House.'" In *Contesting the State: The Dynamics of Resistance and Control*, edited by Angela Hobart and Bruce Kapferer, 87–123. Wantage, U.K.: Sean Kingston Publishing.

De Certeau, Michel. 1984. *The Practice of Everyday Life.* Berkeley: University of California Press.

Deeb, Lara. 2006. *An Enchanted Modern: Gender and Public Piety in Shi'i Lebanon.* Princeton Studies in Muslim Politics. Princeton, N.J.: Princeton University Press.

Delaney, Carol. 1991. *The Seed and the Soil: Gender and Cosmology in Turkish Village Society.* Comparative Studies on Muslim Societies, edited by Barbara D. Metcalf. Berkeley: University of California Press.

———. 1995. "Father State, Motherland, and the Birth of Modern Turkey." In *Naturalizing Power: Essays in Feminist Cultural Analysis*, edited by Sylvia Yanagisako and Carol Delaney, 177–199. London: Routledge.

Dodge, Toby. 2003. *Inventing Iraq: The Failure of Nation Building and a History Denied.* New York: Columbia University Press.

Drieskens, Barbara. 2008. *Living with Djinns: Understanding and Dealing with the Invisible in Cairo.* London: Saqi Books.

Dziegiel, Leszek. 1981. *Rural Community of Contemporary Iraqi Kurdistan Facing Modernization.* Kraków, Poland: Agricultural Academy in Kraków, Institute of Tropical and Subtropical Agriculture and Forestry.

———. 1982. "Hygiene and Attention to Personal Appearance among the Iraqi Kurds." *Archiv Orientalni* 50 (1):43–50.

E., W. L. 1956. "Iraqi Kurdistan: A Little-Known Region." *World Today* 12 (10):417–432.

Economist. 2001. "Broadband Blues." *Economist* 359 (8227):62.

Edmonds, C. J. 1957. *Kurds, Turks, and Arabs: Politics, Travel, and Research in North-Eastern Iraq 1919–1925.* London: Oxford University Press.

Eisenstadt, Shmuel Noah, and Luis Roniger. 1984. *Patrons, Clients, and Friends: Interpersonal Relations and the Structure of Trust in Society.* Cambridge: Cambridge University Press.

Evans-Pritchard, E. E. 1940. *The Nuer: A Description of the Modes of Livelihood and Political Institutions of a Nilotic People.* Oxford: Clarendon Press.

Ewing, Katherine Pratt. 2008. *Stolen Honor: Stigmatizing Muslim Men in Berlin.* Stanford, Calif.: Stanford University Press.

Faurote, Fay Leone, Aerospace Industries Association of America, Manufacturers Aircraft Association, and Aeronautical Chamber of Commerce of America. 1923. *Aircraft Year Book.* New York: Aeronautical Chamber of Commerce of America.

Fernea, Elizabeth Warnock. 2010 [1965]. *Guests of the Sheik: An Ethnography of an Iraqi Village.* New York: Knopf Doubleday Publishing Group.

Fernea, Robert A. 1959. "Irrigation and Social Organization among the El Shabana, a Group of Tribal Cultivators in Southern Iraq." University of Chicago, Department of Anthropology, Chicago.

——. 1970. *Shaykh and Effendi: Changing Patterns of Authority among the El Shabana of Southern Iraq.* Cambridge, Mass.: Harvard University Press.

Field, Henry. 1940. *The Anthropology of Iraq.* 2 pts. in 4 vols. Field Museum of Natural History Publication 469, 631. Chicago: Field Museum.

——. 1952. *The Anthropology of Iraq.* Pt. 2, no. 2: *Kurdistan.*—Pt. 2, no. 3: *Conclusions.* Cambridge, Mass.: Peabody Museum of American Archaeology and Ethnology.

Fischer-Tahir, Andrea. 2009. *Brave Men, Pretty Women?: Gender and Symbolic Violence in Iraqi Kurdish Urban Society.* Berlin: Europäisches Zentrum für kurdische Studien.

Fortes, Meyer. 1953. "The Structure of Unilineal Descent Groups." *American Anthropologist* 55 (1):17–41.

Fouron, Georges, and Nina Glick Schiller. 2001. "All in the Family: Gender, Transnational Migration, and the Nation-State." *Identities* 7 (4):539–582.

Frank, André Gunder, and Barry K. Gills. 1996. *The World System: Five Hundred Years or Five Thousand?* London: Routledge.

Franklin, Sarah, and Susan McKinnon. 2001. *Relative Values: Reconfiguring Kinship Studies.* Durham, N.C.: Duke University Press.

Fuccaro, Nelida. 1999. *The Other Kurds: Yazidis in Colonial Iraq.* London: I. B. Tauris.

Geertz, Clifford. 1994. "'From the Native's Point of View': On the Nature of Anthropological Understanding." In *Culture Theory: Essays on Mind, Self, and Emotion,* edited by Richard A. Shweder and Robert A. Levine, 123–136. Cambridge: Cambridge University Press.

——. 1998. *Works and Lives: The Anthropologist as Author.* Cambridge, U.K.: Polity Press.

Geertz, Hildred. 1979. "The Meaning of Family Ties." In *Meaning and Order in Moroccan Society: Three Essays in Cultural Analysis,* edited by Clifford Geertz, Hildred Geertz, and Lawrence Rosen, 315–391. Cambridge: Cambridge University Press.

Gellner, Ernest. 1989. *Muslim Society.* Cambridge: Cambridge University Press.

———. 1990. "Tribalism and the State in the Middle East." In *Tribes and State Formation in the Middle East,* edited by Philip S. Khoury and Joseph Kostiner. Berkeley: University of California Press.

Gellner, Ernest, and John Waterbury. 1977. *Patrons and Clients in Mediterranean Societies.* London: Duckworth.

Ghanim, David 2009. *Gender and Violence in the Middle East.* Westport, Conn: Praeger.

Gilmore, David D. 1990. *Manhood in the Making: Cultural Concepts of Masculinity.* New Haven, Conn.: Yale University Press.

Gokcumen, Ömer, Timur Gultekin, Yesim Dogan Alakoc, Aysim Tug, Erksin Gulec, and Theodore G. Schurr. 2011. "Biological Ancestries, Kinship Connections, and Projected Identities in Four Central Anatolian Settlements: Insights from Culturally Contextualized Genetic Anthropology." *American Anthropologist* 113 (1):116–131.

González, Roberto J. 2009. *American Counterinsurgency: Human Science and the Human Terrain.* Chicago: Prickly Paradigm Press.

Goodman, Nelson. 2001. *Ways of Worldmaking.* Indianapolis: Hackett.

Goody, Jack. 1983. *The Development of the Family and Marriage in Europe.* Cambridge: Cambridge University Press.

Government of Iraq. 1953. *Iraq Year Book.* Edited by Memdouh Zeki. Baghdad: Times Press.

———. 1973. *Dohuk after March 11* (in Arabic). Translated for Diane King by Ban al Attar. Dohuk, Iraq: Dohuk Press.

———. n.d. Law No. (188) of the year 1959 Personal Status Law and Amendments.

Grant, Asahel, and H. L. Murre-Van Den Berg. 2002 [1841]. *The Nestorians: Or, the Lost Tribes; Containing Evidence of their Identity; An Account of their Manners, Customs, and Ceremonies; Together with Sketches of Travels in Ancient Assyria, Armenia, Media, and Mesopotamia; And Illustrations of Scripture Prophecy.* Piscataway, N.J.: Gorgias Press.

Green, Linda. 1999. *Fear as a Way of Life: Mayan Widows in Rural Guatemala.* New York: Columbia University Press.

Gunter, Michael M. 2008. *The Kurds Ascending: The Evolving Solution to the Kurdish Problem in Iraq and Turkey.* New York: Palgrave Macmillan.

———. 2011. "Economic Opportunities in Iraqi Kurdistan." *Middle East Policy* 18 (2): 102–109.

Hadjiyanni, Tasoulla. 2002. *The Making of a Refugee: Children Adopting Refugee Identity in Cyprus.* Westport, Conn.: Praeger.

Hannerz, Ulf. 1987. "The World in Creolisation." *Africa* 57:546–559.

———. 1989. "Notes on the Global Ecumene." *Public Culture* 1 (2):66–75.

———. 2002. "Flows, Boundaries and Hybrids: Keywords in Transnational Anthropology." *Working Paper Series,* http://books.google.com/books?id=n9WScAAACAAJ.

Hansen, Henny Harald. 1960. *Daughters of Allah: Among Moslem Women in Kurdistan.* London: George Allen & Unwin.

———. 1961. *The Kurdish Woman's Life: Field Research in a Muslim Society, Iraq.* Copenhagen: National Museum of Denmark.

Hardi, Choman. 2011. *Gendered Experiences of Genocide: Anfal Survivors in Kurdistan-Iraq.* Farnham, Surrey, U.K.: Ashgate Publishing.

Harvey, David. 2004. *The Condition of Postmodernity: An Enquiry into the Origins of Cultural Change.* Malden, Mass.: Wiley-Blackwell.

Hassanpour, Amir. 1992. *Nationalism and Language in Kurdistan, 1918–1985.* San Francisco: Mellen Research University Press.

———. 2001. "The (Re)production of Patriarchy in the Kurdish Language." In *Women of a Non-state Nation: The Kurds,* edited by Shahrzad Mojab, 227–263. Costa Mesa, Calif.: Mazda Publishers.

Hay, Rupert, and John Paul Rich. 2008. *Iraq and Rupert Hay's Two Years in Kurdistan.* Lanham, Md.: Lexington Books.

Hegland, Mary Elaine. 2004. "Zip In and Zip Out Fieldwork." *Iranian Studies* 37 (4): 575–583.

Herzfeld, Michael. 2005. *Cultural Intimacy: Social Poetics in the Nation-State.* London: Routledge.

Hiltermann, Joost R. 2007. *A Poisonous Affair: America, Iraq, and the Gassing of Halabja.* Cambridge: Cambridge University Press.

Hirschkind, Charles. 2006. *The Ethical Soundscape: Cassette Sermons and Islamic Counterpublics, Cultures of History.* New York: Columbia University Press.

Hoff, Ruud H., Michiel Leezenberg, Pieter Muller, and Pax Christi International. 1992. *Elections in Iraqi Kurdistan (May 19, 1992): An Experiment in Democracy: Report of a Delegation Sponsored by Pax Christi International, Brussels, Interchurch Peace Council, The Hague, Netherlands, Kurdistan Friendship Society, Amsterdam.* Brussels: Pax Christi International.

Houston, Christopher. 2008. *Kurdistan: Crafting of National Selves.* Oxford: Berg.

———. 2009. "An Anti-History of a Non-People: Kurds, Colonialism, and Nationalism in the History of Anthropology." *Journal of the Royal Anthropological Institute* 15 (1):19–35.

Human Rights Watch. 2012. "World Report 2012: Events of 2011." www.hrw.org.

Îbrahîm, Cemal Welî, Xendan Muḥammad Ceza, Muḥammad Serpaç, and Soran 'Ebdulqadir Koste. 2008. *Oqyanusêk le Tawan: Twêjineweyekî Komełayetiye Sebaret be Diyardey Leşifroşî w Bazirganî Becestey R̄egezî Mêynewe le Komełgay Kurdistanda.* Kurdistan, Iraq: R̄ekxirawî R̄oşinbîrî w Komełayetî Xanzad.

Içduygu, Ahmet. 2003. "Irregular Migration in Turkey." In *IOM Migration Research Series.* Geneva: International Office of Migration.

Inda, Jonathan Xavier, and Renato Rosaldo. 2008. "Tracking Global Flows." In *The Anthropology of Globalization: A Reader,* edited by Jonathan Xavier Inda and Renato Rosaldo, 3–47. Malden, Mass.: Blackwell Publishers.

Inhorn, Marcia C. 1994. *Quest for Conception: Gender, Infertility, and Egyptian Medical Traditions.* Philadelphia: University of Pennsylvania Press.

———. 1996. *Infertility and Patriarchy: The Cultural Politics of Gender and Family Life in Egypt.* Philadelphia: University of Pennsylvania Press.

———. 2003. *Local Babies, Global Science: Gender, Religion, and In Vitro Fertilization in Egypt.* London: Routledge.

——. 2011. "Globalization and Gametes: Reproductive 'Tourism,' Islamic Bioethics, and Middle Eastern Modernity." *Anthropology & Medicine* 18 (1):87–103.

——. 2012. *The New Arab Man: Emergent Masculinities, Technologies, and Islam in the Middle East.* Princeton, N.J.: Princeton University Press.

Iraq Ministry of the Interior. 1936. *The Iraq Directory: A General and Commercial Directory of Iraq, with a Supplement for the Neighbouring Countries.* Baghdad: Dangoor's Printing and Publishing House.

Jacobsen, Thorkild, and Seton Lloyd. 1935. *Sennacherib's Aqueduct at Jerwan.* Chicago: University of Chicago Press.

Jáuregui Bereciartu, Gurutz. 1994. *Decline of the Nation State: Ethnonationalism in Comparative Perspective.* Reno: University of Nevada Press.

Joseph, John. 2000. *The Modern Assyrians of the Middle East: Encounters with Western Christian Missions, Archaeologists, and Colonial Powers.* Leiden: Brill.

Joseph, Suad. 1982. "The Mobilization of Iraqi Women into the Wage Labor Force." *Studies in Third World Societies* 16:69–90.

——. 1991. "Elite Strategies for State-Building: Women, Family, Religion and State in Iraq and Lebanon." In *Women, Islam and the State,* edited by Deniz Kandiyoti, 176–200. Philadelphia: Temple University Press.

——. 1993. "Connectivity and Patriarchy among Urban Working-Class Arab Families in Lebanon." *Ethos* 21 (4):452–484.

——. 1999. *Intimate Selving in Arab Families: Gender, Self, and Identity.* Syracuse, N.Y.: Syracuse University Press.

——. 2000. "Gendering Citizenship in the Middle East." In *Gender and Citizenship in the Middle East,* edited by Suad Joseph, 3–32. Syracuse, N.Y.: Syracuse University Press.

Jwaideh, Wadie. 1960. "The Kurdish Nationalist Movement: Its Origins and Development." Ph.D. diss., Political Science, International Law and Relations, Syracuse University.

Kahn, Margaret. 1976. "Borrowing and Variation in a Phonological Description of Kurdish." Ph.D. diss., Linguistics, University of Michigan.

Kanna, Ahmed. 2011. *Dubai: The City as Corporation.* Minneapolis: University of Minnesota Press.

Karl, Terry Lynn. 1997. *The Paradox of Plenty: Oil Booms and Petro-States.* Berkeley: University of California Press.

Kaufman, Joyce P., and Kristen P. Williams. 2008. *Women, the State, and War: A Comparative Perspective on Citizenship and Nationalism.* Lanham, Md.: Lexington Books.

Keltie, John Scott, and M. Epstein. 1920. *The Statesman's Year-Book: Statistical and Historical Annual of the States of the World for the Year 1920.* London: Macmillan.

Khalife, Nadya, and Human Rights Watch. 2010. *"They Took Me and Told Me Nothing": Female Genital Mutilation in Iraqi Kurdistan.* New York: Human Rights Watch.

King, Diane E. 2000. "When Worlds Collide: The Kurdish Diaspora from the Inside Out." Ph.D. diss., Anthropology, Washington State University, Pullman, Wash.

——— 2005. "Asylum Seekers / Patron Seekers: Interpreting Iraqi Kurdish Migration." *Human Organization* 64 (4):316–326.

———. 2008. "Back from the "Outside": Returnees and Diasporic Imagining in Iraqi Kurdistan." *International Journal on Multicultural Societies* 10 (2):208–222.

———. 2009. "Fieldwork and Fear in Iraqi Kurdistan." In *Violence: Ethnographic Encounters*, edited by Parvis Ghassem-Fachandi, 51–69. Oxford: Berg.

———. 2010. "The Personal Is Patrilineal: *Namus* as Sovereignty." In *Middle Eastern Belongings*, edited by Diane E. King, 59–84. London: Routledge. Paperback edition, 2013.

King, Diane E, and Linda Stone. 2010. "Lineal Masculinity: Gendered Memory within Patriliny." *American Ethnologist* 37 (2):323–336.

Kirişci, Kemal, and Boğaziçi Üniversitesi. 1995. *Refugee Movements and Turkey in the Post Second World War Era*. Istanbul: Boğaziçi Üniversitesi.

Korotayev, Andrey. 2000. "Parallel-Cousin (FBD) Marriage, Islamization, and Arabization." *Ethnology* 39 (4):395–407.

Kreyenbroek, Philip G., and Ulrich Marzolph. 2010. *Oral Literature of Iranian Languages: Kurdish, Pashto, Balochi, Ossetic; Persian and Tajik*. Companion volume 2. London: I. B. Tauris.

Kumin, Judith. 1999. "An Uncertain Direction. Europe: The Debate over Asylum." *Refugees Magazine* (113), http://www.unhcr.org/3b81ode44.html.

Kuper, Adam. 1982. "Lineage Theory: A Critical Retrospect." *Annual Review of Anthropology* 11:71–95.

———. 1996. *Anthropology and Anthropologists: The Modern British School*. London: Routledge.

Kurdistan Regional Government. 2008. "The Act to Amend the Amended Law No (188) of the Year 1959; Personal Status Law, in Iraq Kurdistan Region." In *Act No. 15 of 2008*.

———. 2012. "Fact Sheet about the Kurdistan Regional Government." http://www.krg.org/pages/page.asp?lngnr=12&rnr=297&PageNr=180.

Kurdistan Regional Government Ministry of Planning. 2011. *Regional Development Strategy for Kurdistan Region*. Erbil.

Laurie, Thomas. 1853. *Dr. Grant and the Mountain Nestorians*. Boston: Gould and Lincoln.

Layard, Austen Henry. 1853. *Discoveries in the Ruins of Nineveh and Babylon: With Travels in Armenia, Kurdistan and the Desert: Being the Result of a Second Expedition Undertaken for the Trustees of the British Museum*. New York: G. P. Putnam.

Layoun, Mary N. 1992. "Telling Spaces: Palestinian Women and the Engendering of National Narratives." In *Nationalisms & Sexualities*, edited by Mary Russo, Andrew Parker, Doris Summer, and Patricia Yaeger, 407–423. London: Routledge.

———. 2001. *Wedded to the Land?: Gender, Boundaries, and Nationalism in Crisis*. Durham, N.C.: Duke University Press.

Leach, Edmund R. 1940. *Social and Economic Organization of the Rowanduz Kurds*. London School of Economics Monographs on Social Anthropology, vol. 3. Oxford: Berg.

———. 1961. *Pul Eliya, a Village in Ceylon: A Study of Land Tenure and Kinship.* Cambridge: Cambridge University Press.

Leezenberg, Michiel. 2006. "Urbanization, Privatization, and Patronage: The Political Economy of Iraqi Kurdistan." In *The Kurds: Nationalism and Politics*, edited by Fāliḥ 'Abd al-Jabbār, and Hosham Dawod, 151–179. London: Saqi Books.

Lerner, Daniel. 1958. "The Grocer and the Chief." In *The Passing of Traditional Society*, edited by Daniel Lerner, 19–41. Glencoe, Ill.: Free Press of Glencoe.

Levene, Mark. 1998. "Creating a Modern 'Zone of Genocide': The Impact of Nation- and State-Formation on Eastern Anatolia, 1878–1923." *Holocaust and Genocide Studies* 12 (3):393–433.

Lévi-Strauss, Claude. 1955. "The Structural Study of Myth." *Journal of American Folklore* 68 (270):428–444.

———. 1969. *The Elementary Structures of Kinship.* Boston: Beacon Press.

Lev-Yadun, Simcha, Avi Gopher, and Shahal Abbo. 2000. "The Cradle of Agriculture." *Science* 288 (5471):1602–1603.

Lewellen, Ted C. 2002. *The Anthropology of Globalization: Cultural Anthropology Enters the 21st Century.* Westport, Conn.: Bergin & Garvey.

Lijphart, Arend. 1969. "Consociational Democracy." *World Politics* 21 (02):207–225.

Limbert, Mandana E. 2010. *In the Time of Oil: Piety, Memory, and Social Life in an Omani Town.* Stanford, Calif.: Stanford University Press.

Loizos, Peter, and Euthymios Papataxiarchēs. 1991. "Introduction: Gender and Kinship in Marriage and Alternative Contexts." In *Contested Identities: Gender and Kinship in Modern Greece*, edited by Peter and Euthymios Papataxiarchis Loizos, 3–25. Princeton, N.J.: Princeton University Press.

Longrigg, Stephen Hemsley. 1956. *Iraq, 1900 to 1950: A Political, Social, and Economic History.* Oxford: Oxford University Press.

Longva, Anh Nga. 1993. "Kuwaiti Women at a Crossroads: Privileged Development and the Constraints of Ethnic Stratification." *International Journal of Middle East Studies* 25 (03):443–456.

Luke, Harry Charles. 2004 [1925]. *Mosul and Its Minorities.* Piscataway, N.J.: Gorgias Press.

MacKenzie, D. N. 1962a. *Kurdish Dialect Sudies.* 2 vols. Vol. 1. Oxford: Oxford University Press.

———. 1962b. *Kurdish Dialect Studies.* 2 vols. Vol. 2. Oxford: Oxford University Press.

Malkki, Liisa H. 1995. "Refugees and Exile: From 'Refugee Studies' to the National Order of Things." *Annual Review of Anthropology* 24:495–523.

Marcus, Aliza. 2007. *Blood and Belief: The PKK and the Kurdish Fight for Independence.* New York: New York University Press.

Massad, Joseph. 1995. "Conceiving the Masculine: Gender and Palestinian Nationalism." *Middle East Journal* 49 (3):467–483.

Masters, William Murray. 1953. "Rowanduz, a Kurdish Administrative and Mercantile Center." Ph.D. diss., Anthropology, University of Michigan, Ann Arbor.

Mauss, Marcel. 2002 [1923–24]. *The Gift: The Form and Reason for Exchange in Archaic Societies.* London: Routledge.

McDowall, David. 1997. *The Kurds: Minority Rights Group International Report*. London: Minority Rights Group.

———. 2004. *A Modern History of the Kurds*. 3d ed. London: I. B. Tauris.

McGarry, John, and Brendan O'Leary. 2004. *The Northern Ireland Conflict: Consociational Engagements*. Oxford: Oxford University Press.

Meeker, Michael E. 1976. "Meaning and Society in the Near East: Examples from the Black Sea Turks and the Levantine Arabs (I)." *International Journal of Middle East Studies* 7 (02):243–270.

Mirzeler, Mustafa Kemal. 2000. "The Formation of Male Identity and the Roots of Violence against Women: The Case of Kurdish Songs, Stories and Storytellers." *Journal of Muslim Minority Affairs* 20 (2):261–269.

Mufti, Hania, Peter Bouckaert, and Human Rights Watch. 2003. "Iraq: Forcible Expulsion of Ethnic Minorities." http://www.hrw.org/reports/2003/iraq0303/.

Murdock, George Peter. 1949. *Social Structure*. New York: Macmillan.

Murphy, Robert F., and Leonard Kasdan. 1959. "The Structure of Parallel Cousin Marriage." *American Anthropologist* 61 (1):17–29.

Nagengast, Carole. 1994. "Violence, Terror, and the Crisis of the State." *Annual Review of Anthropology* 23 (1):109–136.

Najmabadi, Afsaneh. 1998. *The Story of the Daughters of Quchan: Gender and National Memory in Iranian History*. Syracuse, N.Y.: Syracuse University Press.

Nakshabandi, Mowafak M. 2007. "Casualties and Deaths from Road Traffic Accidents in Dohuk, Iraq." *Dohuk Medical Journal* 1 (1):15–22.

Natali, Denise. 2010. *The Kurdish Quasi-State: Development and Dependency in Post–Gulf War Iraq*. Syracuse, N.Y.: Syracuse University Press.

Nezan, Kendal. 1996. "The Kurds: Current Position and Historical Background." In *Kurdish Culture and Identity*, edited by Philip G. Kreyenbroek and Christine Allison, 7–19. London: Zed Books.

Niheli, Nasir. 2012. "Students Present Kurdish Culture at Indian University." *Rudaw*, http://www.rudaw.net/english/world/4440.html.

Nikitine, Basile. 1929. "Les Afshars d'Urumiyeh." *Journal Asiatique* 214:67–123.

Nordstrom, Carolyn. 2005. "Extrastate Globalization of the Illicit." In *Why America's Top Pundits Are Wrong: Anthropologists Talk Back*, edited by Catherine L. Besteman and Hugh Gusterson, 138–153. Berkeley: University of California Press.

O'Neal, Colleen G. 1999. " Possibilities for Migration Anthropology." *American Ethnologist* 26 (1):221–225.

Olson, Robert W. 1989. *The Emergence of Kurdish Nationalism and the Sheikh Said Rebellion, 1880–1925*. Austin: University of Texas Press.

———. 2005. *The Goat and the Butcher: Nationalism and State Formation in Kurdistan-Iraq since the Iraqi War*. Kurdish Studies Series. Costa Mesa, Calif.: Mazda Publishers.

Ong, Aihwa 1999. *Flexible Citizenship: The Cultural Logics of Transnationality*. Durham, N.C.: Duke University Press.

Ortner, Sherry B. 1978. "The Virgin and the State." *Feminist Studies* 4 (3):19–35.

Özyürek, Esra. 2006. *Nostalgia for the Modern: State Secularism and Everyday Politics in Turkey, Politics, History, and Culture*. Durham, N.C.: Duke University Press.

Pashew, Abdulla. 2004. "The Free World." *International Journal of Kurdish Studies* 18 (1/2):216–216.

Peirce, Leslie 2000. "Gender and Sexual Propriety in Ottoman Royal Women's Patronage." In *Women, Patronage, and Self-Representation in Islamic Societies*, edited by D. Fairchild Ruggles, 53–68. Albany: State University of New York Press.

Peteet, Julie M. 1991. *Gender in Crisis: Women and the Palestinian Resistance Movement.* New York: Columbia University Press.

Peterson, Mark Allen. 2011. *Connected in Cairo: Growing Up Cosmopolitan in the Modern Middle East.* Bloomington: Indiana University Press.

Pettman, Jan Jindy. 1996[C]. "Women on the Move; Gender, Globalisation and the Changing International Division of Labour." Globalisation Seminar Series, Department of International Relations, Australian National University, Canberra.

———. 2000. "Transcending National Identity: the Global Political Economy of Gender and Class." In *International Relations: Still an American Social Science?*, edited by Robert M. Crawford and Darryl S. L. Jarvis, 255–276. Albany: State University of New York Press,.

Pew Global Attitudes Project. 2007. *Global Unease with Major World Powers: 47-Nation Pew Global Attitudes Survey.* Washington, D.C.: Pew Global Attitudes Project.

Potter, Lawrence G., and Gary Sick. 2004. *Iran, Iraq, and the Legacies of War.* New York: Palgrave Macmillan.

Prados, Alfred B. 1994. *The Kurds in Iraq: Status, Protection, and Prospects.* Washington, D.C.: Congressional Research Service.

Qaradaghi, Mahabad 2007. "The Announcement of the Jury for the Elimination of Violence against Women." *Kurdish Aspect*, 26 November 2007.

Rajagopalan, Kavitha. 2008. *Muslims of Metropolis: The Stories of Three Immigrant Families in the West.* New Brunswick, N.J.: Rutgers University Press.

Rassam [see also Vinogradov], Amal. 1977. "Al-taba'iyya: Power, Patronage and Marginal Groups in Northern Iraq." In *Patrons and Clients in Mediterranean Societies*, edited by Ernest Gellner and John Waterbury, 157–166. London: Duckworth.

Reyna, Stephen, and Andrea Behrends. 2008. "The Crazy Curse and Crude Domination: Toward an Anthropology of Oil." *Focaal* 52 (1):3–17.

Rich, Claudius James. 1836. *Narrative of a Residence in Koordistan.* London: James Duncan.

Richards, Alan, and John Waterbury. 1996. *A Political Economy of the Middle East.* Boulder, Colo.: Westview Press.

Robertson, Roland. 1995. "Glocalization: Time-Space and Homogeneity/Heterogeneity." In *Global Modernities*, edited by Mike Featherstone, Scott Lash, and Roland Robertson, 25–44. Thousand Oaks, Calif: Sage Publications.

Robson, Barbara, and Refugee Service Center. 1996. *The Iraqi Kurds: Their History and Culture.* Washington, D.C.: Refugee Service Center, Center for Applied Linguistics.

Rodman, Margaret C. 1992. "Empowering Place: Multilocality and Multivocality." *American Anthropologist* 94 (3):640–656.

Rohde, Achim. 2010. "The Ba'th Era and Beyond: Revisiting the Republic of Fear. Lessons for Research in Contemporary Iraq." In *Iraq between Occupations: Perspectives from 1920 to the Present*, edited by Ronen Zeidel, Amatzia Baram, and Achim Rohde, 129–142. New York: Palgrave Macmillan.

Romano, David. 2007. *An Outline of Kurdish Islamist Groups in Iraq*. Washington, D.C.: Jamestown Foundation.

Rudaw. 2011. "Airport Director: Erbil Had 500,000 Passengers in 2010." *Rudaw*, http://www.rudaw.net/english/interview/3840.html.

Saadawi, Nawal el. 2007. *The Hidden Face of Eve: Women in the Arab World*. Translated by Sherif Hetata. London: Zed Books.

Säävälä, Minna. 2001. *Fertility and Familial Power Relations: Procreation in South India*. Richmond, Surrey, U.K.: Curzon.

Sabar, Ariel. 2009. *My Father's Paradise: A Son's Search for His Family's Past*. Chapel Hill, N.C.: Algonquin Books.

Sahlins, Marshall D. 1961. "The Segmentary Lineage: An Organization of Predatory Expansion." *American Anthropologist* 63 (2):322–345.

Said, Edward W. 1979. *Orientalism*. New York: Vintage Books.

Savelsberg, Eva, Siamend Hajo, and Irene Dulz. 2010. "Effectively Urbanized: Yezidis in the Collective Towns of Sheikhan and Sinjar." *Études Rurales* 186:101–116.

Schmidt, Klaus. 2008. "When Humanity Began to Settle Down." *German Research* 30 (1):10–13.

Schneider, David M. 1984. *A Critique of the Study of Kinship*. Ann Arbor: University of Michigan Press.

Schneider, Jane. 1971. "Of Vigilance and Virgins: Honor, Shame and Access to Resources in Mediterranean Societies." *Ethnology* 10 (1):1–24.

Scott, James C. 1998. *Seeing Like a State: How Certain Schemes to Improve the Human Condition Have Failed*. Yale Agrarian Studies. New Haven, Conn.: Yale University Press.

Secor, Anna J. 2003. "Belaboring Gender: The Spatial Practice of Work and the Politics of 'Making Do' in Istanbul." *Environment and Planning A* 35:2209–2227.

———. 2004. "'There Is an Istanbul That Belongs to Me': Citizenship, Space, and Identity in the City." *Annals of the Association of American Geographers* 94 (2):352–368.

———. 2007. "Between Longing and Despair: State, Space, and Subjectivity in Turkey." *Environment and Planning D: Society and Space* 25 (1):33–52.

Service, Elman R. 1971. *Primitive Social Organization: An Evolutionary Perspective*. New York: Random House.

Seyhan, Azade. 2001. *Writing Outside the Nation*. Princeton: Princeton University Press.

Shami, Seteney, and Center for Migration Studies. 1994. *Population Displacement and Resettlement: Development and Conflict in the Middle East*. New York: Center for Migration Studies.

Shankland, David. 1999. "Integrating the Rural: Gellner and the Study of Anatolia." *Middle Eastern Studies* 35 (2):132–149.

Sharma, Aradhana, and Akhil Gupta. 2006. *The Anthropology of the State: A Reader*. Blackwell Readers in Anthropology. Malden, Mass.: Blackwell Publishing.

Shryock, Andrew. 1996. "Tribes and the Print Trade: Notes from the Margins of Literate Culture in Jordan." *American Anthropologist* 98 (1):26–40.

———. 1997. *Nationalism and the Genealogical Imagination: Oral History and Textual Authority in Tribal Jordan*. Berkeley: University of California Press.

Soane, E. B. 1918. *Notes on the Tribes of Southern Kurdistan*. Baghdad: Government Press.

Sökefeld, Martin. 1999. "Debating Self, Identity, and Culture in Anthropology." *Current Anthropology* 40 (4):417–448.

Solecki, Ralph S. 1971. *Shanidar: The First Flower People.* New York: Alfred A. Knopf.

Stafford, Ronald Sempill. 2006 [1935]. *The Tragedy of the Assyrians.* Piscataway, N.J.: Gorgias Press.

Stansfield, Gareth R. V. 2003. *Iraqi Kurdistan: Political Development and Emergent Democracy.* London: RoutledgeCurzon.

Stewart, Kathleen. 1996. *A Space on the Side of the Road: Cultural Poetics in an "Other" America.* Princeton, N.J.: Princeton University Press.

Stone, Linda. 2010. *Kinship and Gender: An Introduction.* 4th ed. Boulder, Colo.: Westview Press.

Strathern, Marilyn. 1992. *Reproducing the Future: Essays on Anthropology, Kinship, and the New Reproductive Technologies.* Manchester, U.K.: Manchester University Press.

Swedenburg, Ted. 1990. "The Palestinian Peasant as National Signifier." *Anthropological Quarterly* 63 (1):18–30.

Tapper, Richard. 1988. "Minorities and the Problem of the State. Review of *The Elementary Structures of Political Life: Rural Development in Pahlavi Iran.*" *Third World Quarterly* 10 (2):1027–1041.

Taylor, Gordon. 2005. *Fever & Thirst: A Missionary Doctor amid the Christian Tribes of Kurdistan.* Chicago: Academy Chicago Publishers.

Theodossopoulos, Dimitrios, and Elisabeth Kirtsoglou. 2010. *United in Discontent: Local Responses to Cosmopolitanism and Globalization.* New York: Berghahn Books.

Tosun, Cevat. 1998. "Roots of Unsustainable Tourism Development at the Local Level: The Case of Urgup in Turkey." *Tourism Management* 19 (6):595–610.

Travis, Hannibal. 2010. *Genocide in the Middle East: The Ottoman Empire, Iraq, and Sudan.* Durham, N.C.: Carolina Academic Press.

Tripp, Charles. 2007. *A History of Iraq.* 3d ed. Cambridge: Cambridge University Press.

Tsing, Anna Lowenhaupt. 2005. *Friction: An Ethnography of Global Connection.* Princeton, N.J.: Princeton University Press.

United Nations Development Programme. 2004. "Human Development Report 2004: Cultural Liberty in Today's Diverse World." New York.

United Nations High Commissioner for Refugees (UNHCR). 1992. "UNHCR Report on Northern Iraq, April 1991–May 1992." Geneva.

United Nations Office for the Coordination of Humanitarian Affairs. 2007. "Iraq—Population by Governorate." http://ochaonline.un.org/OchaLinkClick.aspx?link=ocha&docId=1081922.

United States Federal Aviation Administration. 2012. *Prohibition against Certain Flights within the Territory and Airspace of Iraq.* Washington, D.C.: Federal Register.

United States Military Attaché Office. 1944. *Kurdish Tribal Map of Iraq: Showing the Iraq Portion of Kurdistan and the Major Kurdish Tribal Divisions within Iraq.* Tehran, Iran: U.S. Military Attaché Office, from the papers of Archibald B. Roosevelt Jr.

University of Miami Special Collections. 2011. Henry Field papers, 1943–1974. University of Miami Special Collections 2011. http://proust.library.miami.edu/findingaids/?p=collections/controlcard&id=96.

Van Ess, Dorothy. 1961. *Fatima and Her Sisters.* New York: John Day.

———. 1974. *Pioneers in the Arab World.* Grand Rapids, Mich.: Wm. B. Eerdmans.

Vanly, Ismet Sheriff. 1993. "Kurdistan in Iraq." In *A People without a Country: The Kurds and Kurdistan,* edited by Gerard Chaliand, 139–193. New York: Olive Branch Press.

Vansina, Jan. 1985. *Oral Tradition as History.* Madison: University of Wisconsin Press.

Varia, Nisha, and Human Rights Watch. 2010. *Slow Reform: Protection of Migrant Domestic Workers in Asia and the Middle East.* New York: Human Rights Watch.

Varisco, Daniel Martin. 1995. "Metaphors and Sacred History: The Genealogy of Muhammad and the Arab 'Tribe.'" *Anthropological Quarterly* 68 (3):139–156.

Vermot-Mangold, Ruth-Gaby, and Council of Europe Parliamentary Assembly Committee on Migration Refugees and Demography. 1998. *Humanitarian Situation of the Kurdish Refugees and Displaced Persons in South-East Turkey and North Iraq,* edited by Ruth-Gaby Vermot-Mangold. Brussels.

Vinogradov [see also Rassam], Amal. 1974. "Ethnicity, Cultural Discontinuity and Power Brokers in Northern Iraq: The Case of the Shabak." *American Ethnologist* 1 (1):207–218.

Wahlbeck, Östen. 1999. *Kurdish Diasporas: A Comparative Study of Kurdish Refugee Communities, Migration, Minorities, and Citizenship.* New York: St. Martin's Press in association with Centre for Research in Ethnic Relations, University of Warwick.

Weber, Max, and Sam Whimster. 2004. *The Essential Weber: A Reader.* London: Routledge.

Weiss, Wendy A. 1990. "Challenge to Authority: Bakhtin and Ethnographic Description." *Cultural Anthropology* 5 (4):414–430.

Welling, Dominic. 2012. "Incheon to Manage $200m Kurdistan Gateway Project." *Airport World: The Magazine of the Airports Council International,* http://www.airportworld.com/news-articles/item/1360-incheon-to-manage-$200m-kurdistan-gateway-project.

Wolf, Eric R. 1966. *Peasants.* Foundations of Modern Anthropology Series. Englewood Cliffs, N.J.: PrenticeHall.

Wright, Joanne H. 2004. *Origin Stories in Political Thought: Discourses on Gender, Power, and Citizenship.* Toronto: University of Toronto Press.

Yalçin-Heckmann, Lale. 1991. *Tribe and Kinship among the Kurds.* Frankfurt am Main: Peter Lang.

Yavuz, M. Hakan. 1998. "A Preamble to the Kurdish Question: The Politics of Kurdish Identity." *Journal of Muslim Minority Affairs* 18 (1):9–18.

Zaken, Mordechai. 2007. *Jewish Subjects and Their Tribal Chieftains in Kurdistan: A Study in Survival.* Jewish Identities in a Changing World. Leiden: Brill.

INDEX

Abdulhamid II, Sultan, 229n.3
Abdul Rahman, Bayan Sami, 213
Abdul Rahman, Sami, 55, 147–148, 164, 213
Abu Afif confectionery, 55
Abu-Lughod, Lila, 78–79
accent, as cue to place and lineage, 84
accidents: automobile, 105–106; fatal, and blood reprisal, 106, 173
Acton, Lord (John Emerich Edward Dalberg), 205
Adelkhah, Fariba, 11
agency, through belief in binaries, 221
*agha*s, 70, 92–95, 237; as antitheses of nouveaux riches, 83–84; *chete* payments funneled through, 167; dating from early 1800s, 87; *diwans*, 139; mountain, 99; as patrons, 81 (*see also* patron-client relationship); status of, *vs.* peasants, 81
agnation, 3, 78–79. *See also* patriliny
agriculture, 13; early, and accumulation of capital, 16; Iraq loses self-sufficiency in, during Iran-Iraq War, 21–22. *See also* foodways; herding
AIDS, 127
'a'ila, 7, 237. *See also* patrilineage
aircraft, non-Iraqi, in no-fly zone, 208
air pollution, from cooking fires, 233n.3
alliance, marriage as, 129
Al-Qaeda, 180
alterity, and zero-sum contests, 196
Amed, 233n.6. *See also* Diyarbakir
"America" and the West, fetishization of, 192
American University of Beirut, 170
"American Village" development (suburban Hewler), 222
Amn al Amm, 224
Amnesty International, 224
amulets, 121–122, 233n.5
Anderson, J.N.D., 75
Anfal campaign (1988) against Kurds, 62, 172, 176
anthropology: of globalization, 208; immersion and embodied research,
232–233n.4; kinship studies, 77–80; poststructuralist, 78; "salvage ethnography," 223; of the state, 208. *See also* methodology
anthropometry, 230n.11
apical ancestor, 77, 80
Appadurai, Arjun, 11, 217
apple orchards, 90, 99
Aqre, border community, 157–158, *158*
aqueduct of Sennacherib, 15–16
"Arabization" program, Iraq, 93, 156–157, 176
Arabs: concerns over chastity, 133; patrilineal succession patterns among, 75
"Arab Spring," 28
Aras, Ramazan, 233n.8
Arendt, Hannah, 182
Aristotle, on monogenesis, 67
Armenians: in Iraqi Kurdistan, 5; massacred by Turks, 229n.3
Article 140, of 2005 Iraqi constitution, 156, 159–161
artisan class, 82
asayish, 149
Assad, Bashar al-, 215
assassinations: raid on Hewler in 1996, 46, 148, 151; of Sami Abdul Rahman, 55, 213; Turkish complicity alleged in, 192
Assyrians, 18: Christian, 233n.4; identity through patriliny, 75; massacred at Simel, 21; nationalist movement in Iraq, 158
asylum, 182; seeker of, *vs.* refugee, 174
asylum/refuge regimes, complicated by Kurdish migrations, 40
Atran, Scott, 129
Austrian Airlines, 9, 231n.20
autochthony of citizens, state's claims for, 154
automobiles: accidents, 105–106; women as drivers, 103–111
autonomy: female, limiting of, 7; regional, in Iraq, 156

Kuper, Adam, 77–78
Kurdish Autonomous Region, 230n.8
Kurdish dress, traditional, and the
    Kalashnikov rifle, 219
Kurdish language, dialects of, 19–20, 154
Kurdish music, clandestine in Turkey,
    58
Kurdish National Council of Syria (KNC),
    215
Kurdishness, 2; aghas an abiding symbol
    of, 95; Iraqi Kurdistan as embodiment
    of, 56, 212
"Kurdish Question," 19
"Kurdish refugee," imaginary of, 190
Kurdish Textile Museum, 216, 217, 218
Kurdish uprisings, 41–42, 42, 143, 222
Kurdistan: as both democracy and
    oligarchy, 39; British colonial period,
    19–21; collective memory of
    patrilineage in, 79–80; economic
    activities and connections in, 12–13,
    21–29; ethnogeographic, 3–4;
    ethnographic studies of, 6; foreigners
    in, 24, 31–32, 54, 210–211; gender
    system, 102–137; history of violence,
    172; impediments to social research in,
    53; maps, 4, 42, 42, 92, 94; Neanderthal
    life at Shanidar Cave, 15; negotiates
    modernity and globalism, 2–3;
    nouveaux riches of, 83–84; Ottomans
    impose direct rule, 86–87; passageways
    through, 150; post–Gulf War relief
    effort, 9; recent sense of safety in,
    53–54; as state (see Kurdistan Region);
    as unlikely haven, 55–61
Kurdistan Democratic Party, see KDP
"Kurdistani," 229n.1
Kurdistan Islamic Union, 95, 120
Kurdistan National Council of Syria
    (KNC), 238
Kurdistan Region, 2, 4–5, 205, 230n.8;
    autonomy of, 40, 203; as focus for
    Kurdish nationalism, 211–216; fuzzily
    defined sovereignty of, 170; industry,
    55; as mercantile "gateway to Iraq," 55;
    parliamentary ethnic/religious seat
    quotas, 152–153; as remedy to
    statelessness, 6; as site for
    experimentation with modernity, 212
Kurdistan Regional Government, see
    KRG
Kurdistan Workers' Party, see PKK
Kurd/Kurdish, as ethnic identifier, 229n.1
Kurds: increasing awareness of outside
    world, 29; as Middle Eastern
    counterpublic, 169–171; mistreatment
    of, by dominant state ethnic groups, 5,
    56; oppressed by Turks, 57–60; out-
    migrating, 5–6, 168; patrilineal

succession patterns among, 75;
    population estimates, 4, 101, 230n.7,
    235n.11; as a "postcolonial" people, 222;
    religious identity, 5; returning
    migrants, 30; settled in West, 30, 40;
    social and symbolic life, 7–10; violence
    against, in modernizing Iraq, 61–62
Kurmanji Kurdish dialect, 19, 154
Kuwait, Iraqi invasion of, 177

land: complex ownership, 184–185;
    husband's, 128; inheritance law
    reform, 70, 131; likened to honor, 66;
    lineages linked to, 80–81; as men's
    wealth, 197; redistribution of, by KRG,
    82; as religious territory, 75–76;
    transfers of, restricted to co-
    religionists, 75–76
land mines, 45
land reform, 13, 93, 98
language: accent as cue to place and
    lineage, 84; describing ethnicity,
    229n.1; Kurdish dialects, 19–20, 154;
    pronunciation of Kurdish Roman
    alphabet, xiii–xiv; references to God,
    119; virginity terminology, 235n.6
Layard, Austen Henry, 18
Layoun, Mary, 119
Leach, Edmund, 6, 78, 94
leaders: land-connected, as connectors of
    people, 98; noncosmopolitan Kurds,
    170; tribal and urban, 92–98
League of Nations British Iraqi Mandate,
    20, 87
Lebanese: doing business in Kurdistan,
    31–32, 232nn.24–25; Kurdishness
    stigmatized by, 61
Lebanon: American University (Beirut);
    PKK strongholds in Beqa Valley, 61
Leezenberg, Michael, 168
Lemkin, Raphael, 21
Levene, Mark, 227
Lévi-Strauss, Claude, 129
Lev-Yadun, Simcha, 15
licenses for businesses, and party
    membership, 83
life course, and migration events, 193
lifestyle changes, and influx of capital to
    Kurdistan, 27–28
Limbert, Mandana, 212
Lindsay, Sir Ronald, 19
lineal masculinity, 116
literacy, women's, 37; vs. men's, 102
liwas, 101, 156, 237
logistics, epistemology inseparable from,
    43
Longrigg, Stephen, 24
Longva, Ah Nga, 116
"low intensity panic," 63, 64

ABOUT THE AUTHOR

DIANE E. KING is an assistant professor of anthropology at the University of Kentucky. She is the editor of the volume *Middle Eastern Belongings* (2010; paperback edition, 2013) as well as scholarly articles and journalism on collective identity, kinship and descent, gender, and the state. Since 1995, she has been conducting ethnographic fieldwork in the Kurdistan Region of Iraq. Her Ph.D. (2000) is from Washington State University. She previously taught at Washington State University and the American University of Beirut. Her research has been supported by her employers and by the Wenner-Gren Foundation, the Hewlett Foundation, the Howard Foundation (of Brown University), and the British Council.

CPSIA information can be obtained at www.ICGtesting.com
Printed in the USA
BVOW04s0222190115

383911BV00001B/112/P